Defending a Way of Life

SUNY Series in American Labor History
Robert Asher and Charles Stephenson, Editors

Defending a Way of Life

AN AMERICAN COMMUNITY
IN THE
NINETEENTH CENTURY

Michael Cassity

State University of New York Press

307.74
C 34d

Published by
State University of New York Press, Albany

© 1989 State University of New York

For information, address State University of New York
Press, State University Plaza, Albany, N.Y., 12246

Library of Congress Cataloging-in-Publication Data

Cassity, Michael J.
    Defending a way of life : an American community in the nineteenth
century / Michael Cassity.
        p.   cm.—(SUNY series in American labor history)
    Bibliography: p.
    Includes index.
    ISBN 0-88706-868-5.   ISBN 0-88706-869-3 (pbk.)
        1. Labor and laboring classes—Missouri—Sedalia—History—19th
century.   2. Sedalia (Mo.)—Economic conditions.   3. Sedalia (Mo.)—
Social conditions.   4. Labor and laboring classes—Missouri—Pettis
County—History—19th century.   5. Pettis County (Mo.)—Economic
conditions.   6. Pettis County (Mo.)—Social conditions.   I.   Title.
II. Series.
HD8085.S433C37   1988
307.7'4'0977845—dc19   88-12324
                                                                         CIP

10 9 8 7 6 5 4 3 2 1

for Connie

all right we are two nations
　　　　　—John Dos Passos, *U.S.A.*

Contents

Preface / *ix*

PART ONE
OF DREAMS AND REALITIES BORN

Chapter I: Origins and Purposes   3

  i. *Dwellers of the Inland* / *3*
  ii. *A Birthright Reclaimed* / *6*

Chapter II: The Pattern of Community   10

  i. *Economy* / *10*
  ii. *Polity* / *19*
  iii. *Bonds of Mutuality* / *33*

Chapter III: The Crisis of Change and War   36

  i. *Prometheus Bound* / *36*
  ii. *A New Society* / *45*

PART TWO
THE RISING PATTERN OF INDUSTRIAL MARKET SOCIETY

Chapter IV: The Engines of Economic Growth   53

  i. *Social Discipline* / *53*
  ii. *The Juggernaut* / *64*

Chapter V: God and Mammon: The Birth of East Sedalia   69

Chapter VI: A Vale of Tears: The Experiences of Change   79

    i. *More Than a Machine* / *79*
   ii. *Visible Destruction* / *82*
  iii. *The Corruption of Eve* / *84*
  iv. *Of Faith and Fear* / *87*

PART THREE
THE AGENCY OF THE PEOPLE

Chapter VII: The Businessmen and the Market   97

    i. *The Social Contract* / *97*
   ii. *Competition: The Lifeblood of Freedom* / *100*
  iii. *The Curse of Consolidation* / *103*
  iv. *The Imperative of Autonomy* / *107*

Chapter VIII: The Community of Workers   115

    i. *The Wellsprings of Vigilance* / *115*
   ii. *Responsibility: Moral Vision and Social Need* / *120*
  iii. *Amity and Equity* / *125*
  iv. *The Sources of Discipline* / *131*
   v. *Ishmael* / *145*

Chapter IX: The Agrarian Commonweal   149

    i. *Arcadia and the Scourge of Nature* / *149*
   ii. *Sowing the Wind* / *157*
  iii. *Toward the Cooperative Commonwealth* / *162*

Chapter X: The Travail of Sisterhood   170

    i. *The Ordeal of the Doyennes* / *170*
   ii. *The World of Women and the World of the Market* / *189*
  iii. *The Redeemers and the Seeds of Feminism* / *193*

PART FOUR
CONCLUSION

Chapter XI: A Way of Life Forsaken?   205

A Note on Historiography / *213*

Notes / *224*

Index / *254*

Preface

From time to time as I have thought about the questions guiding this study I would imagine a man and a woman, whose names I never knew but whose lives and whose passage through this world always attracted me and seemed crucial to an understanding of the large process of social change which they witnessed and felt and in which they participated. I would imagine them at the end of the day when the chores were done, when they had a moment to themselves, as they sat quietly gazing into the fire that warmed them and as they gazed into each other's eyes. The gaze was not one of looking and examining, but one of remembering and pondering. The silence might be interrupted by the shrill whistle of the train in the distance, or by the low moan of the wind, or by the muffled night sounds of a child in the next room. But the introspection remained unbroken in its essentials as those sounds kindled reflections rather than disturbed them. What these people pondered was life itself, what their lives had been and where they were going. It is in exactly such intimate and quiet moments, after all, that the largest questions are raised, the questions that the institutions of society seem almost inherently incapable of addressing, whether those institutions are businesses or legislative bodies or labor unions or universities. And, I wondered, what did they think as they reflected upon the past they knew, the past that brought them to their present? What did they hope and what did they fear as they speculated about the future? Since these people lived, as do we all, between the past and the future—sometimes with comfort and sometimes with awkwardness and apprehension—these questions were natural enough and possibly even unavoidable. Perhaps the ultimate question they pondered, though, as the others came together, was: Just how much *alone* were they? A powerful, frightening, and hard question to pose in the past, it is also a question that we often avoid in our own times. For their part, this couple may have found one answer to that question in the touch of each other's hands, another come sunrise as they faced again the challenges of keeping body and soul together in a world not of their own making. In this study I try to determine what their answers, and the answers of others like them, were to these fundamental questions of life.

It is possible now, perhaps more than ever before, to undertake such an inquiry for the day is past when historians could write about the history of American workers from the exclusive perspective of the trade union or strike. Because of the efforts of historians like E. P. Thompson, Eric Hobsbawm, Raymond Williams, Herbert Gutman, David Montgomery, and others, few are content with calling the growth of labor institutions aspiring to collective bargaining a social movement. The focus has shifted away from the purely episodic and institutional to the broader trends of the experiences and the culture of workers. And the result has been a dramatic broadening of the potential in the history of the American people wherein their lives and aspirations need not be reduced to the imperatives of the cash-nexus.

Similarly it is no longer plausible to generate a chronicle of the growth of businesses and their institutional order and call it community history. The community, where human issues and opportunities and tensions find their most immediate expressions, has proven to be where the nation lives. Indeed the community focus has turned out to be far more revealing than centralized arrangements in uncovering the structure, values, and relationships characteristic of American society. It is in the community, also, where people lived and died, labored and loved, and where workers and others confronted life in the process of the rise of industrial capitalism that the relationships formed and sundered need not be reduced to a rigid schematic. It is there that the analytical categories hold a greater potential for emanating from the patterns of relations formed by real people over time than from the ready-made, but ill-fitting, apparel on the historians' shelf.

The beginning point for such an inquiry, therefore, is not with a sense of ambition and confidence, much less with the self-satisfaction that often accompanies efforts to find the origins of our own society. It is rather with an acute sense of one's own limits and the recognition that such questions as I have posed have no final answers. The mystery of what the introspection of the unassuming couple I described above yielded will not be resolved, ever, to the satisfaction of all. But to approach that mystery and to gain a glimpse into what these people believed about their lives and about the world around them seems to me an imperative and even urgent task. I should note that this is a journey to which others would take exception. I would concur, however, with E. P. Thompson, who, when confronted with similar circumstance, argued that they are instead "those questions of satisfaction, of the direction of social change, which the historian ought to ponder if history is to claim a position among the significant humanities." Unanswerable these questions may always be; unasked they must never be.

This is not to suggest that sheer speculation and idle rumination is sufficient. It is not. Indeed, to promote a meaningful discussion of such large questions requires a sensitivity to precise theoretical concerns and possibilities. The approach that I have chosen, therefore, is one that focuses on the broad patterns of change in the social structure, an approach that seeks to determine the coherence and direction of the pattern of change in the institutions we think of as making up organized society. With an eye to the pre-eminent results of those changes, this approach also beings with a consideration of industrial capitalism as an entire system of developing social arrangements and patterns of life, not just as a form of economic organization. The central concept in this pattern is one that can best be associated with the market—the market not just as an institution of exchange but as a conception of human relationships that emphasizes the individual as an independent marketing, or bargaining, agent in the determination of his or her own fate. The freedom implicit in this conception finds expression socially in fluid, contractual relationships which ostensibly emphasize the ability, and certainly the responsibility, of the individual, but which all too often, indeed even systematically, underscore the role of concentrated power and control of resources in the determination of the fate of individuals and society. As social organization itself becomes a bargaining process, individuals are forced to rely on whatever resources or property they have as something to market simply as a matter of survival; often their capacity to labor itself winds up a commodity of necessity in the exchange. This process, which involves the subordination of other values and priorities to materialistic impulses, is one that E. P. Thompson has aptly termed "the annunciation of economic man." How this transformation, essentially a social phenomenon despite the narrow economic goal, came about in an American context is one question that I address in this study.

The consequences of and the popular response to the development of market society also demand analysis. Since the change from a premarket, preindustrial form of social organization to a society organized around the principles of the market involved an attempt to narrow the role of people to economic units to be regulated by markets (free or controlled), the costs came in broad terms. Whether considered in terms of the life of the community or the life of the individual, such change comes not to one part of life alone, in isolation from all else, but to the entire structure, purpose, and pace of that life. Thus changes in the work system, in the possession of initiative, in the internalized standards and compunctions, and in the power relationships were part of the larger process. So too were challenges mounted to traditions, customs, community obligations, and even morality weighty elements in this transformation of life. The total effect is not something that can be added up in the calculable terms of wages and hours, but in the loss of a way of life that defies precise measure. Logic dictates then that the response to this transformation would not be restricted to the arena of economics but would traverse the entire spectrum of political, economic, religious, literary, fraternal, and personal experiences. Sometimes the responses, expressions of social consciousness, come in well developed, articulate statements of theory about the operations of societies and alternatives to them. This, however, is not the most common form. I have found it more useful to seek less articulate expressions of social awareness by examining patterns of collective behavior. By focusing on what Raymond Williams has termed "the structure of feeling," the common purpose expressed by the unity of popular institutions, community values, patterns of discipline, and theories (or coherent assumptions) of a particular, identifiable group of people, I have been mainly concerned with what would certainly appear to others as incidents of minor importance compared to the purportedly more articulate activities of political and economic elites.

There is an assumption basic to this approach that I feel obliged to make explicit. It is my conviction that the ways in which people respond to the pressures of the world they live in reveal deeply held values concerning relationships they deem important. On one level this is simply acting on the basis of a coherent world view; on another it is an effort to fulfill basic human needs. This does not mean that by so acting they are always fully aware of the ultimate implications of their behavior in any kind of explicit sense. In fact, the process that I examine is one in which precisely this sense of social consciousness develops an articulate form. In this I mean no derogation of the human condition. In the final analysis it is they, those involved in the change, in their relationship with material change, not material things alone, who shape that consciousness.

The choice of Sedalia and Pettis County, Missouri, was not deliberate. I started curious about two strikes that centered in this community in 1885 and 1886. What was particularly significant about these strikes was that the first held the support of the workers and the community while the second collapsed because precisely that support was absent. This presented the intriguing situation of workers and townspeople acting in ways in which they were not, by conventional social and economic theory, supposed to act. There was something, some hidden factor, some unidentified but powerful drive, that transcended the quest for money and gain. The search for that factor then took me deeper and broader into the history of the community than I originally anticipated.

One of the justifying considerations in pursuing this quest for such driving forces at the level of the local community is the opportunity there, absent in the larger picture, of capturing the wholeness of the life of the community instead of reducing that life down to its material contours and narrow economic connections. Even so, I also recognize that my effort to reconstruct that whole life is not complete and that there are substantial omissions. In particular, I would observe the neglect in these pages of groups defined by gender and race. While not addressing those cultures with the sustained attention given to others, I hope to suggest a pattern in which their institutions, values, priorities, and collective behavior might hold a different meaning from that traditionally understood.

It was with a sense of fascination and caution that I originally approached this study. It is with a sense of humility that I bring the work to a close. I am aware, more so than when I began, that such an inquiry as this will never be truly concluded. Yet, as I have contemplated the process of social change, the experiences involved in it, and the responses of people to those changes, I have become impressed with the limits of analyses that assume that the whole is but the sum of the parts or that hold that by reducing life to standardized quantifiable terms and categories it is capable of being fully understood. Part of my humility thus derives from my perception of the solemn mystery of the subject. And part of it derives from my conviction that no final answers will ever be found.

But the subject is too important to ignore. This is, after all, an effort to understand the lives of people at a crucial moment in the past, not to make light of them, not to use them as object lessons, and not to praise or censure them. In that regard it is also an attempt to understand the meaningful legacies of their experiences for our own times. Which all suggests that I have attempted, above all, to raise questions, questions about the past, about prevailing interpretations of the past, and therefore questions about our own lives today. Thus again the image before me of the couple gazing into the embers of the fire late at night pondering the mysteries of life, of satisfaction, of loneliness, of the purpose and course of organized society. With that in mind the possibility has occurred to me that perhaps they could see more clearly where their society was headed than we can see where we have been.

This study has been a long time in the making. In the process I have received generous assistance from many people and institutions. I wish to thank them all and to extend my apologies for drawing upon them so persistently and so often. My first debt is very simply to David Thelen. This is a huge debt and it goes back nearly two decades to the time when he introduced me to intellectual exchange in a way I had never experienced or anticipated. Since then, in this work and in others, he has proved an invaluable source of energy, insight and encouragement. I am grateful and fortunate.

A wide range of people read earlier versions of this manuscript, commented on it, and thereby helped shape what it became: Lewis Atherton, Numan Bartley, Richard Bienvenu, Nancy Dye, Gary Fink, Peter Gardner, William F. Holmes, David Montgomery, Edward Purcell, and the late John C. Rainbolt. David Thelen saw it in its most primitive form and saw it in its most recent construction, being supportive and perceptive in both instances and between. Susan Flader read and reacted to my earliest attempt to make sense of this community and has since provided a sounding board for particular points and issues of a much broader nature. Robert Asher proceeded well beyond the line of duty for an editor and offered advice in the creation of this manuscript that I have found most helpful. Priscilla Evans demonstrated a thorough knowledge of nineteenth century Missouri and its historical sources and always shared her knowledge of both with me.

A group that includes a rare and wonderful assortment of talented and honest people has learned that this work is much of my life; they have indulgently tolerated both. Russell Duncan, Jean Friedman, Leann Grabavoy, Dale Grinder, David Kathka, Susan Laser-Bair, Margaret Murdock, Randy Patton, Sarah Poole, David Potenziani, Lynn Questel, Fred Rich, Christina Strobel, Curtis Synhorst, Richard Vietor, Kirk Willis, Dan Woods, and Lee Ann Yannotti all shared with me their thinking on the issues raised in this study, sometimes directly and sometimes with a more subtle and less obvious connection, but always with original perspective and imagination, and in so doing contributed to the formulation that has emerged in these pages. They have offered insights, criticism, and commiseration constantly and freely. I have never felt alone in what could otherwise be a labor of solitude.

The staff at the State Historical Society of Missouri and at the Western Historical Manuscripts Collection, both in Columbia, and at the Missouri Historical Society, in St. Louis, were invariably cooperative, resourceful, and gracious. I was fortunate to receive financial assistance from the Woodrow Wilson Foundation and the Ford Foundation, and faculty research grants from the University of Missouri-Columbia and the University of Georgia. Aside from the encouragement that support represented, it also made a substantial difference in the kind of effort I could make at crucial moments. The staff in the University of Wyoming in Casper typed and otherwise made possible the preparation of this manuscript in ways that spared me grief and frustration. The *Journal of American History* has kindly permitted me to include in these pages portions of my essay that appeared in that journal in 1979.

There is another group that deserves special mention. These are the people of Sedalia and Pettis County who shared their community and their lives and their understandings of the ways of history with me and did so asking nothing in return. Those people who sat in a cafe talking with me, who walked down dusty paths showing me places and marks of the past with a nearly sacred meaning to them, who took me into their homes to show me patterns of construction and wear that reveal something of the lives and character of those who came before them, who opened strongboxes hidden deeply away to share important documents of their heritage, who walked with me through pastures and fields reconstructing the lives of people who walked the same ground a century or so before—those people have given more than can ever emerge on the written page. There have been many and I am indebted to them all.

Mr. W. A. McVey is a very special person. Sharing his intimate knowledge of the county, he revealed an enormous generosity and appreciation for the heritage of the county that transcends the approach ordinarily assumed by the local historian and professional as well. Moreover, he knows many a good story. I will long remember the times he and I spent following the back roads of the area, sharing new discoveries and comparing notes on what each of us had already unearthed. Likewise, William Claycomb unhesitatingly shared his knowledge and his time taking me to places I would never have been able to visit or appreciate otherwise. Karen Chamberlin not only extended every courtesy as we traversed the northern portion of the county but responded to a number of pointed questions later. Mr. McVey once told me that it is remarkable what a person can do if only he or she is not so concerned about who gets credit for it. That spirit is abroad in Pettis County as much now as a century ago, and more; those people deserve much credit. And they deserve far better than what I have done. Indeed, in the sense that they deserve better than the world has handed them, they have much in common with earlier generations.

Through it all, my family has borne the load with patience and equanimity. Now I can only offer my daughters Rebecca Rose and Jessica Mariah and my wife Constance my apologies and gratitude, knowing that that is not enough.

PART ONE

Of Dreams and Realities Born

I

Origins and Purposes

There may have been a time when fantasy and reality were not separate, when work and play merged together in a single realm, when the material and spiritual worlds knew no distinction, and when the individual and the community formed a complete unified whole unmarred by organized strife. Whether such a harmony could last would depend not on nature, which after all defined and dominated that harmony, but on the people who would root their lives in those circumstances. Their actions to preserve or destroy that organic harmony would in turn depend on their visions of what life ought to be, either a vision of the past (as it really was, as it was embellished and imagined to have been, or as it was feared to have been) or a vision of the future, itself characterized by either hope or fear. Such has been the universal pattern of history as promoters of change have continually encountered a resistance, sometimes feeble, sometimes articulate and powerful, to their visions of the future. The ultimate origins of that resistance, the dreams of the past that opposed innovation, could lie in a reversion to a primordial subconscious or in real experience. To the extent that actual experiences shaped the resistance to change, and especially to specific patterns of change, so much would the resistance offer a telling commentary on the course of change wherein that harmony became increasingly a dream of the past.

i. Dwellers of the Inland

Rousseau himself could have picked the area that would become Pettis County, Missouri, as one where people could fulfill their potential in harmony with nature and with one another. Located in west central Missouri, away from the rivers, on the road to nowhere, white settlers came later here than to the north along the Missouri River or to the south along the Osage River. It was not especially different from the surrounding country; nor was it naturally foreboding like the Ozarks to the south. But the streams and creeks that drained the area did present obstacles to

3

commerce more than avenues. Those creeks would run year round but they were not deep and they were often overgrown with wild flora in narrow valleys. The Blackwater River, Heath's Creek, Muddy Creek, and Flat Creek all drained the county in a general easterly and northeasterly direction ultimately reaching the Lamine River which itself only skirted the edge of the county before darting into its northeastern corner and back out, then moving in its characteristically winding way on toward the Missouri River. Along those creeks the land tended to be hilly and wooded, sometimes with steep bluffs where the waters had etched courses through the centuries. Occasionally the valley would broaden out into a fertile strip of rich bottomland. Aside from the country around the main streambeds, the county generally consisted of broadly rolling hills and gentle prairies. For all but the intrepid who sought the isolation this out-of-the-way land offered, it would be easier to go around, to stick to the main waterways. It would not even occur to others to bother with the country until after it had been tamed and offered the kinds of opportunities for commerce and profit that only settled areas can promise. So the land remained virgin, subject only to the natural processes of change for centuries on end. Unchanging in its essentials it seemed to hold neither past nor future.

The Indians who came seemed even to prefer other areas. Various groups would come here occasionally to hunt the game that found it so inviting. The deer, elk, buffalo, and even bear continued to populate the area well into the nineteenth century. But several mounds along the streams indicate that Indians did in fact visit the area to hunt, to gather fine clay for pottery, and to fashion points for arrows from the deposits of chert and flint. Still, they established no permanent settlements. The mighty Osages remained mostly to the south, though they considered this part of their natural territory for roaming and hunting. The Missouris and Otos, like the Pawnees, would also come into the area although they more commonly remained farther north in the area of the Missouri River.[1] The purpose of these native American visits into this country, however, suggests that the attitude of these tribes was not so much that of mastering the land as working within a natural framework in a non-acquisitive way. That way would change, in its systematic formulation, only with the intrusion of white people.

The first whites to penetrate the region that would become Pettis County did little to work such a change. These hunters and trappers who began filtering through these woods and prairies in the late eighteenth century were rare and represented a different group from the *coureurs de bois* who traveled the rivers and prairies in organized parties and the entrepreneurial sorts seeking land and fortune. The going was not always gentle, profitable, or linked to any kind of a market. The opportunity sought was not the commercial prospect but the freedom and independence of nature, a freedom lacking in the confines of organized society. In a way, those who came did so not with a vision of the future but as an escape into the past. And like the panther that stalked the deer, the hunter fit in. That solitary life represented not a force for change but another part of an intricate ecology. But change followed nonetheless.[2]

The change came from outside. It came when others representing larger forces than separate individuals roaming this land, in societies characterized by claims to possessions, began to lay claim to this parcel of nature. The earliest claims here, those stemming from the discovery of the New World in the fifteenth century, proved to be irrelevant. Just as the claimants had no idea of what and whom they figured to possess, those native inhabitants had no idea that their land and water—their world—had been staked out by someone else. It would only matter when those outside forces attempted to take possession. At first those efforts came to naught. Probably the first contact in this area came when a Spanish caravan coming east from Santa Fe in 1720 made camp just north of the future county. The reception this encampment received was portentous. Thinking the group of Indians at that place to be Pawnees, an ally, the Spanish offered them the instruments of change and defense: guns and ammunition. The Indians, however, were Missouris, bitter enemies of the Pawnees (partly because of that Spanish alliance) and during the night the Spanish expedition was decimated. Only a priest survived to tell the story of the expedition's misfortune.[3] A decision in a far away country could not automatically be realized without encountering some measure of local resistance. This much would never change.

Nor did matters alter significantly when Spain yielded control of this territory to France. News of the change of hands did not even reach the settled areas along the Mississippi River until two years after it came in 1769. Effective control by the French came even later and to the dwellers of the inland it never really mattered. Not even the transfer of the territory to the United States with the Louisiana Purchase in 1803 registered locally. After that transfer, however, the United States government began to take steps that would ultimately lead to the penetration of a new kind of society into this hinterland. Establishing a trading post at Fort Osage to the west on the Missouri River, the government, using the Chouteau brothers as factors, introduced systematic trading into the area which then meant the opportunity for profits and the ultimate demise of the domain of the Osages themselves. This was the form of change that was noticed and resented and resisted locally. During the War of 1812 this became evident. The various groups of Indians in the area joined the British effort against the United States. But like the British, the Indians lost.[4] After the war settlers began to filter into the area. Unlike those who came before, their intention was to stay. And to build a particular kind of society.

ii. A Birthright Reclaimed

The forces at work reshaping the nation in the early nineteenth century made this land an especially attractive haven. It possessed qualities that were fading in other more established and settled parts of the country. A nation that was changing from a localized, non-commercially oriented form of social organization produced frustrations as well as rewards. To many it came as a loss of power and purpose—a loss of the birthright of freedom. As the forces of a larger society began to intrude into the back areas of North Carolina, Tennessee, and Kentucky—areas where many had gone from more urbanized areas in the first place—the response of some was to flee, to relocate in hopes that the birthright they had known or sought could at last be fulfilled. That dream, in fact, would be sufficient to keep a number of Americans on the move for coming generations. At one level this was the dream of individuals and families for peace and freedom; at another level it was the agrarian dream of Thomas Jefferson writ into the dreams and actions of the American people.

The first permanent settlement in what became Pettis County obliquely reflected these pressures and these aspirations. As early as 1808 and 1809 Hiram Jenkins of Murfreesboro, Tennessee, came to this place. A hunter by instinct and tradition, and an occasional trader by necessity, Jenkins viewed this inland setting in a way that revealed something of his hopes and also his fears. He was looking for a new place to live. When Jenkins' father had moved his family from Pennsylvania into the hills of Tennessee nearly twenty years earlier, settlements were sparse, game was plentiful, and the woods were more open and far reaching. Now that the home in Tennessee was suffering the fate of the earlier home in Pennsylvania, the course seemed obvious. The younger Jenkins stretched his hunting trips farther and farther from Murfreesboro as he looked for game and a new home. He made several hunting expeditions into the country between the Missouri and the Osage and he became particularly attracted to the area along Heath's Creek in the northeastern part of the future county. Indeed, he even hunted with and helped John and Robert Heath ship the salt kettles up the river from St. Louis to their salt works at the mouth of the creek that soon bore their name where it joined the Lamine River. As he hunted along Heath's Creek and Muddy Creek—which Jenkins named after being mired there—he came to a gradual decision. But other factors intruded for a while. In 1811 and 1812, Jenkins returned to Tennessee and the Heaths abandoned their salt operations as the hostility of the Indians increased and the pressures of war mounted. After the war, in the winter of 1816–1817, now at the age of forty-five, Jenkins set out again for this county. He led his own family of seven and two other families who shared his feelings. Thomas Marlin and John Bowles took their families too and

Jenkins wound up leading a group of twenty-six people up the Missouri River, south along the Lamine, and into the country below Heath's Creek. There the families began to build a hamlet that would become theirs when the land books opened in 1823.[5]

The proper explanation of this small migration will remain highly speculative. Dealing with questions of individual and collective motivation and satisfaction, the possible explanations are many. The evidence and the documents sustaining those interpretations, however, are scant. Indeed, given the depth of the problem of individual motivation, such documentation, if available, could only hint at, or even obscure, the answers to the questions. Several points are clear, nonetheless. One is that this was not a part of a literal frontier safety-valve in which the poor of the urban East found refuge on the frontier. These people, their economic well-being aside, came not from the urban society, but a society beginning that process of urbanization, a conceptual point at which the tensions of social change are exceptionally visible and acutely felt—as careful observers like Charles Tilly have noted. Another framework, that of the expectant capitalist moving onto the frontier with visions of profits, enterprise, and fortunes, is even less appropriate. That small group of individuals, organizers, and incorporators, whose number can probably be counted on the fingers of both hands, would be more accurately represented by promoters like William Henry Ashley. And even Ashley chose to pass by this unpromising region and to stick to the rivers that provided the avenues of commerce to harvest the lucrative resources of the Far West. Those who migrated to this area understood as well as Ashley the enormous isolation it held, the distance to markets and to sources of authority, the distance to the main traveled roads. Commercially, this place promised little. What it promised, rather, was by its very isolation the opportunity to reconstruct the kind of life these people valued, that comported with their individual personalities and physical abilities, and that met their own conception of their physical and spiritual needs. What it promised was not a fortune in riches nor even just a new job. What it promised was a birthright to be reclaimed.

In some particular instances the sheer determination and strength evident in the relocation suggests the power, the attraction, and the urgency of that birthright. Consider the Widow Hieronymous. In the early 1820s she and her husband, John Hieronymous, set out from Kentucky on their Missouri trek. Like many others they followed the river and finally settled in 1822 and 1823 in Howard County, already a growing commercial point on the Missouri River. That place itself proved to be growing, crowding, and uncongenial, and in 1825 John Hieronymous died there. The next year the widow moved her twelve children to a place along Muddy Creek with the same strength her husband had shown in leaving Kentucky. And they stayed there.[6]

Over and over again this was the story. From the same middle region—Tennessee, Kentucky, and North Carolina—settlers came to carve a niche for themselves and villages and the rudiments of civil society began to emerge here. Between 1815 and 1825 the scattered households in the eastern portion of the future county began to form a pattern of settlements along the creeks and trails, moving from north to south. Most of these villages were tiny, holding but a handful of settlers, farmers all, in little more than spread-out neighborhoods. But by the early 1830s definite social centers had emerged at Pin Hook, Arator, Postal, Buncombe, and Longwood. Some, like Arator, had a tavern and a blacksmith shop. Pin Hook, however, had more; it stood clearly as the most prominent of the early villages. Nestled in the valley of Muddy Creek, the site of Pin Hook remains one of the most picturesque of the county. By 1832 the site had so developed that it could claim a water mill operated by Thomas Wasson, two stores, one operated by Marmaduke and Sappington out of Arrow Rock, the other by Clifton and Watson Wood, and a smithy.[7] In 1833 the state set aside Pettis County from the other counties that had previously contained this area and it also designated St. Helena, as Pin Hook was by then more commonly known, as the temporary county seat. There, near the mill, on the flood plain, the county court dispensed justice for four years. St. Helena, however, did not grow and in fact this change in political status seemed not to alter the circumstances of life in the new county. It is almost as if the local residents wished this change to have no such impact.

Migration proved to be the greater force shaping the society emerging in this young county. Settlers continued to move into Pettis County in the 1830s and 1840s. By 1850 more than five thousand people lived in the county. These settlers, like their predecessors, traveled in small groups usually from the same area, usually dominated by connections of kin. One of the most visible and revealing of those migrations was that conducted by General David Thomson from Georgetown, Kentucky, in 1833. What makes this instance so signifying is that unlike many who came, Thomson had choices. In 1833 David Thomson, at the age of fifty-eight, had achieved a certain measure of fame, glory, and wealth. A hero of the War of 1812 who competed with his nephew, future Vice President Richard M. Johnson, for the honor of killing Tecumseh, he had reached the rank of brigadier general in the Kentucky militia. One of his sons would become lieutenant governor of Kentucky. Thomson himself served nine years as state senator and another year as sheriff of Scott County. As a prosperous planter he owned around seventy slaves. General David Thomson would not be pushed out of his home country for trivial reasons. Nonetheless, Thomson decided in 1833 to move into Pettis County taking with him most of his sons, daughters and their families. He had lived more than four decades in Georgetown, Kentucky, and the decision to move came as no light event and only after much deliberation. The difficulty increased given that Thomson's best years were now behind him. Yet in a way, that is exactly what motivated him to move in 1833. He wanted to recapture those golden times of the past. When he had first moved to Kentucky the population was sparse. The good land was plentiful and much land had not even been entered. More importantly, Thomson was sensitive and a romantic through and through who valued the demands of a vigorous life rather than a commercial calling, who loved and praised the adventures of war and disdained the commonplace of business transactions. But the years of romance and challenge had faded for him. The central theme of the society around him was its increasing commercial nature, a burgeoning population, and an intensifying competition; an ever more expansive and demanding market and the interdependence implicit in it was replacing the social organization Thomson valued. At the same time, the inflated land values created by active speculation and the availability of cheaper land in a less trafficked area made a move of the dimensions Thomson had in mind a viable possibility. The land in Pettis County seemed ideal. It held little promise for development. Transportation and communication there, like governmental links to the rest of the world, ranged from primitive to nonexistent. Such a location encouraged the development of a pattern of life the Thomson family valued. They would be free, it appeared, from the forces that had undermined that way of life in Kentucky, changes would be resisted, and the past would be reconstructed. In the autumn of 1833 Thomson and around eighty-five others, including his slaves, settled along Muddy Creek in Pettis County, well upstream, to the west of St. Helena. They would be followed by more family later. It took time and sacrifice, but the reconstruction began to emerge. When Thomson built his large home at Elm Spring he planted the grounds with the cedars and locusts that reminded him of his earlier Kentucky. When the county laid out a new county seat in 1837 near the Thomson holdings, the old patriarch received the honor of naming the new town. He named it Georgetown after his home of four decades.[8]

But the larger question remained unsettled by the actions of any individual or family. That question revolved around what kind of society this new country would host. Would these people be sheltered from the forces that had prompted them to move to this land? What would happen when the same forces of change again caught up with them? How long could such a pattern of change be resisted? The future remained clouded. But the people seemed to hint at an answer even in the earliest years, even as they made their separate decisions to come to this land: in order to resist social changes of the magnitude that could transform the nation in the early nineteenth century, an alternative would have not only to be dreamed but to be moved closer to realization by the people themselves.

II

The Pattern of Community

To live in Pettis County in its early years could have been the best and the worst of lives. In its essential harmony with nature, in work, in ecology, in mutual dependence and collective self-reliance it could well have been a satisfying existence. In matters of social authority, race relations, gender roles and limitations, individual liberties and economic opportunities, that same society could also generate enormous frustrations and disappointments. It could simultaneously appear to be even an oppressive society. That such opposite qualities could emerge reveals much about the nature and purpose of the society that took shape in Pettis County. For in this society no single individual achieved his or her exact wants, yet each received something larger. Those frustrations and oppressions were the costs of a larger harmony and community. Obligations rather than rights defined social relations. The aspiring Promethean would be sharply at odds with this society that stressed the well being of the community more than that of any individual, that emphasized individual limits rather than individual ambitions. The ability to suppress the tension between the individual and the community probably stands as the supreme accomplishment of that society and later the inability to suppress that tension its greatest failure.

i. Economy

The limits placed on the early economy were altogether natural, in keeping with the basic demands and forces of nature, although their precise origins in many instances were social. The economy served not to dominate life or to give purpose to activities but to fit into a larger pattern of life. As such, the early settlers of Pettis County developed a system of production and distribution that was not uncommon in its time and that sharply opposed the market mechanism that would later become so pervasive, if not popular, in the area. Whether conceived as an arrangement for the mobilization of individual efforts in society's conquest of nature through competition for limited resources or as a broader framework for

10

the just dispensation of rewards and penalties, the market never knew free reign and was indeed systematically warrened at every point in this early society.

In its most literal sense, Pettis County's isolation made the temptations and burdens of the marketplace peripheral to life. Only by the most deliberate effort could the large market connections be made. The nearest markets were those of Arrow Rock and Boonville on the Missouri River thirty-five or forty miles from Georgetown.[1] To the south, it was even farther to commercial points on the Osage River. The roads failed to reduce the distance when they could be traveled and absolutely eliminated the possibility of commerce at other times. In 1837 Absalom McVey complained to his wife that even the mail was uncertain in those parts for "there are no bridges, and the creeks and rivers in the winter season are impassible every week or two."[2] George Smith's biographer noted the same phenomenon: "What roads existed were atrocious, being mere bridle-paths through forest and prairies, abounding in quagmires and rough with stumps and hillocks . . ."[3] Not surprisingly it was a monumental occasion when, in 1851, George Smith bought his daughters a piano in St. Louis and had it delivered. The piano was shipped from St. Louis to Jefferson City by boat on the Missouri River. There he hired a wagon to carry it the remaining sixty-five miles to Georgetown, an arduous trip that required several days with the wagon's wheels "digging deeply into the mud" when the general's daughter met it. Another sign of the isolation of the area was the lack of stage coaches, leaving either foot traffic or horseback as the prime systems of transportation, a fact that, as Smith's daughter Martha explained, "made travelers very rare."[4] On those rare occasions when the annual trip to market was made, it was made only by a few. In 1847 Absalom McVey figured that it would usually be six or eight farmers—or at the most eighteen to twenty people— who would do the marketing for ten to fifteen farmers for the year.[5] The isolation of the place put severe limits on the commercial nature of the economy. This is understandable considering the circumstances which caused many to relocate to this area; they would usually not be seeking out the market, the institution that had been responsible for displacing them once already.

It was this determination to avoid the market that probably most accounts for the nature of the economy in the area. Few, after all, bothered to make the trip to the markets. Most produced what they needed for their own consumption. Absalom McVey described his brother-in-law and neighbor in Pettis County thus: "Caleb Edmondson would not think of carrying eggs and butter to market tho he could sell them at as great profit . . . he eats all such like."[6] Ten years earlier, in 1837, when McVey first visited the area, he noticed the same phenomenon, though on a more primitive level: "The present settlers appear too lazy for work, so they have and can get as much bacon and cornbread as they can eat, and appear satisfied. [A]lthough the country is as good for vegetables as any place in the temperate zone, a great many of them have neither milk or butter, nothing but bread and meat and call that a fine living."[7] A fine living indeed. Ten years later it was more sumptuous—but still a living dependent only upon nature and free of the constraints of the market. Placed in more positive terms than suggested by a focus on the absence of market relations, the general purpose expressed in the structure of the Pettis County economy was subsistence, or more properly, production for use instead of for profit. That purpose, and the social and natural implications of it, was manifest in every part of production, consumption, property relations, technology, and commercial exchange within the county.

The economy of the area, of course, was agricultural; but it was a particular kind of agriculture. The production and harvest of food and fiber, indeed the capture and processing of energy from the sun, was in a very real sense organic with a deep sense of human dependence on nature, a certain respect for natural forces and elements, and an appreciation for the limits of individual enterprise. People were indeed limited in this area to what either grew naturally or what could be made to grow. One side of that effort would be the intensity of endeavor involved in husbandry. The other side was a certain independence. Just as the opportunities for growth were neither present nor wished by the Pettis Countians, neither were the onerous demands of the market visible. The intensity could be seen in the ingenuity of utilizing nature to its fullest. When buffalo, deer, bear, and turkey were hunted and killed, the game was used as fully and practically as in aboriginal custom. The deer supplied buckskin for clothing and venison for food. Even the bear's tough but pork-like meat furnished the table, the thick fat supplied tallow for candles, and the hide made warm blankets. Beeswax and honey could be harvested and cultivated. The forests provided not only wood for houses but furniture. The streams provided water for energy and fish for food. And this intensity could be seen as well in the conscious and deliberate efforts of each family to provide for its own wants. In a region that lacked trained medical assistance, these families grew the herbs that they would need in such emergencies. Aside from keeping a set of medical scales and some bottles of quinine and packets of calomel, they would keep dried bunches of "boneset, rue, mint, nervine, hoarhound, lobelia, ipecac, and rhubarb." The clothing, not surprisingly, was almost entirely of home manufacture. Buckskin was the order of the day for men. The cotton and wool goods were likewise home made. General Smith's daughter recalled one particular dress her sister received from a neighbor: "a white cotton dress, home-grown, home-spun, and home-woven."[8] Even the raw materials provided for the local crafts and shops came locally:

sawlogs, clay for the potter, coal for the blacksmith's fires, the hides and bark for the tanners, the furs for the hatters, the wool for the carders, and the grain for the mills.[9] From other perspectives the outstanding quality of this society would be its restraints, its material limits. But from within the society the valued and precious characteristics were the freedom, the independence, and the responsibility it generated.

Diversification and a collective self-sufficiency were the watch-words, not just of an organic economy, but of democracy. Wealth, in such a system could not be the standard of success. The wealthy families engaged in precisely the same endeavors as the least "prosperous," and sometimes with less success. Virtually all farmers in the county by 1850 produced enough milk and butter, hogs, potatoes, corn, oats, and honey for their own families. Most had their own slaughter cows for beef and sheep for wool. By that standard it is difficult to say that David Thomson with three hundred of his thousand acres of land in cultivation was substantially better situated than Mary Stotts who had seven of her forty acres in cultivation. Thomson had seven horses, eleven milk cows, six oxen, twenty-five other head of cattle, forty-five sheep, and one hundred-fifty hogs. He grew corn, oats, wool, potatoes, sweet potatoes, butter, hay, and beeswax. Mary Stotts kept two horses, three milk cows, two slaughter cows, ten sheep, seventeen hogs, and farmed corn and potatoes, and produced her own wool, butter, and honey. She valued her own domestically manufactured goods for the year at thirty-five dollars. General Thomson's home made goods were placed at twenty dollars.[10]

This diversification of agriculture, like the self-sufficiency that characterized it, was important for what it meant in ecological terms and for what it meant in social terms. The land was not being mined for profit nor was it exhausted through the single crop farming so characteristic of commercial agriculture. It was being used to provide the needs of people and animals in ways that blended well with nature. The extractive qualities that would later become paramount were yet unseen. Moreover, while these farmers were not routinely concerned with replenishing the resources they used, neither was there great reason for them to be so concerned. They used but little; most of the land in fact remained, in the terminology of the market, "unimproved." In social terms the meaning was never lost: local freedom and independence. In an ironic way this harmony with nature in the system of survival generated a social harmony that prevented the dominance of materialistic ends over social organization and assured the survival of a culture that placed values and standards above material considerations.

In the very conception of work evident in this society and the system of production the harmony with nature was visible and valued. The implements and machinery were not destructive of the soil. They were not capable of it. Indeed, it is a commonplace that the tools of agricultural production were largely the same as the tools and methods of Biblical times. They were slow, hand–held, and permitted only a limited harvest. The basic tool was the hoe. There was simply no other way to plant corn than by using the hoe. Sometimes the unbroken virgin prairie would not yield to the plow; a gash made by a hoe would provide a place for the seed. The cultivation of the corn was left to nature; the hoe would not help. Indeed, this system may well have been more efficient than the barren-land farming practices of later generations that, by weeding the area, remove the grasses that hold in the moisture. But even the plow had its limits. First, very few had a plow; "if a man owned a wooden board plow he was quite an aristocrat."[11] Moreover, there were some parts of the thick sod of the prairie that would not yield to the mouldboard plow. When it was used, though, it was not used with the abandon and reck-lessness that would make it a later folly. When the prairie was broken and turned, the lush prairie grass was left to rot and decay, thereby nourish-ing the soil for the planting of crops.[12] Other horse or oxen-drawn tools might occasionally be found, but few farmers had oxen or mules. And often it would take four or five span of oxen to break the ground. Most relied on the hand–held tools like the hoe. When harvesting, the hand held cradle and scythe remained the basic instrument for cutting oats and wheat. Wheat was seldom produced, but when it was harvested it was cut by hand and trampled out by horses, resulting usually in a "loss" of about a third of the harvest.[13] Of course, it was not lost, it went back into the ground. There were no cultivators, nor reapers, nor double shovel plows. Farming had to be slow. It had to be deliberate. And it had to be careful. At its fastest it would be at the pace of the oxen, a pace that was "majestically slow."[14]

The pace of nature mandated the pace of work and of life. Whether perceived in a longer framework, annually, or in its immediate form, daily, the apprehension of time was itself organic and bound the society that much closer to nature. The seasonal basis of the work is obvious; the farmers could not have, even if they had wished, altered the time framework of their work any more than the cycles of life and death, of hustle and rest. Planting, cultivating, harvesting, and preparing the ground for the winter were stages of the year as unchangeable as the seasons themselves. Even the winter required certain activities. The farmer turned from husbandry to cabinet making, to tool making, to equipment repair, to hunting, to butchering, to trapping. The craftsmen too were especially busy in the winter as the demand for their work in-creased and as their own farming activities also subsided [15] But it was more than the seasons which set the pace of life. Even the pattern of weather altered and shaped the routines of the community. A dry spell would mean that the water mills would not turn. A wet spell would mean that it might be impossible to cross the steam to the mill on the other

side. A prolonged drought or flooding steams could hold the community in peril, at least in some material concerns. In 1841 David Thomson began to build a bridge for the county near his mill. The work progressed unevenly, with stops in sawing logs at the mill caused by low water causing delays in construction. By the fall of 1842 the principal timbers were in place, but the project was not completed and work had been halted for some time. By May 1843 the work was still incomplete, but the water had risen in April. By July 1843, the bridge was finished. For two years work had been stopped because of low water. But when it was finished, a grand bridge it was. The quality of the work was superlative; the bridge commissioner declared it "certainly the best I have seen in the state and I think should be a standard by which other bridges . . . should be required to come up to. . . ."[16] The frailty and constant dependence on nature made Pettis County a poor place to be for the impatient. It may have been a good place to be for those who accepted their limits.

This natural perception of time pervaded every aspect of life. The basis of it was the measure of time by the standard of work, not the measure of work by time. The job could not be hurried; nor could it be started or stopped anywhere but at the beginning and the end. To do otherwise was unthinkable. Thus the day made sense as a comprehensible unit, marked at one end by the milking of the cow and the beginning of daily chores and at the other end by the milking of the cow again and the cleaning of tools. Thus too was the year a comprehensible unit, one that conformed socially to the patterns of work and production. Not surprisingly, debts would be settled annually, or seasonally, not monthly.[17] That only made sense. And the day was not marked off so rigidly into hours, but into periods separated by meals and the approximate location of the sun. A community meeting would not begin at a specific hour; instead, for example, a church service would begin "at the early lighting of a candle."[18] The clock of nature may possibly be superior to that of organized society; at any rate it was more influential in the determination of patterns of living and working.

Nor was there a sharp distinction between work and recreation. Many individual activities were thus blurred. The sense of accomplishment or fulfillment appears to be the discriminator. For example, hunting would become an onerous task only when it became desperate, and even then as future generations would also attest, the despair and cold and frustration could quickly be erased by success. But in the 1830s and 1840s that frustration was not common: according to one old settler, wild game was abundant: "they were as plentiful as domestic stock in our pastures, and could be killed just as easy."[19] The settler's memory may have been embellished with age. Had it been an onerous chore, however, that part would no doubt have been emphasized. Likewise in the building of furniture: the pride and sense of accomplishment that went into the task was sufficient to cause even people not otherwise noted for their commitment to manual labor to work with the hickory and black walnut to fashion chairs, tables, chests, and bedsteads.[20] In a host of other individual or family tasks—quilt making, berry gathering, crafts—work and play merged into an activity that could not be neatly pigeonholed.

Some tasks, of course, demanded hard, brutal work. To build a house or barn could be a back-breaking, muscle straining, and blistering chore. To wash, card, and pick wool was dirty, smelly, and altogether distasteful. To shuck corn chafed bare hands and was boring. The answer to the challenge presented by each of these and more was to turn them into cooperative celebrations. The shucking bee, the barn-raising, the apple parings, and the wool processing became gala occasions that would bring neighbors from eight to ten miles distant prepared not just for a cooperative work effort but a community event. Children and adults alike would join in the tasks. "After the work was done a great feast would follow, and often a long-necked gourd filled with apple or peach brandy would be produced and partaken of, while stories of hair breadth escapes by flood and field would be narrated by each in turn."[21] Not only were work and play effectively united, but society and nature worked together into this collectively self-sufficient, cooperative relationship.

That organic relationship was not restricted to the farming population of Pettis County. Those craftsmen in Georgetown were equally bound to nature and society. Few were exclusively craftsmen. They also farmed. When Absalom McVey visited the area in 1837 he was contemplating moving to the county. He was a skilled carpenter and joiner and indeed contracted to do substantial work on the courthouse while there. But even though he was an experienced and valued carpenter and was training his sons in the same skills, he set up his farm. This was a common arrangement, and the seasonal nature of the work made both possible.[22] The supply of raw materials used by the craftsmen came locally, and thus depended upon the same system of production attuned to the flux of nature. And the need adjusted according to the time of year also, except for the carpenter who made the coffins. His task was an all night task that added to, not took the place of, his regular duties.[23]

The craftsmen were able to maintain a particular reverence and respect based upon their ancient traditions and skills. Their skills were prized possessions. They knew the right way of production and in the eyes of the community nothing else would suffice. In 1835, as plans were made for the construction of the court house in Georgetown, George R. Smith proposed a brick construction. That proposal, however, according to Smith's daughter, "met with great opposition, for no brick had even been made in that portion of the country, and it was thought there was no one there who understood the art."[24] An intricate art it was. The ancient, slow, brick-on-brick method of construction symbolized much of the nature of work in the community. The size and weight of the brick that remained essentially unchanged through the centuries, was scaled to human dimensions. The rhythm of work developed by the master mason as he established his balance and picked up a brick with one hand and a trowel of mortar with the other was a perfectly natural rhythm. The knowing eye and touch of the mason was necessary to determine not just the level and plumb of the course of bricks, but the proper saturation of the bricks with water to create just the right bond with the mortar and the actual content of the brick itself. The result was, of course, something that held the respect of the community. It was also something built to last. The brick courthouse withered with the town of Georgetown. Its materials lived on in another building. But the brick house of David Thomson, built in 1840 still stands, a testament not just to a way of work, but a way of life.[25]

The learning of the skill was in itself a reflection of basic assumptions of this society. The process by which the skills were learned, like the skills themselves, was ancient, passed down from generation to generation. The apprenticeship system was still common in Pettis County in the 1830s and 1840s. It seemed especially appropriate in those instances in which the father was unable to pass the craft on to his sons. Thus John Miller in 1839 applied to the Pettis County Court and secured articles of indenture to bind out his ward, Nancy Gabriel, as an apprentice to John G. Newbill. In 1842 when Miller's other ward, Aaron Gabriel, reached the age of apprenticeship he too was bound out, to Morton Thomson and Richard Hurt, to learn the art of wool carding. Lelitha Cooper bound out her son William to George M. Pemberton at the age of eleven to learn the art of husbandry until age twenty-one. But more was involved in the apprenticeship than the learning of a skill. The master who agreed to take on an apprentice also agreed to provide for the youth and to supply him or her other necessary education. And the county court enforced these obligations and annulled the indenture articles when the skill had been learned or the need fulfilled.[26] The master's obligations to his apprentice were, then, not just to teach a skill of production but to teach a way of living. In this sense the classic description of that obligation, *in loco parentis*, suggests the subordinate level of economics to other parts of life and goals in the county.

Like the system of production, the system of exchange and distribution also placed limits on the role of the economy in society. The basis of exchange was simple: the exchange of one commodity for another. The point of this was equally simple, the acquisition of a different commodity. It was not a speculative venture in which money was invested in a particular commodity for the purpose of securing more money. To that extent, it was not a growth or profit oriented system of exchange. It would have been, for instance, unthinkable to offer to pay one's neighbors who had helped at a barn raising or corn shucking. They knew that they would be expected to return the favor the next time they needed help. Those who possessed specific skills, like the carpenters, and wool carders similarly would not charge for their services; they would instead swap work.[27] On one level, this could be called a system of barter, even when money was used to facilitate the exchange of commodities. On another, it could be considered a system based upon a labor theory of value: a labor exchange.

One characteristic of the society and economy encouraged this pattern of exchange. There was very little money in circulation. In 1837, C. M. Cravins wrote M. M. Marmaduke that he could not pay his note to the latter since he had for two years been hard put for money but that he would send along "the next money that comes to hand."[28] As late as 1848 the main currency was "such articles and commodities as were used in every day life." It was not uncommon for a farmer to have, as one did, between sixty cents and a dollar and a half as working capital for a year. With a self sufficient farm and a self sufficient community little more was needed.[29] The claims against estates being settled were frequently remarkably low. When Samuel Marshall died he left debts amounting to $14.07. The largest debt was $8.98. The others were $2.77 and a half, $2.18, and $.12 and a half.[30] William Boeker, who had served an apprenticeship for three years as a wagon maker, in the 1840s ran a farm of more than a hundred acres. On one occasion as he and his wife were despairing of being unable to attend church meeting since they would not be able to help pay the expenses of the minister, a neighbor needed two bushels of seed potatoes and was willing to pay him fifty cents for the load, "as there was no market in this part of the country," with which Boeker was able to pay the preacher and buy coffee too.[31] What is so telling about this experience is partly the small sum involved in the transaction and how that reflects the money shortage in the area. Also, though, the transaction stands out as an exception. In other societies the fifty cent transaction is usually not so significant as to be recorded and passed on to generations. This one was.

This system was also distinguished by another phenomenon. With cash so unavailable debts were common. Few, save the poorest and most isolated farmers, were free from debts. Quite commonly the settlement of estates showed this as page after page of court records would list the debts of the deceased. In life these debts could be paid back by swapping work or crops. In death it often meant a parceling out of the estate to settle accounts. There was no central source of funds to control indebtedness. It was too widespread and decentralized. Put another way, everybody was into everybody else for something. Just as a person would owe many people, so too would many people in turn owe that person. It was circular; it was self-contained; and it relied on a lot of good faith.

It also created a set of bonds, or, perhaps more accurately, reflected a more fundamental set of bonds of community. This was truly a group of people beholden to one another in a variety of ways.

In reflecting on the organization of the system of economy in Pettis County in the 1830s and 1840s, perhaps its most striking feature is the total scheme of things and its essential unity. Not dependent upon the outside for either markets or supplies that economy did comprise a virtual whole. And as an organized entity the economy did not constitute ways to wealth or opportunities for individual ambition defined in acquisitive and material terms. Instead the economy operated within stark limits that restricted such ambition and emphasized an ecological and social harmony. Production for use and the expenditure of effort according to need provided not just redeeming qualities for this economy—they gave it a purpose and a reason for existence. Thus did economy fit into the pattern of community. Like that community the economy demanded a respectful observance of the limits of nature and the limits of the human condition.

ii. Polity

The structure of authority that dominated life in Pettis County in the 1830s and 1840s could almost wholly be defined in a passive tone. Its purpose, after all, was not to alter or reform relationships between people or between people and property, but to crystallize or facilitate the relationships that already existed and in fact to prevent any great change. While it is true, as a later generation of people in this county would discover, that any time authority acts it both helps and hurts, it generates both victims and beneficiaries, that perception had not arrived in the early years of the county and it had not arrived for good reason: during the 1830s and 1840s the overweening emphasis on the protection of the community both restrained individual actions that would impact negatively on others and reminded individuals of the necessity of sacrifice for the common well being. And somebody would indeed have to sacrifice given the fact that different parts of society often stood opposed to each other in the determination of the common good. The system of authority held, therefore, a dual capability; it was able at once to promote the public welfare in way that often appears paternalistic and also to reflect, not a consensus, but an equilibrium between mutually suspicious—if not openly antagonistic—elements of society. In this way the system of power operated at two different levels to two different purposes. The system of politics, narrowly conceived, operated in such a way as to promote community and harmony. The system of social relationships from which those politics derived, however, the system of power relations in the broader conception of politics, maintained a delicate balance between rulers and ruled that kept both the prisoners of each other. The will of the people proved to be a powerful notion.

The character of the political institutions themselves sheds light on their purpose. The critical agency in the decentralized system of government was that of the county court and the responsibilities of that body were solemn and consequential. They were, however, administrative rather than jurisprudential responsibilities and they certainly did not revolve around an adversary system in the determination of public decisions. Even so, the court's general object proved to be the dispensation of justice and equity and even amity. Thus the court would issue licenses to merchants, a practice bequeathed from mercantilistic regulations and maintained for its utility in protecting the public from an unrestrained system of commerce. It would also administer county property, appoint assessors and collectors, control school lands, lay out townships for school and election districts and offer a reward for killing wolves.[32] It also held jurisdiction in matters of probate and charity, responsibilities that occupied much of the energy and attention of the early court and that reflect its character and purpose. The records of the early court fail to reveal a single case of probate hearings and resolution involving the claims of disgruntled heirs. Instead, the large number of probate cases resolved by the court simply passed estates from one generation to the other and in the process satisfied creditors, usually neighbors and usually with small debts of long standing. This was the time for the final settling of accounts and perhaps the only time that could be counted on with any certainty. Charity too loomed large in the purview of the court with the frequent necessity of determining the fate of orphans and other minors and of those they called insane. Again the court assumed an attitude more closely linked to chancery proceedings than adversary procedures as it would literally act "in the interest of" the particular ward of the public.[33] In matters of probate, in matters of charity, the court expressed an attitude of frank paternalism and in so doing attempted to fulfill its obligation to the public.

Even in the complex and potentially contentious realm of road building, a responsibility that could hold great opportunity for competition and strife, the purpose and design seems to have been not that of promoting commerce but that of promoting amity. To say that the roads did not move in a direct fashion would be to understate and misapprehend the pattern of the road network in the area. The roads that the county built sometimes followed old Indian trails. They often connected points of natural significance—a ford across a creek, a spring, or a clearing for a campsite—with one another or they might connect a mill with surrounding farms. But the pre-eminent pattern demonstrates an effort to connect farms with one another. The result was an often confusing array of roads and trails that wound around and circled back and then moved on in a

seemingly unpredictable direction. W. A. McVey, the foremost authority
on the early years of Pettis County and especially on its roads, once commented that "You wonder how those early travelers knew where they
were and where the road was going." He quickly adds that it is no wonder really. The roads suited them.[34]

The court that administered these responsibilities formed part of a
larger system of local government that served as the core of the explicitly
political relationships. In addition, the affairs of the county were performed by county surveyors, coroners, and assessors. Aside from the obligation to meet the needs of the public each of these offices carried,
the common bond uniting them emerged from their popular accountability in the electoral process. Yet the meaning of that process is not immediately apparent. Thus too is the nature of the system of authority
clouded.

One quality and one quality only is clear about the elections conducted in Pettis County in the 1830s and 1840s: they were celebrations.
In these celebrations substantial numbers of people would gather, join the
festivities, express their preferences for public office, and watch others
do the same. In most accounts of those elections the celebration process
occupies much more attention than the specific elections or their out-
comes. To some, as to the daughter of General George Smith, the elections were "those afflictions that had to come to all towns, like whooping
cough and measles to children: and were primarily noted for the intoxi-
cation they produced."[35] Mentor Thomson, who had a much more charitable view of the practice, noted that "men went to the polls to stay all
day, eat ginger bread, drink hard cider, etc., and have a jolly time."[36]
Indeed, when one examines the election paintings by George Caleb
Bingham, who frequented these parts, the first impression is not just of
celebration and conviviality but of downright drunkenness.[37] Obviously
the significance attached to this element is itself subject to dispute.
While Mentor Thomson seemed to regard all this as benign, Smith and
his daughters viewed the entire elective process with some disdain because of its inherent corruption by unprincipled and unlettered men. So
too did Bingham's paintings find favor with Smith, and especially the
close mutual friend of Smith and Bingham, James Rollins in Columbia.
Whigs all, leaders all, too often they found the elections controlled by the
opposition. Smith continually failed of election to the state legislature
with but one exception before the Civil War. Bingham, apparently the
narrow victor in adjoining Saline County in his 1846 effort to secure a
seat in the state legislature, had his election invalidated by the state legislature when his opponent contested the results of the poll. But the elit-
ism that caused some to cherish Bingham's portrayal of the election
caused others to rebuke it. One critic argued that while such an election
may be characteristic in remote parts of the country, one painting

"defamed one of the most valuable of our political institutions" by not depicting the soberness and refinement and purity that ought to obtain in the electoral process.[38] In other words, that critic suggested the painting was too true. The celebration, like it or not, proved central to the election experience.

The very crudity and unrefined nature of the electoral process, however, raises questions about the actual function of the electoral process as a device for enforcing the popular will on leaders and policy or as a device for maintaining a planter hegemony through the enticements and allurements of entertainment and drink. In the quest for the forces that dominated the local campaigns and elections, the substantive issues never surface, in part because the focus on the style and practice tends to obliterate the issues and content, and in part because the issues may never have been there. Again, Bingham's art provides insight. In both the *County Election* and *Stump Speaking* Bingham endeavored to show his mid-Missouri neighbors subject to all kinds of persuasion besides the force of logic and argument on an issue. The drink, the obsequious courtesies, the physical transportation to the poll, and the fatigue evident in the election scene he composed all bespoke a popular immunity to issues and logic. Even the *Stump Speaking*, depicting a debate, proved empty of substance, as in Bingham's words, "a wiry politician, grown gray in the pursuit of office and the service of party" spoke before "a shrewd clear headed opponent, who is busy taking notes, and who will, when his turn comes, make sophisms fly like cobwebs before the housekeeper's broom."[39] Not that Bingham was critical of such a scene, since he had participated himself in it recently, but his casual assumptions that sophistry and allegiance to party dominated the political scene and quest for office suggest again that cleverness, personal traits and loyalty proved far more powerful than issues in the electoral process. What Bingham's work suggests and what no other evidence contradicts is that personalities were far more important than issues in the elections.

The actual function of the election process is further clouded by the fact that it seldom mattered, in significant ways, who won the elections. Court policy and the policies of the county officers never changed in the 1830s and 1840s as a result of the elections. Some officers maintained a hold on their positions with a long duration. Mentor Thomson managed to retain his office as County Surveyor from 1835 to 1866 standing for re-election every two years. William R. Kemp won election as sheriff three times and James Kemp to the same office twice between 1833 and 1852.[40] It is a distinct possibility that these elections were not fought on issues, and in fact were not even hotly contested. Yet the elections came and went. The first Monday of August continued to generate excitement and participation and to provide an event of unquestioned significance locally.

That significance, though, likely had little to do with the determination of the fate of the county in an explicitly political context. The significance derived more from the nature of participation and the kinds of people gathered for the occasion. The nature of the event did in fact revolve around the celebration it inspired. Yet the festivities provided less opportunity for the swaying of votes, in an area where access to polls at designated places in the townships proved difficult and required only the most deliberate of purposes to justify the trip, than they did opportunity for celebration after the civic duty was performed. The socialization with neighbors no doubt provided a basis for renewing larger community relationships. One of those relationships, perhaps the most important, found expression in the balloting itself. The vote cast by voice before and in the midst of one's neighbors, indeed usually at a neighbor's house, was subject to far more pressure than alcohol could bring to bear. Or it could be that the alcohol relieved some of that pressure. But the pressure of neighbor and fellow citizen witnesses was undeniable. Its effects could be twofold. It could possibly influence the choice of some in the election one way or the other. Or, more likely, it could have a greater impact simply by binding not just partisans together, but members of the larger community as well, by virtue of the profound experience involved in stepping forward to announce a decision, knowing that the support or condemnation of neighbors would be forthcoming. This bond-generating function becomes all the more significant in light of the varieties of people and stations united under the aegis of universal white manhood suffrage. On that day the red-shirted, rough-cut citizen balloting in Bingham's depiction became the equal of the dandy supplicating votes behind him. On that day the squire with polished carriage and finery would be reduced to the equal of his least propertied neighbor. What was involved was a vast ritual that reminded all of the elements of democracy, and their own power and obligations as individuals and citizens within that society of sovereigns. When they cast that vote they confirmed to themselves and to their neighbors that a final check remained on government officials. And while the people gained from their participation feelings of unity and power, the leaders themselves derived a sense of legitimacy for their own efforts. The election was both more and less than the expression of the will of the people. It was a ritual that bound leaders and followers the more tightly together and that brought citizens and sovereigns together. Indeed, it brought purpose and power together.

The extent to which this ritual served as a charade to propagate a vibrant myth and artificial sense of importance remote from the reality of power is difficult to gauge. So long as the ritual generated satisfaction, it bolstered the system of power relations as they were. Indeed, given the breadth of participation, it would not be unusual for the driving force making the event attractive to lie in an equally broad sense of powerlessness.

But there remain too many discordant elements for such a complete picture of cultural hegemony. Both the caricature of the dandy begging a vote (for what he must surely believe his due) and the contrast in styles evident in the election suggest limits to the hegemony.

In fact, the closer one examines the election scene the more the conclusion emerges that there were two groups represented there: the nabobs and the people they obviously considered their inferiors. And, moreover, it is at this point that the emotional charge, the apprehensions of the elite, the supplications, the wheedling, the cajoling, and, indeed, the *begging* start to make sense. A ritual it was; a harmless, innocuous ritual it was not. The elections masked a contest of fundamental importance, not between individuals or even on issues but between different parts of society. In this contest there were two winners: those who were elected to office and those who exacted a price from those to be elected.

In a slave society the obvious measure of status is the number of slaves owned by an individual. And by any other measure as well, the slave-owning portion of the population of Pettis County formed an elite. The public officials themselves came from this elite as eleven of the seventeen county court judges and sheriffs who served before the decade of the 1850s owned slaves. Usually they owned two or three, a few held eight slaves, one a dozen, and another twenty.[41] If there were a dividing line between the gentry and the masses it could well have been at the line of slave-owning or not. With that line it would appear that the gentry had all they wanted: positions, power, and respect.

Yet there is another group of public servants that needs to be considered as well, those who did not hold a permanent public office, those whose tenure was short but critical, those who, in fact, emerged only at election time. These were the judges of the elections, those officials to whom each franchise was sworn and to whom each vote was spoken and by whom each vote was tallied. Up to 1844 there were only five municipal voting precincts in the county. In the election of 1838, for which the names of the judges are preserved, the composition of the panel of judges can be explored. In Elk Fork township two of the three judges of the election, in fact, owned slaves. In Blackwater township one judge owned two slaves while the other two owned none. In each of the other three townships not a single election judge owned slaves.[42] Perhaps only in Elk Fork township did the nabob feel comfortable in waging his effort for election at the poll. The places where the elections were held could have intensified the discomfort. In Elk Fork township where the election was held at the house of Mason Pemberton, the sheriff, who owned a dozen slaves, it was one thing. It may have been less hospitable a place in Blackwater where the poll was held at the house of a man who owned a single slave. But it was certainly something different, a different world even, in each of the other townships where the election was held at the home of a non-slave-owner or on neutral ground—the mill or the court-house. Perhaps the candidates were in foreign territory, being refereed by foreign judges, being voted upon by foreign constituents—indeed, having to cast their own votes before that crowd and to those judges. Perhaps, just perhaps, Bingham was right—right, not in his contempt for the people, but right in his fear that the people did not automatically oblige their betters in the system of power. This would certainly explain his jaundiced view of the electoral process. No wonder the supplication. No wonder the drink and hospitality. No wonder the begging. The elite won the offices but to do so the candidates and officials had to submit to periodic review and approval, to what people like Bingham and Smith considered the humiliating judgment of their inferiors. The people de-manded a price for their support of the system. The price was the loss of self-image of omnipotence and the humbling of the high and the mighty. This was not the hegemony of the planter class; it was an equilibrium between the gentry and the people.

This is not to deny the genuine paternalistic impulses that some-times existed. They were present. The wellsprings of such paternalism lay deep in tradition and in public and private relationships. Those rela-tions can be clearly seen in the case of the grand patriarch of Pettis County, General David Thomson, and his family. Exactly what consti-tuted his family was itself defined in paternalistic terms as, according to one member of a later generation of his family, "the term family to him included all who looked to him for care and maintenance." Once Thom-son recorded in his diary that the measles had hit his family in 1829: "About twenty of our family had it, whites and blacks."[43] His own family proper was large enough with five sons and five daughters. True to form, most of them moved with him to Pettis County. Sons Milton and Mentor settled adjacent to his property with their own families. His daughter Mildred settled with her husband, Lewis Redd Major, almost within sight of the Thomson home. His daughter Melita settled with her hus-band George Smith and their daughters also next to the Thomson place. His daughters Marion and Melcena were young enough that they were still in the household at Elm Spring as were Morton and Monroe. Appar-ently only the oldest son, Manlius, a college president and later lieuten-ant governor of Kentucky stayed in that original settlement. This was not only a large, even extended, family but a tightly knit one and one that demonstrated unmistakable respect for the patriarch. Thomson's authority in the family went unquestioned. That two sons-in-law would take their families with him suggests the power of the deference.[44] And when they constructed a society in Pettis County those relations would persist.

From the moment of their first arrival, not to mention their trip it-self, this paternalistic family relationship became evident. They all stayed at first in cabins closely arranged on the elder Thomson's land, crude and crowded though they were. But the next year David Thomson built better, larger structures, though not elaborate, in a row connected together by a roofed, open passageway, and in these all the families took up residence for several years. All the while, as one of Thomson's grand-daughters recalled, the patriarch took great pains to tend to the needs of his large family. His store of household supplies was open to them. His slave weaver made rugs for them. His geese provided the initial flock for others. When George Smith took his family on to his own land, it was still Thomson's slaves who built their cabin there. And when the cabin burned, taking with it all the Smith family's possessions, again the family returned to Thomson's home, where, in fact one of Smith's daughters had been staying anyway.[45] When Milton had to leave his family for a trip west, it would be Melcena who would tend to the baby while his wife depended on her help in others ways as well and on the help of the other relatives.[46] For nearly two decades Thomson's home (after 1840 his elegant Elm Spring house), served as the physical and moral center of the life of the family—the location of shelter, amusements, and the rites of passage. Education came in a cabin on his land half way between his home and that of his oldest daughter. Milton Thomson was the teacher.

Throughout one sees evidence of Thomson's paternalism based in love and duty. Toward his wife and children the manifestations of the paternalism found expression not only in material forms but in more spir-itual ways as well. The crusty old general would write love poems to his wife and he would alter songs of the day to sing to his daughters in praise of them. He found one especially meaningful verse he preserved that revealed much of his passion:

> In vain surly Pluto declared he was cheated,
>   For justice divine could not compass its ends;
> The scheme of man's fall he maintained was defeated,
>   For earth becomes Heaven with wife, children and friends.
>
> The soldiers whose deeds shine immortal in story,
>   Whom duty to far distant latitude sends;
> With transport would barter whole ages of glory,
>   For one happy hour with wife, children and friends.[47]

Inspired by love, Thomson's paternalism must have been powerful. What that meant for him was that final authority rested with him, and so did final responsibility.

That paternalism could well have been stifling for others. Certainly it was for the women. With others assuming the right and the power to make decisions for women, the female role knew serious limits. Martha Smith recalled—notably not of her own experience but of that of others around her—that women "were too modest to sing or read in public. . . . Reticence, modesty, and virtue formed the triple crown of a true and noble woman. . . . They were encouraged to be delicate and absurdly modest."[48] The county history placed the responsibility for this on the isolation of the families, but the effect seems to have been the same: "The girls of a few families were bashful and timid and in their homes perfect prudes. The hoiden was unknown. However, the better classes brought up their children with great vigilance, training them in home etiquette, domestic economy, and love for religion."[49] But that paternalism knew bounds in this regard. Martha Smith was, after all, a woman nurtured in this system of relations and who came to condemn such subservience. The elder Thomson established a school for his children and in fact sent his youngest daughters to Boonville to the girls' school there. He also inculcated vigorous habits of work and industry in his daughters and granddaughters. To do their work instead of depending on slaves came to be not just a habit but almost a fetish by the time the practice reached Thomson's granddaughters. This independence bordering on the work ethic could later prove to be a factor undermining the whole set of paternalistic structures and values.

The spill-over effect of this paternalism beyond the immediate family took a number of forms and knew the same sources. But in this more public aspect the motivation of duty loomed larger than familial love. Thomson's heroes were military heroes because sacrifice characterized the military experience and that virtue of selflessness was the noblest. Sacrifice and duty—these ideals generated and defined a person's relationship to society in Thomson's view. "I am sensible of my duty to society," Thomson once wrote in response to an inquiry about public education, "especially in this particular, as it accords the warmest feelings of my heart."[50] And indeed, he did advocate public education. Though able to see that all his sons received college education, his daughters had formal schooling, and tutors were provided for his own, he also saw that the children of his neighbors as well as direct kin went to the same school as his own. When a relative received a position as county surveyor, he wrote instructions by way of his son that he should pay "attention to the duties devolving on him, [and that] one thing, it will be necessary for him to be accommodating to all who may require his official services."[51]

This sensitivity to public and private obligations brought Thomson to sharply rebuke an old friend who had become a Shaker and left his family to join their society. This man had forsaken everything, Thomson said, and even to remember the old times "must give you pain because they have passed away not to return." His friend had been, he told him, "the kind and obliging husband, the affectionate father, the friendly neighbor and the worthy citizen." Now, though, in place of being a kind and obliging husband, you have without cause dissolved the sacred ties of matrimony, falsified your vow made on the altar in the face of your country and in the presence of God. You have discarded the wife of your bosom, the mother of your children, dissolving the tie of blood and kindred, and the decree of heaven which gave woman to man as a helpmate, you have set at naught. In place of being an affectionate father, the tender offspring is abandoned, or what is worse, driven by a parental authority beyond the confines of reason and prosperity into a state of mental slavery and brutal drudgery totally subversive of human character. And in place of being a friendly neighbor, you have withdrawn yourself and your means beyond the reach of neighborly friendship, and sunk below the cheering horizon of sociability and that happiness which is the sure reward of deeds of charity.[52]

By rejecting the obligations that Thomson so valued in favor of the free, narcissistic associations of his new communal life, his old friend, Thomson figured, was degraded, polluted, and worthless. Naturally, Thomson's paternalistic duty and deep concern required him candidly to inform his friend of these shortcomings.

The extent to which those paternalistic values and assumptions characterized the larger realm of social relations emerges most conspicuously in the institution of slavery. Again those relationships stemmed from assumptions about the extension of family relationships and the notion of duty. Even George Smith around 1840 figured the higher reward people could aspire to would be the "welcome plaudits of 'Well done, thou good and faithful servant.' "[53] For others this point of reference could be taken casually perhaps, but for Smith it is far more revealing. In another decade and a half, Smith would find servitude of any kind humiliating and contrary to human nature. But in the 1840s even Smith believed servitude to be the pivotal and unifying force of the community. And as David Thomson glorified sacrifice in his own life and urged it on others, so too did the same logic compel sacrifice from a whole race of people. That Thomson would refer to his slaves as members of his family suggests an explicit paternalism; that he would act in such a way gives the paternalism depth. When preparing to leave Kentucky for Pettis County, the leader of the clan arranged to leave or take entire families of slaves. That they had intermarried with blacks on neighboring plantations meant, as his granddaughter recalled, buying where he could and selling where he had to, a difficult and complex task. This involved between thirty and forty of his more than seventy slaves. Thus flowed the obligations of the slaves to their master; thus flowed the obligations of the master to his slaves. It should come as no surprised that George Smith's daughter recalled "the bonds that bound us in twofold slavery," the powerful obligations of each race to the other.[54]

That paternalism naturally dominated the prevalent picture of slavery in Pettis County. Admitting that it was a superficial view, and that "our Eden was nursing the serpent slavery," Martha Elizabeth Smith nonetheless painted this picture of the institution:

> A picture of greater beauty lies nowhere in my childhood memory than the one at my grandfather's home. The older negroes had their comfortable houses, where each family would sit by their own great sparkling log-fires. The younger negroes were engaged, in the day-time, at the work of their master, while the children out in the sunshine laughed, played, and frolicked their time away. Like the lilies of the field, they were all without thought for food or raiment; indeed, of raiment they often had but little! They sang their plantation songs, grew hilarious over their corn shuckings, and did the bidding of their gracious master. Their doctor's bills were paid; their clothing bought, or woven by themselves in their cabins, and made by their mistress; their sick nursed; and their dead laid away—all without any thought or care from themselves as to expense.[55]

In this picture Martha Smith would later argue that it was this benevolent paternalism that was wrong for denying the slaves individual responsibility.

Even so, serious limits remain because of what is neglected and what is concealed. The paternalistic picture makes no mention, after all, of the slave camp William H. Powell set up to deal locally in slaves. Or that the Thomsons themselves would sell slaves.[56] There is no mention of the coercions of slavery either, to which other kinds of inculcations and imprecations were but alternatives. As Martha Elizabeth Smith herself wrote to her family, while on a trip in 1855, "How much I would give if they would only be good, and the sound of the lash might never again be heard on our place." The alternative to the lash: be "smart" and obey ("Tell them not to try to hide anything from mistress and master for God can see them all the time and he will punish them for every sin.") or be sold: ". . . tell Harriet if she will make Lilly smart, I will always keep them both and treat them kindly."[57] The specter of the market would always hang over the lives of slaves, protected only by a paternalism that knew real bounds. Even in the most benevolent of households, the slaves could be property to be auctioned in the process of estate settlement. While the court continually took pains to specify that families should not, if possible, be disrupted in the sale, only the larger circumstance of the estate would determine for sure their fates.

Yet another shortcoming of such a picture revolves around the thoughtlessness of the slaves. Given their mandated chores of producing food and fiber, the notion that they went without thought for the expense of food and raiment seems odd. Give the skills involved it seems preposterous. And considering the accomplished artisanry represented among some of Thomson's own slaves—a carpenter, a stone-mason, a millwright, a weaver, a spinner, and cooks—the picture of thoughtlessness tumbles further.

But aside from the particular skills involved in their work, the attitudes and values of the slaves can be seen in other ways, ways that do not necessarily mirror the preconceptions and images cast upon them by their masters. In some regards the culture of blacks in Pettis County closely paralleled that of whites. Where Martha Smith would note that blacks "grew hilarious in their corn shuckings," a similar statement could be made about whites who shucked their corn. This communal work experience that brought people together not only formed the basis of a grand party in which recreation and work merged, where friendly competition and pride and singing combined, but it also bespoke a traditional work culture characterized by natural rhythms, spontaneity, and alternating periods of intense work and play. In that work culture blacks and whites found a common bond, a bond that emphasized nature and tradition.

So too did a parallel pattern run in family structure. While later generations would deny the existence of the black family in slavery, or even among blacks in any condition, there is every reason to believe that slaves held on to their family relationships with every bit the same tenacity as whites. Even a cynical reading of David Thomson's motivation in avoiding the disruption of families when he moved his family to Missouri would come to this conclusion by suggesting that he did so to prevent dissension and even to avoid the threat of runaways seeking to reunite families after the move. That was in 1833. As late as 1859, more than a quarter century later, a slave named David was sold from his parents in Pettis County and taken to Texas by his new owner. So strong were the family ties between David and his parents that the son's new owner sanctioned and penned a letter to his parents to preserve those ties, or at least to respect them.[58] Whether it was paternalism or fear that generated that sanction is less to the point than is the fact that family bonds among slaves were important enough to require serious attention from all concerned. In the ways of making a home and performing their work, blacks and whites seemed united by a common pre-industrial culture.

But the differences separating the cultures ran deep, if ambiguously, and served to keep the cultures apart and to foster discrete habits and beliefs that would follow racial lines. The chasm between black and white began with a fundamental difference in color apprehension as whites, like centuries of whites before them, emphasized and cherished the paleness of their own skin color. A few sentences after she described slave life in Pettis count, Martha Smith observed that among the white women of those years "sunbonnets, veils and gloves were worn to protect the complexion." With such a goal those people with black skins seemed inherently deprived of something good and honorable. Indeed there often appeared a spectrum of values that moved from white women at the pinnacle down through various color and sexual gradations to slave men. Moreover, blacks themselves often seemed to hold aspirations and orientations to which their white associates usually proved insensitive. The very commonality of a black culture broader than that represented in the family surfaced occasionally as in the exodus from Kentucky. Although Thomson had managed to make the move with a minimum of disruption in the family life of his slaves, still those slaves held to "dear old 'Kaintucky' memories [that were] to them hallowed things of the beautiful, irrevocable past."[59] What had they left in Kentucky? The white people they had known mostly came with them, except in the case of those slaves that were purchased so that they could be with their families. But the black people and families they had valued and married into, the black culture they had known, now formed a large part of that "beautiful irrevocable past." The components of that culture that they carried with them into their new homes, subtle and obscure as they often had to be, can be glimpsed in the areas of music and religion. On a large scale, the plantation songs that Martha Smith remembered so vividly provided the vehicle for the expression of a vast array of themes ranging from the yearnings for freedom or a return to African shores in a religious symbolism, to subtle or bald satire of white masters, to a song used for pacing their work. In all three respects, the "plantation songs" sounded distinctive enough to whites to forever identify them with blacks. For blacks, those same songs would continue after slavery to express the same lamentations, hopes, and sources of pride.

The music often fused with the religious impulses of the black community, itself another distinctive and racially identifiable cultural element. For much of that religious expression the songs form the only visible evidence, other manifestations of the spiritual beliefs being restricted to either the slave cabins or to attendance at a white dominated church to be exposed to doctrines of submission and patience.[60] But part of this lack of evidence is also the result of an overly narrowed conception of the spiritual, or of the proper spiritual attitude. It should come as no surprise that part of the African legacy remained through the generations finding expression in ante-bellum Pettis County either in forms that merged with Christianity or that provided a black alternative to the religion of their masters. Thus, again, Martha Smith recalled five "aunts" and "uncles" among her grandfather's slaves "who, as I remember them, were oracles of wisdom, holding direct communication with spirits, wizards and witches." Or in a much different vein, though again broadly construed as evidence of the superstitious nature of black people, a recollection of the first night in Pettis County of the large body of travelers in the Thomson migration focuses on the spectacular meteor shower that illuminated the skies all night while the crowd was camped along the Lamine River. The slave who provided the recollection gave the spectacle a religious, indeed, a Christian significance: "we-all thought judgment had come. Could hear the stars falling like hail on the tops of the tents. The old folks all prayed, and we children 'hollered.' The elements were ablaze. It done lasted for hours, and we-all never expected to see daylight no more."[61]

The separateness of black life in Pettis County may be inferred from yet another quality: the masters were never convinced that their hegemony had actually been internalized by their slaves. Despite their coercion, despite their preaching, despite their praying for the slaves and warnings of perdition for disobedience, the masters still suspected that their wards would try to make a run for it. Again, Martha Elizabeth Smith provides the chronicle: "The law of the country was to keep the patrol out for the purpose of detecting negroes who might leave home without a pass; and all, the good and the bad, had to obey."[62] There was a real tension between black and white life. They may even have lived in fear of each other. George Smith, shortly after arriving in the county, had built a home for his family, and that home was shortly thereafter burned. The source of the fire was not a mystery, although it is only mentioned once in the various biographical accounts of General Smith. The family was gone overnight while the fire burned and, according to Smith's friend and confidant Bacon Montgomery, "it was supposed to have been set by one of his negro boys, who had been whipped for disobedience of orders. The loss was almost irreparable. . . ."[63] Like the county's political system which exuded an aura of paternalism but which in reality seems to have reflected an equilibrium between the governed and the governing, so too does the broader system of paternalism in slavery seem to have represented not a hegemony but a balance between two opposing forces.

It would be easy to overstate the significance of these scraps of evidence bearing on slave life in Pettis County. But at the very minimum they make clear that in important ways the paternalism of the masters did not always find reciprocation or even acceptance among the slaves. That culture was far too ambiguous to be blithely characterized as one of acquiescence or conformity or even to assume that when slaves "did the bidding of their gracious master," they demonstrated an unthinking deference—deference yes, unthinking no.

In the system of polity, in the system of power in this society the hallmark was not paternalism, though that was there, nor was it democracy, though that was there. The hallmark was restraint, universal restraint that kept sovereigns and dandies in a political equilibrium, prisoners of each other, and a restraint that kept masters and slaves in a system of "two-fold slavery" as Martha Smith called it. The restraint was, in and of itself, even, a virtue. Sacrifice and self-denial, the virtue of serving, the glory of duty and the beauty of harmony and community were qualities that pervaded the entire society and qualities that prevented the tensions in society from taking explicit, articulate form. In a society where everybody had obligations and where sacrifice for the moral unity of the community was expected as a daily feature of life, the issue of freedom could not emerge. The reason for this, in reflection, is obvious: to liberate one group from its restraints and obligations would also be to liberate others. The consequences of that would be unthinkable. Such a development, when viewed from the operative assumptions guiding this community, would threaten to transcend the limits of the human condition in organized society.

iii. Bonds of Mutuality

Once when Milton Thomson wrote his wife in 1851 he mentioned a minor frustration and then promptly fell back on the solace of an aphorism he stated almost as a self-evident, eternal truth: ". . . but man is born to disappointment." Such resignation to a limited fate in life seldom finds so explicit a philosophy. Yet such acceptance produced constant expression and justification in the early decades of Pettis County and that acceptance becomes significant in ways larger than revealing something of the temper of the people. Especially is it important in revealing the priorities of the society and in underscoring the essential static nature assumed in social relationships. The central element is this: such routine disappointment could become tolerable because it juxtaposed personal disappointment with community satisfaction. The restraint of the individual seemed to redound to the benefit of the community. A foreboding implication, though, ran through the same logic: the unleashing of the individual to no longer suffer a fate of personal disappointment could undermine the marrow of the community.

A poignant example of this phenomenon cropped up as soon as George R. Smith arrived in Pettis County. Trained in the law in Kentucky and with a mind to achievements and glory as great as those of anybody else, he expected to follow that calling in Pettis County. But that did not work. As his daughter noted: "There was no occasion to use his knowledge of law. In this new country there was no litigation. Everybody was everybody else's friend." Smith's disappointment was enormous. He had, of consequence, to turn to farming, an occupation that he disliked and that he would try to escape so long as he practiced it. And he was not the only one. The first lawyer in the county, George Heard, who preceded Smith, had suffered a similar fate, only Heard set up a school to make his way in this amicable country that deprived lawyers of the opportunity to resolve conflicts.[64] Cooperation rather than competition seemed the order of the day.

This cooperation surfaced constantly in the various relationships that served to prevent the emergence of issues and to protect the community. In economics this could be the substitution of a barter and cooperative system for that of the market. The task of raising a cabin would more likely be done by joint effort than by contract. The resulting life style would stress not greater material accomplishments and style but the homilies of cooperation and subsistence. In politics these relationships could be seen in the development of a system of elections that minimized issues and maximized the pressure for consensus and unity. The assumed obligations of individuals and races underpinned that cooperation. Even in matters of criminal justice as it was informally dispensed, this is evident. The "ill-will of the community," according to one source only a generation removed, "was more terrible than the law."[65] In religion a frequent emphasis on human depravity and a humbling powerlessness required a conscious, deliberate effort of the individual to rise above that natural condition though never on terms designed by mortals. And in a society where individuals knew personally those with whom they did business and conducted public affairs, and into whose families their children would marry, the incentives for cooperation remained always high.

What is so striking about this cooperation is largely its pervasiveness and the casual manner in which the limits of individuals would be assumed. So deeply did the assumptions and expectations of cooperation run that in fact they found little extended defense or explanation. Yet time and again references to the early years in the county focus not on pride of individual families or personalities but on community or neighborhood endeavors. As Martha Elizabeth Smith, daughter of the proudest man in the county, expressed those relations: "Everybody was everybody's friend. They helped each other. If a house was to be built, all the neighbors went to the 'raising.' If any were sick, the neighbors helped take care of the invalid. Any misfortune to one called forth the sympathy of the neighborhood."[66]

The limits on individuals, the bonds of mutuality, produced harmony on some occasions but generated cooperation regularly. An individual depended upon neighbors for satisfaction, commiseration, aid in hard times, joy in living and loving, and in all things that gave worth to life. In turn that person's own respect would come to the extent that sacrifice for the well-being of neighbors was freely offered. The alternative, to ask those neighbors for their sacrifice without reciprocating, and to live for oneself and for oneself alone would not only have been next to impossible given the network of community associations in the area, it would also be unthinkable.

In this way it appears that the limits on individuals as perceived by Pettis Countians in the 1830s and 1840s proved less restrictive than a modern perspective might suggest. Indeed, such limits endowed that society with a precious freedom that marks it as discretely pre-modern. That freedom, born from individual and local responsibility in decision making, and experienced in material and nonmaterial choices available, could perhaps explain the series of ironies that pervaded life in Pettis County. In that society it was the most powerful who held the greatest obligations and the poorest who were the most debt free. It was a society that contained much isolation, yet little privacy. The society required sacrifice for others but also offered the assurance that such sacrifice would be reciprocated. Those who accepted their limits could find commiseration, help, and a sense of satisfaction as well as the freedom that comes from the absence of a competitive structure pitting individuals against each other. Those who saw in those same relationships—the bonds of mutuality—nothing but obstacles to their own ambition, and who saw themselves as possessed of talents and qualities that put them at an advantage over their neighbors, were probably the most frustrated and the most oppressed. Put differently, to view those relationships as restraints on human potential would require a fundamentally different view of humanity from that dominant in Pettis County in the 1830s and 1840s: such a view would center around an acquisitive, atomistic being with the material ambition of the individual the sole standard of judgment of how a society meets its obligations.

The suppression of self-centered behavior and the sufferance of individual disappointment could be made tolerable only by the understanding and knowledge that the community would be stronger and more satisfying for it, and when it was made thus tolerable the potential issue separating two different views of individual and society would be suppressed. To allow that issue to emerge, to allow the rise of a view that sanctioned individual oriented behavior which emphasized personal prerogatives at the expense of others and that transformed the individual to the center of social relations would undermine the basis of the community. To allow that to happen would generate the same conflict between dreams and realities the deliberate and purposeful suppression of which had caused the community to take the shape it did. That conflict, once set loose, would be a long-lived feature of life in America.

III

The Crisis of Change and War

In the 1850s Pettis County changed. The signs of the change were subtle and the contours of the transformation were not always clear. But in retrospect those who knew the area saw the decade as a turning point of some kind. Martha Elizabeth Smith saw the change plain enough when she noted that ". . . different issues came up in the political field, and our little district, apparently pure at first, began to contribute its quota of evil to the world."[1] Others began to make connections with cause and effect, linking such disparate phenomena as the building of a railroad and the pattern of criminal avarice. The historian of Green Ridge township observed tersely three decades later: "Few crimes have been committed in the township and none whatever were committed until the railroad was built."[2] What happened in the 1850s was indeed subtle, but powerful, and went to the very core of the organization of life. In that decade some attempted to overcome what others viewed as natural and proper limits and in the process they began to work a revolution in society. That such a change would generate deep issues is entirely understandable since in that new society sacrifice would no longer be accepted by all, obligations would take on a new meaning, and in that society the community would become subordinate to the aspirations of separate individuals. In those times all that had been would be lost.

i. Prometheus Bound

One person, and, as it turns out, almost one person alone, represented the forces working such an enormous change in life in Pettis County.[3] George R. Smith, a son-in-law of General David Thomson and one of the most prominent men in the county, by the 1850s felt uncomfortable and limited by the society that had emerged in this area. Since his first arrival in Pettis County, Smith had followed a line of development that was bound to conflict, sooner or later, with the distinctly non-growth oriented community around him. While General Thomson came

36

to Missouri to recapture a past society, Smith had in mind something different. Still a young man when he moved, trained as a lawyer, ambitious, and a speculator by temperament, Smith had already been active in the burgeoning market of Kentucky both as a shipper and land speculator. He viewed the undeveloped, commercially untouched land of western Missouri with an enthusiasm born of dreams of the future. The life of the plantation was not the life for Smith. Increasingly it grated on him. Partly this disaffection came from the growing pervasiveness of the closed relationships of that society and partly it resulted from an internal magnification of those relationships as his own assumptions developed in a contrary direction. With little enthusiasm for the life of the plantation, his farm suffered. "It was a standing joke among his neighbors—and it was true," his daughter recounted, "that he had to buy feed for his cattle and family every year."[4] This, in a society that prided itself on its self-sufficiency and independence, could well have been cause for more than casual joking. The line between humor and derision in such instances is a fine one. In either case, Smith was anything but a typical farmer of Pettis County.

Smith's activities and his heart truly lay in other areas, areas that revolved around the market. From his first entry into the county George Smith made his mark as a man of the market, entering into real estate deals, contracting to build the new court house, and serving even as a purchasing agent in securing pork for the distant navy. This course he continued with relish. He would constantly be involved in freighting and in buying land warrants from veterans of the Mexican War. In 1840 he supplied provisions to the tribes in Indian Territory and drove a large herd of hogs from Pettis County to Fort Gibson "where they were disposed of at a good profit."[5] His Whig political affinities, although seldom paying off locally, enabled him to receive a handsome patronage plum in 1843 as Receiver of Public Moneys at Springfield, an office, however, that he lost when the Democrats returned to power.[6] The more enduring efforts came in his attempts to forge linkages with the national market. His successful bid to secure the contract for delivering the mail from Jefferson City though Georgetown to Springfield embodied not just his competitive spirit but his appreciation for the links established by transportation and communication systems in commercial development, and the role of government support as well. There must have been some profit in the enterprise too; he subsequently bid on and received eight additional mail contracts.[7] On a visit to Washington in 1846 Smith observed an invention that he thought "unquestionably surpasses all that has ever yet been discovered, or perhaps that ever will be." He had seen operating first hand the telegraph. It, like steam, could bring countries, even worlds together. From his perspective of the world of communications and transportation, it represented the "*ne plus ultra* of our age."[8]

After the Mexican War Smith immersed himself in his freighting operations along the Santa Fe Trail. The way of George Smith was the way of the market. And the way of the market was the way of the future.

Smith's regard by the community where he lived was perhaps accurately reflected by his failure to be elected to the state legislature in both 1836 and 1840. His status was substantial nonetheless. Indeed, in 1838 following the Mormon War, in which the Mormons were driven from Missouri by a voluntary militia, Smith's managerial and supervisory abilities were recognized when the governor named him a brigadier general commanding troops in a four county area.[9] But that status came from outside, it was more honorific than functional, and the young General Smith valued material growth more than the trappings of protocol.

General Smith's aspirations remained for a long while simply a subject for joking and happy diversion or suspicious contemplation among his neighbors. In the early 1850s, however, his effort to bring the railroad to the area set the course of his increasing divergence from the people of Pettis County. Two routes were possible for the Pacific Railroad in its traverse of western Missouri. One proposal would have the railroad follow the winding course of the Missouri River and the other would leave the river at Jefferson City to move more directly to Kansas City. Smith quickly championed the route that would cross Pettis County, the inland route. His arguments in favor of it were plausible. In the first place the river counties did not need the railroad so much as the inland region since commerce, transportation, and communications were already well developed and were adequate for these counties. Moreover, he explained to his neighbors that the railroad could connect them with the national market, break down the isolation that hung like a pall over their society, and stimulate economic growth and immigration for the county. The railway company, for its part, simply agreed to follow the route offering greater financial support.[10]

General Smith moved rapidly, if without competition, to become the leader of the local railroad effort, actively circulated petitions seeking state assistance for the railroad, and initiated an engrossing campaign to bring the line into the county. The early successes in attracting the railroad grew directly from his energies. In early 1852 he called a meeting of county citizens to consider voting a subscription to railroad stock. Initial opposition to such a venture proved both natural and widespread. The meeting dragged on, defeating each proposed amount of subscription all the way down to ten thousand dollars. Finally, after sitting in silence, Smith rose and delivered a two hour speech extolling the virtues and necessity of the railroad for the region and subsequently secured an endorsement from the remaining audience for a one hundred thousand dollar bond issue. Then he vigorously campaigned for the issue, crisscrossing the county mobilizing support and daunting the opposition. The issue passed in the ensuing county election. The next year the railroad announced that an additional four hundred thousand dollars was needed from the several counties along the inland route before the company would accept that route. Once again Smith willingly accepted the position of chairman of the "Pacific Railroad Committee for Pettis County" to secure these commitments.[11]

Smith's singleminded devotion to railroad promotion dramatically revealed the kind of society he was trying to build. It was a society centered around economic growth, the free activity of the market, and an intense individualism. On one level, this meant simply reducing the isolation of the county with a convenient outlet to the national market. The commercial benefits were obvious. But on another level, the coming of the railroad entailed a much larger change as the logic of the market extended to subtle relationships that traditionally had been inherited or prescribed by social position and that could become subject to negotiation and competition only with a severe dislocation. The bargaining posture of the marketplace threatened to undermine and replace the values of the community, values that General Thomson and his family and others had moved to Missouri to preserve, values that had been woven into the very fabric of this local society. The railroad, General Smith argued, would release individual ambition and energy in a market society.[12]

In 1854 some of the implications of the changes involved in the market society came into view as the railroad first became linked with the power of the state and then with even larger issues. In that year the Pacific Railroad began to threaten with law suits those people who had originally pledged financial support but who were now balking. In that situation General Smith became an agent of the company to help them collect subscriptions between Jefferson City and the Kansas border. He also became one of the directors of the Pacific that year. But even more significant, he finally won a seat in the state General Assembly in 1854 as a representative from Pettis County. Not quite making up for his earlier defeats, he now won only by a plurality created by the bitter split between the Benton and anti-Benton factions of the Democratic Party, and was elected, as his opponents persistently claimed, "by accident rather than by the choice of the people."[13] In a state government dominated by the uncompromising opposition of its governor, Sterling Price, to internal improvements, Smith's main purpose was to promote the interests of the railroad through legislation.

Compounding the associations of the railroad, Smith's political affiliation linked his ardor for that system with larger forces of which he approved but hesitated to embrace too passionately in a slave society. During the 1854 campaign, a friend advised him to renounce his Whiggery; every victory for a Whig was considered a victory for abolitionism because of the close ties of that party to Free Soil. The Whig Party, his friend urged, was not the same as it had been: "there is only a sectional Whig party at war on the institutions of the South." Though vacillating on the question of slavery, General Smith remained a Whig for a while longer.[14]

Smith was visibly bothered by slavery, though, and this irritation stemmed from the same set of values that led him to promote the railroad and the changes it would bring. In the first place, as one of his daughters recalled, "Slavery was conducive to indolence and immorality. God has so arranged this life that if we are bread-eaters, we must be bread-winners; each individual for himself, must earn his bread 'by the sweat of his brow.' " The problem was that the institution of slavery brought unearned leisure to those not slaves. "Our young men had nothing to do and our young women had no aim in life except marriage . . . ." And if the immorality produced by such life was immoral only within the context of the work ethic, the guilt generated by slavery was the denial of slaves the individual responsibility in life necessary for productive goals. The guilt was not over the harshness of the life but over the very benevolence of the plantation: ". . . where was the justice and where the mercy in such an aimless life?" They had no ambition. Slavery, as an institution, a particular form of social relationships, violated the precepts of the market society. But General Smith was not yet ready to free his own slaves. That remained, with the railroad and the Pettis County metropolis, a dream.[15]

In the view of his neighbors, though, the general's dreams were already being fulfilled, if not by him. The convergence of circumstances in western Missouri in the mid-1850s highlighted the connection between the railroad as an agent of social change and the antislavery impulse. The market society began to take shape. The debate over Free Soil had been watched with keen interest in Pettis County, and the final decision in 1854 in the Kansas Nebraska Act to repeal the Missouri Compromise and allow popular sovereignty on the question of slavery in the territories put that slave society on the defensive, particularly since New England organizations for land speculation and "emigrant aid" were already active in Kansas. At its most literal their anxiety could be interpreted as just an effort to prevent the location of a haven for freed slaves less than a hundred miles away. No doubt this was a real fear. Throughout the state the fear of slave escapes, and more, slave abductions, reached overwhelming proportions.[16] But such motivation by itself would hardly have produced the breadth and intensity of effort actually generated to resist the onslaught of the antislavery forces. As the very real nature of the threat increased, the implications of the argument that their local railroad propagandist, General Smith, had been using while touting the future became all too clear and assumed a more immediate importance.

The critique of market society before the Civil War took strange forms. Perhaps the most explicit analysis came from George Fitzhugh who with great pains and intellectual strength contrasted the organic, paternal, even aristocratic relationships of slave society with those of the ruthless competitive capitalist society he saw developing in the North.[17] It would be futile to hope for a more penetrating critique at that level of analysis from his compatriots in Missouri, for most of them operated in worlds vastly different from the abstract realm of the Port Royal polemicist. But the issues Fitzhugh addressed were felt and argued with equal, or even more, intensity and passionate commitment, by those involved at the rawest level of the conflict. In the breadth of expression and variety of defensive measures taken, it is clear that the Civil War, or more revealingly in this instance, the War for Southern Independence, in western Missouri began as a resistance movement to the penetration of market society from within and without and escalated into general warfare.

The general phenomenon of resistance took shape, in the eyes of General Smith and some of his legislative colleagues, as a problem of unbridled demagoguery. Major James S. Rollins of Columbia warned his friend Smith, quite unnecessarily, that if they did not stand firm "and resist the spirit of reckless and unprincipled fanaticism which a few dangerous demagogues are now inciting, there is positively no predicting what is to become of our institutions."[18] Indeed, it did seem that the institutions of law and order were breaking down as men openly flouted the law, violence became an instrument of conflict, and the most "unprincipled"—those who opposed internal improvements and defended slavery—usually won the elections. To an extent the question was the very style of social and political activity since it was intimately related to the issues involved. But the general pattern of behavior suggests that more was at stake than gullibility.

When the threat of Kansas as a free state became a real possibility, the formation of secret societies, Blue Lodges, swept the area. These organizations, created "for the protection of all," were simple in form but assumed a sacred mission as the members swore on the Bible to do all in their power to make Kansas a slave state. Clandestine in their nature, the Blue Lodges bound members together with secret oaths, passwords, signs, grips, and penalties for violating rules or revealing secrets. Apparently even written minutes were kept of lodge meetings.[19] On the face of it these lodges were innocuous enough but they consciously incorporated some of the important aspects of the society valued by the membership: obligations, a purpose above the limits of secular laws, a sacred aura, and the defense of slavery which had been revalued from a part of society to the very basis of society. They also provided a forum for the discussion of issues and the mutual reinforcement of attitudes, an effort made doubly effective by the instruments of secrecy. Although the secret nature of the lodges has concealed from historical investigation much of their operation, it is quite apparent that they contributed substantially to the mobilization of pro-slavery forces from the area across the line into Kansas in the fall of 1854 and the spring of 1855 to vote for a Congressman from the territory and then to elect a state legislature which would write a constitution including a slave code.

As Missourians poured into Kansas, the territorial population more than doubled, and as a result Kansas at first harbored slavery. Whether the absence of a residence provision for voting had been intentional or not in the Kansas-Nebraska legislation, these voters reasoned that if they were close enough to be immediately affected by the form of government Kansas developed, then they should have a voice in the government. The conflict inside Kansas then increased as the antislavery forces formed their own constitution and government and the "border ruffians" conducted raids on the antislavery settlements. Pettis County made its contribution. A group of prominent countians approached General Smith to try to persuade him to join their efforts to make Kansas a slave state, "and fall in with the prevailing sentiment." He refused, just as he had refused to join a Blue Lodge. The general did receive considerable notoriety for his actions on the other side, though. Brinksly Hornsby in Independence wrote his friend Smith in August, 1855, that "I believe the people in this section award to George R. Smith no small part in putting the ball in motion, and if I am not mistaken will properly appreciate his valuable services." Other people had a different appreciation of the general, and four months later, Hornsby informed Smith that the "border ruffians" were increasing their attacks with considerable success; Smith as it turned out, far from a hero, was now a "marked object."[20]

If by this time General Smith could be singled out as one of the enemy by the proslavery gangs along the border, he did not fare much better in his home county. What is more important, there the system of laws and values he represented were under vigorous attack. In 1853 as the tension mounted over the fate of Kansas, and thus Missouri, and the prospects of the railroad became more real, General Smith once again made a stand against the rule of the masses, favoring instead the less direct course of due process by law. In nearby Heath's Creek township, a mob threatened to take a prisoner from jail to lynch him only to meet the intercession of Smith who attempted to persuade them to abide by the provisions of the law for his trial and punishment. The man, named Sam, was black and the crime of which he was charged was the attempted rape and the murder of a white woman, symbolically the ultimate affront to white values. Despite the general's efforts, the crowd took the man from jail and ceremoniously burned him at the stake, gathering their own slaves to witness the spectacle as an object lesson. According to one witness, George G. Vest, later U.S. Senator, the scene lacked the usual tinges of the irrational element so frequently associated with mass psychology; the mob, he explained, "was composed of cool, determined men, and all appeals to them were in vain." Were it not for the striking combination of impulses in this incident and the particular social context in which it transpired, its main significance would be as the only such happening in the county, if one of the most grisly anywhere. But it has a larger meaning. For these people the elaborate system of determining justice through a series of procedures and channels missed the point. They knew he was guilty, or at least felt they knew, and to wait for a confirmation of that guilt by an established court of law with the distinct possibility that such confirmation would never come, made little sense. In fact it may well be argued that the whole question of guilt was secondary to the greater concern for what the victim was—a slave in a society being challenged by the very institutions that were for the moment protecting him from a traditional conception of meting out justice. (It was only much later that witnesses to the mutilation attached any importance to the confession and then it came at different points in the affair.) What did make sense to them was that General Smith would intervene with this particular legal system to protect a slave. Their original intention before Smith's protests had been to hang the man. After that, hanging was not enough.[21]

While the activity beneath the surface increasingly narrowed the ground held by General Smith in his community, the general himself hastened the estrangement. From his vantage point in the General Assembly, Smith continued to fight for even more benefits for the railroad. One of his main goals was to have the state drop its lien on the physical property of the company in favor of putting it on the Pacific's private stock. Only with such action could the railroad attract foreign capital, he argued. And this was at a time when the railroad was faced with increasing resentment from within the state and the consequent loss of original subscriptions at many points. So strong was sentiment against the Pacific that the *Jefferson Inquirer* lamented, "We are, sometimes, almost forced to the conclusion that there is a regular organized opposition to the Pacific Railroad Company, west of this city." Smith's effort failed. His wheeling and dealing in Jefferson City on behalf of the Omnibus Bill, a measure to secure a state appropriation of ten million dollars for all the railroads, thereby reducing competition for funds among the railroad partisans, brought further bitterness. In an all out effort the supporters of the bill prepared a fabulous banquet for legislators who could be persuaded to vote for the bill. Smith made the grand speech of the affair on the duty of the state to use all its power to develop the material resources of Missouri. This successful effort, as the assembly even managed to pass the bill over Sterling Price's veto, brought Smith additional prominence in high quarters. He finally received encouragement for the course he had chosen, but it came from outside his own district.[22]

His activities in the legislature made General Smith a likely candidate for Congress in 1856. The support he received was impressive; some of the best, most forward looking men in the state were pushing him. He entered the contest in the American Party convinced that this party offered the best possibility of preserving the Union without too great a strain. In each of the two American Party conventions, he failed because of his lukewarm views on slavery and what many perceived as too much zeal for internal improvements. He tried again in 1858. This time many of his own friends and relatives offered their personal sympathies but balked when it came to the principles he supported. The only support he received came from distant parts of the state. Out of touch with his own people, Smith even issued a circular calling on the people of his district not to make an issue of slavery. This was in 1858, when the western part of the state was virtually in arms, federal troops were maintaining an antislavery government in Kansas, and the threat of disunion grew day by day. Once again he lost. He was, however, re-elected to the Board of Directors of the Pacific Railway that year.[23]

The railroad, as always, remained his pet project. As it came closer to Pettis County his anticipations brightened and became more specific. The surveyors and company officials working on the extension of the road frequently stayed at his home while in the area. Bringing their families along, the visits would last for weeks at a time, and the officials with their stories and manners of the Northeast generated even more enthusiasm, if only in Smith's family. "We revelled in dreams of the future," recalled his daughter of those experiences, ". . . when we should see the same culture brought into our own land." And the contrast, already quite real, became more evident. As the progress of the road increased and it approached Georgetown, Smith learned that it would pass several miles to the south of the community. He pleaded with his neighbors to take out additional subscriptions to bring it directly through. But just as the benefits of the railroad were becoming obvious and the prospects of a market society within grasp, the people of Georgetown refused. They did not want it.[24]

Undaunted, Smith set out to build a new city where the market society of the liberated individual would be welcome. Feverishly borrowing money wherever he could, be began buying up large blocks of land around the proposed route of the railroad. After securing as much land as possible, negotiating with the railroad for the location of the depot, and trying to attract settlers, Smith filed the plat and moved to Sedville, named after his daughter, Sarah, who was nicknamed Sed. This arrangement seemed to satisfy many as Smith began to devote most of his effort to the internal development of the town and no longer tried to involve the people of Georgetown in his own vision. He was also free to build the society he wanted and could follow a more independent course in the development of his own ideas of social organization. The ideological divorce that had extended to a physical separation from his community widened as the general became convinced that a compromise of the issues involved locally and nationally was no longer feasible or even desirable. To this extent he had caught up with the sentiment of his neighbors. But, unlike them, he attached his support to the cause of the industrial market society of the North.[25]

ii. A New Society

The firing on Fort Sumter was anticlimactic in this region. Sporadic fighting had existed since the early Kansas troubles and had never really subsided to any lasting degree. As recently as the winter of 1860–1861 when the railroad tracks had reached a point short of Sedalia by about five miles, the tracks were surreptitiously destroyed in an effort to prevent further construction. Now, though, the fighting merged with the larger warfare of the nation. As the movement for a permanent division of the country mounted, the position of the state of Missouri seemed certain to be for secession. The Governor, Lieutenant Governor, Speaker of the House, both U.S. Senators, and most of the members of the General Assembly all favored withdrawing from the Union. But a convention elected to decide the question voted to remain loyal. George G. Vest, then representing Pettis County in the General Assembly, and supporting secession, described the members of that convention as "political cheats, jugglers and charlatans." He appears to have reflected the mood of his county. At a mass meeting in Georgetown, General Smith spoke for the union side of the question. Even for the general, who had quite a reputation for it, his bitterness was unprecedented. Mentor Thomson, who had moved to Pettis County with him three decades earlier, was a candidate for the convention and was willing to vote for secession if the people wanted him to. General Smith, greeted with hisses and jeers, made clear the distance he had come since that early settlement and how far from his neighbors he had moved when he was asked if he would vote for Thomson: "No! If a rope were tied around Mentor Thomson's neck, and my vote would save him, I would not vote for him. Furthermore, if every man, woman, and child in the [United] State[s] should go except Massachusetts, I would go to Massachusetts, if I had to crawl on my hands and knees to get there!" That Mentor Thomson was Smith's brother-in-law seemed to count for naught.[26]

This break with the Thomson family coincided with other developments that severed the family bonds and that emphasized the dramatic contours of the change that was underway. One by one, the blood lines connecting the two families and the opposing visions of society they represented were sundered. In April of 1861, Smith's wife, the daughter Melita of the old Thomson, died of pneumonia. An obvious tragedy for her husband and daughters, as well as for her own father, the circumstances of the time and the enormous tension evident in society meant that this might even be a blessing. As one of her daughters recalled, "we were sometimes almost glad that the sweet little mother had been removed from the perils of the hour." Three months later Smith's only grandson also died, still an infant. Then in October of that year, David Thomson himself, beset with grief for his daughter and his wife (who died in 1857), also met his demise. He was, as a descendant described it, "saddened by the destruction of the world he had helped to create." The precipitating crisis bringing his death is clear enough. At midnight a group of Union soldiers showed up at his door at Elm Spring. "The shock of their sudden and unexpected appearance in the middle of the night and the ensuing excitement were too much." He suffered a paralyzing stroke and died not long afterward.[27] He had truly seen the end of the world he valued and loved. The most visible personal symbol of the world that had been Pettis County was gone. And George Smith turned his back on that past and on Georgetown and moved into a new society.

Prometheus was truly unbound. General Smith had no ties, whether family, ideological, or even physical, to the culture he had been living within. Outspoken as ever, he set out to fight the war and started to organize a Union company, a task fraught "with great danger and difficulty in that section." He kept in touch with the Committee of Safety in St. Louis which had engineered the convention against secession and which provided the early center for direction of the Union war effort in Missouri. As threats increased against the general, he moved his family to Jefferson City and from there to St. Louis with the retreat of the government. The convention had deposed the recently elected officials and appointed new ones who were Union oriented. To the new governor, Hamilton Gamble, Smith offered his services and was appointed Adjutant General. This only lasted a few months as Smith fell into a dispute with Gamble, quitting his position because he felt the governor was not prosecuting the war vigorously enough. After sending his daughters to live with relatives in Ohio for a while, General Smith eventually returned to Sedalia when it was occupied by the Union army.[28]

Sedalia's existence in its early years depended almost exclusively on the military. During the war at various times up to eight thousand federal troops occupied Sedalia. One of those soldiers wrote home to a friend that he was stationed "away out here, in the Wilderness, . . . where you see nothing but Soldiers." In Sedalia proper, he wrote, "there is so few Houses and inhabitants, that it does not seem like a town."[29] This Union military dominance was not completely natural, however. The prevailing

sentiment of the area around Sedalia seemed to be decidedly anti-Union. Some locals went south to serve under General Sterling Price; others joined the wide ranging bands of guerrilla raiders; still others simply held tight in Pettis County, fighting or resisting when the situation required or the opportunity emerged. "Treason stalks unseen and unmolested," Union officer James E. Love wrote home in 1861. "There are troops in quantity here & below—marching all over the country, with all the pride & pomp of Glorious War—& there are secessionists, who swear fidelity to the union once a day to get passes &c, who ride hither & thither reporting our every movement to the prowling armed bands who are so ready to pounce when occasion offers, & to run when it don't. . . ."[30] The situation had not changed materially by the autumn of 1863. At that time, a prominent citizen of Sedalia later recalled, "many rumors of raids about to be made on Sedalia or vicinity prevailed, which kept the residents of the town in more or less of a commotion. . . ."[31]

The conflict between the partisans ran deep and surfaced often. The chief obstacle to the Union forces came in the sporadic forays of small bands of bushwhackers. These bands, proud but weak, undisciplined, lacking trained or experienced leadership or even coordination with others, remained a serious and embarrassing thorn for the Union forces. The decentralized, amateurish nature limiting their effectiveness also reflected fundamental tendencies contributing to the encouragement and logistical support provided by the local population. Though holding the town, the Union was unable, try as it may, to suppress completely the resistance. And it tried virtually every tactic. With the Union headquarters in his own house, General Smith frequently rode with the troops to point out rebel sympathizers and activists among his neighbors. That, like the exercise of martial law in an area accustomed to government by consent and deference, the expropriation of supplies widely viewed as plunder, and the constant threat of the selective imposition of a tax on rebel sympathizers to pay for damages as a counterinsurgency tactic only backfired. The resistance lived on and, indeed, thrived as the federal forces took the shape of an invading, oppressive army.[32]

Personal experiences gave shape to the larger systematic perception of oppression. Typical of such experiences would be that of the wife of Thomas Prince Earl Rees. She kept a running ledger of goods taken from the family by the federal forces. In 1861 and 1863 Union soldiers took all kinds of food from her house, including eight hogs, four hundred fifty barrels of corn, thirty or thirty-five stacks of timothy, seven stands of bees, seventeen turkeys, a hundred fowls, forty three geese, all the sausage, between fifty and a hundred bushels of apples, two stacks of oats, "a fine mississippi rifle and cartouch box," a horse, three fat cows, and even "they then searched the house and took at least 50 dollars worth of money." They did not get, however, her prized apron. This apron's design followed the stars and bars of the Confederate flag.[33]

Possibly less common was the experience of Mentor Thomson. One night in May, 1863, Mentor Thomson's wife was awakened by a banging at the door. Discovering men trying to force their way into the house she summoned her husband; she took refuge with him in his room. When one of the band forced his way there, Thomson shot and killed him. When another waiting in the hall started to attack Thomson killed him too. Yet a third barely escaped after Thomson, his shotgun empty, wrestled him down furiously. Three others escaped completely. Thomson was left with a wounded arm where one of the intruders' bullets tore away the flesh. The problem was that the band was a group of Union soldiers. That this was an unauthorized predation seems obvious, given the attempt of the soldiers to disguise themselves and their repudiation by the local commander. It is nonetheless clear, however, that only the violent resistance of Mentor Thomson and the official disclaimer of the commander separated this incident from others.[34]

Perhaps the most extreme case was that of William H. Field. Field, a farmer north of Georgetown, had long been known for his pro-Southern sympathies, and was also one of the most prominent planters around. A wealthy slave owner with more than fifteen hundred acres, his position was that much more galling to the union forces occupying the area. On June 5, 1862, a squad of US Cavalry rode to Eldon, the home of Field. They summoned him and directed Field and one of his sons to ride with them. The father and son became separated and the son was later told to return home. After that, according to the testimony of one of the soldiers involved in the episode, Field was taken into the brush and summarily executed. The point of this cold-blooded murder was not the simple removal of a figure of resistance. It probably more accurately revolved around the affect it produced. As his son recalled, the murder "struck terror in the neighborhood where he lived."[35]

The resistance to Union occupation remained scattered, unorganized, and spontaneous and seldom presented a real threat. Even so, the town fell to Confederate control briefly in October, 1864. General Sterling Price's force came close and a part of that regular force, under General Jeff Thompson, approached Sedalia. One of Price's officers, Major James C. Wood, was from Georgetown, knew the area well, and led a scouting party to determine the strength and location of the local union fortifications. After surveying Sedalia's security force, Wood went to Georgetown where he was received warmly by old friends, put up in the local hotel and feasted. Not surprisingly, the Union prisoners that his force captured talked freely and provided much information to their captors. The next day he made his report to the larger force and plans for an assault on Sedalia began. As it happened the Union forces normally occupying the place had withdrawn and in fact orders were sent to the local militia supporting the Union that they too should evacuate the area, leaving Sedalia to the obvious fate. The local militia, however, chose to make a battle of it. The force that was mobilized included not only the firebrands among the Union supporters, but even "a few men of southern sympathies who were willing or forced to unite with them . . . ." The battle itself, when the attack came, was short but furious. Not accurately assessing the size of the force upon them (a large force with possibly up to 1500 men), some of the militia determined to fight it out. A few even proposed to shoot two women who were waving a white flag to secure a truce in the fighting. But defeat came surely. And, after the customary foraging and pillaging (tempered by personal acquaintance in many instances), the Confederate force moved out before night had settled on the town. Around midnight around twenty-five hundred Union forces appeared and the town returned to its normal activity, under the protection of the federal forces.[36]

In the case of Sedalia it could well be, as Charles Beard argued in a larger context, that the fighting of the Civil War was but a fleeting incident; the larger social revolution contributing to the war and propelled further by the war was in fact the essential portentous outcome. By 1864 Sedalia rested on a permanent foundation that was not likely to collapse with the end of army protection. With a general commercial growth that had been spawned by the needs of the garrison, the city had a population of nearly a thousand. The political change accompanying this growth was equally portentous as the market society envisioned by General Smith pushed aside the prevailing regime. In 1862 Smith had run for the legislature again, this time as a Radical Republican. Though trying to be elected to the seat from Pettis County, he remained in St. Louis, a safe distance from his prospective constituency, denounced the local "traitors," and failed. The following year he presided over the "Charcoal Convention" of Radicals and helped formulate a petition to President Lincoln seeking assistance in pushing the state government to a more aggressive posture on emancipation, the disfranchising of Confederate sympathizers, and military action. He even went to Washington as part of a committee to present the petition to Lincoln. Eventually Lincoln refused all their requests except the proposal to restrict the franchise to loyal Union supporters. It was with the restricted franchise that the general entered the elections of 1864. And that factor made all the difference in the world. Smith's personal success was unequalled that year as he was elected a State Senator, President pro tempore of the Senate, and became chairman of the committee on elections. He also was an official elector for Lincoln. The most lasting and most symbolic victory of that year, however, came when Sedalia received a charter naming Smith the first mayor of the city.[37]

But this was only the beginning, and a very formal beginning at that. As difficult as it had been up to the founding, the hard part remained. The city had been born under the most inauspicious of circumstances. From the perspective of General Smith those circumstances, involving armed force, disfranchisement, and the imposition of a different pattern of life on the local populace, were justified by the general's own dreams of the future. For the others, the methods and the goals they had encountered held much less claim to legitimacy. And in that lay the problem of the future. General Smith still had not really achieved what he had set out to do. Sedalia was a city with a legal basis for existence and with a railroad and a small population living there; but the future remained far from certain and the city a far cry from the metropolis Smith sought. He had in mind a particular kind of city, a city with the qualities of the market that the people of the area had been fighting for more than a decade, and there was little reason to believe that they would quit the struggle. The ultimate fulfillment of General Smith's dreams involved the creation of institutions and the propagation of values that would foster commercial growth, discipline a work force, and extend the role of the market further and further into the surrounding areas and into the lives of the people subject to it. It involved an entire transformation of relationships—and a transformation of dreams.

PART TWO

The Rising Pattern of
Industrial Market Society

IV

The Engines of Economic Growth

i. Social Discipline

The growth of Sedalia in its early years was less dramatic than the conflict which had given birth to the city. The conflict persisted in different forms, however, and it became one of the duties of the victors to secure a sufficiently broad base of support to allow the city to progress unhindered. At the same time, and inextricably bound up with this duty, it was necessary to begin the enormous process of developing an entire system of social organization—of working a social revolution. The choices that were made in this process and the framework within which they were posed set the pattern of urbanization that would alter the entire orientation of society in the area.

In part a new group of people emerged into power with the end of the war; more significantly, a new ideology came into power. Those few who had been on the outside previously now wielded a great authority. One consequence of this was an intensified suspicion even of those within their own ranks. Fellow Unionists, people who had been comrades during the war, could now be singled out as "lukewarm Radicals" because of the fear that their commitment was not sufficiently pure. These were people, according to General Smith, who now balked as the Emancipation Proclamation worked on some "the same disease that it did upon hundreds."[1] Those erstwhile allies could no longer be trusted. The end of the war witnessed an incredible narrowing of accepted orthodoxy.

If supporters of the Union were now suspect, those who had sympathized with the Confederates or who had simply resisted Union subjugation were humiliated and silenced. With loyalist troops under General Bacon Montgomery to preserve order, those who had protested and resisted to the point of making war now saw their society being undermined at every point: the system of slavery they had come to accept as the core of society collapsed with emancipation; the railroads and telegraph broke down the isolation that had been honored for its protective features as well as for the extremely local commitments and loyalties it generated. And they were powerless to do anything about it. Armed resistance by this point could only be counterproductive and the formal channels of protest were open only to those who could prove their allegiance to the Union. The new regime, emanating largely from the state government under a new constitution, effectively squelched the opposition first by disfranchising all those who had at any time held sentiments or conducted themselves in a manner favorable to the rebels. This was the enforcement of the notorious Ironclad oath. Further, that same oath restricted all possible access to the legal machinery to loyalist attorneys. The debilitation proceeded to a more subtle level as the oath became a prerequisite to holding a teaching position. Even the relationship with the churches assumed a definitely secular and political tone as members of the clergy also were required to swear past and future allegiance to the Union before they could deliver sermons or perform marriage ceremonies.[2] Sometimes the penalties for contrary beliefs were severe. In October, 1865, John R. Staley, "for many years a prominent citizen," according to the county history, stood indicted for treason.[3] Or consider the fate of H. M. Ramsey, buried in the Heath's Creek Baptist Church cemetery on the county line. Almost eighteen years old when killed, his gravestone reads simply: "Murdered by the Mo. State Militia." The sword of the conqueror knew no rest.

In the sheer effort to change the orientation of society by thoroughly undermining the props of the old order and creating a dependence on new institutions, it had become evident how immense the task would be as even more loyalists began to balk. Over the protests of long-time county residents, the Radical legislature moved the county seat from Georgetown to Sedalia in 1864 in an action fraught with symbolism. A striking change in political leadership accompanied the physical removal. Even with a severely restricted suffrage, the people of Pettis County had elected to the county court, their administrative as well as judicial forum, men questionable from the Radical viewpoint. Empowered by the new Radical constitution of 1865, the governor began a systematic purge to cleanse the government throughout the state of all influences of the slave regime and his ukase soon reached Pettis County. One Sedalian, a loyalist, described the reaction to the governor's capricious removal of the circuit court clerk: "How much his forcible removal was distasteful to us we proved by our loud protestations; but when a stranger and a man without ability or *prestige*, succeeded him against our expressed wishes, we were almost mute from astonishment." It was this *prestige*, or legitimacy, that the writer emphasized, that the new government lacked.[4]

To many of the proponents of the new society it had seemed that such legitimacy, like the physical growth of Sedalia as the commercial center of the area would come naturally. Consequently, the first years of the new city were characterized by a complete lack of systematic effort and planning for growth. After destroying the old regime the victors offered nothing as a replacement. In this vacuum the forces of a free swinging, wildly competitive raw market of supply and demand began to operate without governmental guidance or restriction. The signal tendency, though, was for the momentum of past accomplishments, in particular the railroad, to loom more important than new directions for future gains. That momentum, of course, was nothing to be slighted. Already as the western terminus of the railroad, Sedalia had begun to suck in the commerce of a large region by making possible and attractive economic activities that would have been unthinkable without the access to the market provided by the railroad. Besides the extensive commerce initiated to the immediate vicinity and the upper valley of the Osage River, the coal mines near Granby in the extreme southwestern corner of the state utilized Sedalia as a shipping point as well as their chief supply station. The postwar cattle drives from Texas to Sedalia have become legendary despite the fact that few of the drives ever actually made it all the way to Sedalia. Most, after encountering hostile Missourians who feared the introduction of Texas fever into the region, chose to head for rail points farther west. Still, the cattle trade in Missouri began to expand at a rapid rate and Sedalia was the logical and convenient target for their drives. At the same time, though, the constant westward movement of the terminus with the consequent shifting of the market center farther away provided a vivid lesson of what could happen without a sustained, conscientious effort for planned growth.[5]

But this neglect of planning for growth seemed desirable to many. Even with a restricted franchise the political life of the new city was dominated by forces urging restraint in economic growth and emphasizing thrift and economy. Taxation was already high due to past railroad bond investments, but more important, tax assessment was for many, their first contact with new demands of the market society. It was unfortunate for the promoters of growth that the first identification with, and the first concrete participation in, the fate of Sedalia should come in the very negative form of taxation. And the positive contacts, those services which their tax money provided, often had a similar repelling quality as they centralized functions that either the individual had performed independently or had been superfluous to a differently oriented society. In such circumstances even the most ambitious city fathers were reluctant to make more appropriations for more services. Just the routine costs of running a government regularly forced the city into debt and just as regularly brought a new city administration pledged to retrenchment. And as they feared to impose higher taxes, they also feared, or at least shunned, the use of credit for growth. As one editor observed when he tried to nudge the board of aldermen into approving expenditures for a new fire engine, useful cisterns, improved streets, a market house, a city hall, street crossings, culverts and sewers, as well as other projects considered essential to the operation of the city, indebtedness was different for a public institution than for a private citizen. For the individual, it gave easy evidence of a willingness to overextend personal capabilities. For the city, on the other hand, indebtedness was not just respectable but necessary since only money would attract more money. But the city refused to issue bonds for even the most mundane and seemingly necessary obligations of Sedalia.[6]

The fruits of this retarded development suggested widely accepted limits on urbanization. A few paved streets, mostly financed by private investment, some culverts, a county highway to Warsaw built by a road tax often paid by labor on the road instead of with money, a few bridges, and a set of standard weights and measure to ensure fair trade made up the positive side of the ledger for both county and city. The limits were conspicuous. A laughable fire engine that could not shoot a stream of water twenty feet, very few cisterns for the engine to use anyway, unanswered petitions for more public roads, a bridge built without a right-of-way secured beforehand that then had to be dismantled and sold for junk, and the simple absence of services that a concentration of people required, all testified to a deep unwillingness to engage in speculative public growth. This was made vividly, and disastrously, evident in November, 1867, when a fire swept the business district of the city. Because of inadequate fire protection, the blaze raged unabated until the gale that drove it died down. And even this catastrophe only temporarily broke down opposition to an enlarged role for the city administration in social development. The city bought a new expensive steam engine and hose only to have the hose slashed when an alderman in a bit of raucous merriment called out the fire company to water down a local brothel in the middle of the night. The lasting responses were not by the city but by private merchants who rebuilt their businesses in brick. There still was no sustained, disciplined effort for growth within the city government.[7]

The important arena of economic activity as yet remained independent of the local government. Unlike the city's role, this was an impressive beginning. Within a short period following the war Sedalia could boast, in addition to the railroad and telegraph, a ponderous number of mercantile, trading, and real estate enterprises and two large banks. But it was unplanned and haphazard. The aggressive spirit that before the war had envisioned a metropolitan commercial center faded into an acquisitiveness that forced the city's development to come as a byproduct of the market, not the market as a result of development. The chief forms of activity were efforts at quick profits and often involved intense competition, efforts that seemed directly opposed to planned economic growth.[8]

Not surprisingly, the germs of planning emerged in those parts of the market where competition was felt most. An association of Sedalia realtors emerged immediately following the war to organize and rationalize control of the market in land. This control, that grew ever tighter and more effective with a rising rate of immigration, pressed land values in the area to unprecedented heights. Within the brief period of four months in 1867, the going price of land rose twenty-five percent. And the realtors spurred more immigration by publishing their own newspaper to advertise the possibilities for settlement. The situation reached such proportions that one of the leading boosters called upon the land profiteers to ease up: "You are actually making yourselves and our city poorer by your avaricious instinct." Those instincts were shared by others. The Pettis County Board of Immigration began active recruitment of tenant farmers and laborers through a contract labor system. The physicians in the county organized to standardize prices and profits, as did the region's newspapers.[9]

The main thrust of all this activity, however, remained random, uncoordinated, and reckless. Ultimately, this thrust was disciplined and forced to organize when it sought public support at the same time that it violated precepts of thrift and responsibility. As had been the case earlier, the issues precipitating the confrontation came with efforts involving the extension of Sedalia's role as a market city by the construction of new railroads. By their very nature, the railroad projects which attracted business leaders of the city following the war required larger financial support than that small group was able to provide. The necessity of public involvement loomed large, given the number of projects presented. One effort, the Sedalia, Lexington, and St. Louis Railroad, would connect Sedalia northwest with Lexington in Lafayette County with prospects of extending it in the near future. Another, the Tebo and Neosho (later the Missouri, Kansas, and Texas) Railroad, would send lines southwest to Ft. Scott, Kansas, through Clinton in Henry County. A separate effort proposed the extension of this line to the northeast eventually all the way to Chicago but initially only to Boonville and Moberly. But if local citizens had consented to the acquisition of an operable fire engine only after the business district was razed by fire, their consent to an even larger, more portentous, investment would be even slower coming.[10]

The opposition had neither the organization nor the resources to mount an effective challenge. However, if that resistance was in the shadows, its presence was nonetheless felt by the promoters of the railroads. In 1866 General Smith, in one of his last public actions, travelled through the county calling meetings to drum up support for the Tebo and Neosho Railroad. At a typical meeting in the northeastern part of the county around Longwood, Smith met an unreceptive audience. One person expressed the sentiments of those at the meeting when he observed that "The road will advantage ONLY this little cormorant city [Sedalia], which has already swallowed up the once beautiful and flourishing village of Georgetown, the county seat of Pettis, and imposed on the county heavy burdens of taxation." General Smith offered to pledge ten or twelve thousand dollars himself if the others would subscribe, but this offer was taken as further evidence of the malproportion of benefits and expenses: "As the road will benefit him ten times that amount, he can afford it." The meeting was a failure for the general. The president of the railroad, T. L. Wilson, in a visit to Sedalia shortly afterwards expressed severe disappointment that subscriptions were going so poorly in the county.[11]

And popular opposition to the railroad projects became evident in the campaigns for bond issue elections. The intense opposition caused the proponents to secure a delay in at least one election to allow them more time to mobilize support. They focused their campaign on the farming community in the county where the resistance was most entrenched. The outlying districts had even provided sufficient strength in county elections to keep the county from building a new court house and jail in Sedalia. Convincing these rural people that they would benefit by participating in the national market proved difficult. Accordingly, only one aspect of the introduction of the market received attention in their propaganda. The effect of wider competition was passed over as the Radical Sedalia *Weekly Times* advised the farmers that "Your land will raise more corn and wheat; that is, you will get more money for everything you raise for sale by means of having a market." After the concentrated campaigns of propaganda and booster meetings, the elections themselves were anticlimactic. In fact, the amount of the bond issue and the conditions set forth were often heavily qualified during the campaign to make them more acceptable. In 1868 Sedalia reduced a proposed $100,000 bond issue to $30,000 and stipulated that these bonds could only be issued once the other cities and counties along the line had issued theirs. And, as it happened, the city refused to issue those bonds until a local banker, Asa C. Marvin, became the chief executive of the company.[12]

For good reason the county reflected a distinct fear in consulting public opinion. In 1869 it authorized the issuance of $200,000 bonds *each* for the Lexington road and for the Tebo & Neosho route without public warrants. It then increased taxes to pay for the expenditures. As these new claims on the citizens of Pettis County reached further and deeper, they encountered and provoked to action a resistance that had been largely inarticulate if not completely passive. Accustomed to meeting in secret in these years of Radical domination, the conservatives began a campaign of quietly circulating petitions demanding the recall of the judges of the county court. Like the impact of the taxes, the movement spread widely across the county and into Sedalia and across the ranks of the loyalists until finally the maneuvers erupted into public meetings. To maintain broad support the public assemblies appointed a committee, respectable by virtually any standard, to investigate the county court. The investigation revealed, to the surprise of few, that the court's disregard for the public will converged with the apparent corruption and misman-agement in the court clerk's handling of funds. The clerk, former Radi-cal mayor of Sedalia, Bacon Montgomery, began to spread the guilt by charging General Smith with having offered a secret slush fund from public monies to one of the railroads as an enticement to locate in Sed-alia. As the charges and counter charges followed, the incident seemed to have grounded the boundless speculative spirit that had been rampant. One observer described this aspect of the situation in verse:

> A reckless spirit's been unearthed.
> And all the records show it,
> The people's will has been defied,
> It's well the public know it.
>
> A petition has been sent forth,
> The people, willing, sign,
> Asking the Court, also the Clerk
> Their offices to resign.[13]

But there was even more involved than an effort to replace the offic-ers of the court. The petitioners also demanded that the collection of the taxes for the railroad bonds be ceased and pledged themselves to donate money instead for the legal fight to prevent collection of those taxes. At this point the Radicals, embarrassed since "the Ring" included two former Radical mayors of Sedalia, and because the officials responsible for the crisis had all been Radicals, insisted that the problem was simply one of inefficiency and decried the behavior of the insurgents who con-sidered it a question of representative government. As one Radical put it, "the temper of the last meeting was more that of an anti-bond meeting, whether legal or illegal, than that of a united counsel to devise means to reduce taxes."[14] Indeed, this was an understatement. Some of the revolt-ers went so far as to advocate the complete institutional abolition of the county court, replacing it with a provisional government with complete accountability and responsibility to the public.

On this problem of objectives, the movement began to fall apart. Most clearly the division became apparent between the leaders and the followers, between the people who had initiated the movement and those who had been recruited for the respectability they furnished. Upon con-sultation with an expert on the law of bonds from Boonville, who com-mitted himself in the abstract and not in the particular situation, the leaders accepted the view, which was identical to the defense presented by the court, that that body did, after all, have the legal right to issue bonds without public approval. Frustrated by an apparently arrogant action of the court, then by the leaders' acceptance of an interpretation of court decisions to the effect that the people had no business requiring the court to follow their will, the insurgents made their position plain. They pledged, law or no law, to resist the taxes. And many refused to pay to the end. Years later the county found itself in federal court as the railroad companies forced complete collection to pay for the bonds.[15]

The long range effect of the tax revolt is difficult to calculate. The abiding distrust of legal institutions, including the law itself and the officials administering the law, the nascent rebellious spirit, and the division between polished leaders and more direct citizens, all would persist and crop up in different circumstances in the future. But the immediate impact was less promising, and in a way counterproductive: it had simply forced the speculative spirit to discipline itself, not to abate, but to proceed with more caution in regard to procedures and technicalities to avert the threat of insurrection. The basic impulse was still there. On the other hand, the impulse of the insurgents was frustrated and debilitated. Less than two months after the tax revolt, in January, 1870, the city council voted to issue city warrants at a discount of ten percent and bearing ten percent interest to pay off a debt that was bearing no interest. After the vote, the president of the Board of Aldermen, Thomas J. Montgomery, urged his fellow councilmen to reconsider the move: "I protest against it as being a species of class legislation—favoring one class of city creditors to the detriment of other classes." After which the other aldermen reminded him that their action was legal and consistent with the long range interest of the city. And that ended the dispute. Disciplined economic growth was coming into its own.[16]

By this point—1870—it was clear, that, as Montgomery suggested, a ruling class was emerging. It was a ruling class, rather than an elite, because it was made up not simply of well placed individuals but of men sharing certain values and ambitions that separated them from the rest of society and because it had its own system, however informal, of enforcing and perpetuating those values. By pointing out the economic aspect of the city council's action, Montgomery indicated an outward manifestation of class, a power relationship. By pointing to the technical provisions of the law and expressing their concern for the long range dimensions of Sedalia's growth, his fellow aldermen hinted at some of the inner workings of class.

The ways in which this nascent class progressively separated itself from the rest of society pervaded all realms of social relationships. The restricted franchise, the most obvious delineation based on social attitudes and commitments, even proved too broad and too inclusive for the unhindered orderly progression of commercial development, as the protests of loyalists demonstrated. But it did confer certain status almost by default on the only ones with a voice in the decision making process. The honorific military titles added a deferential quality to this status. Although the pattern of housing segregated mainly the blacks from the whites and the workers from the merchants, "the bloods" were able to control admission to their exclusive neighborhood. Originally, the four houses of General Smith, Colonel A. D. Jaynes, Albert Parker, and Cyrus Newkirk (all involved in banking and railroad promotion), "which would do credit to St. Louis," were the model of exclusiveness not simply on the basis of wealth (no residences were allowed to be constructed on the lots for less than twenty thousand dollars), but for status as well.[17]

The social institutions they created provided the emerging class the ready opportunity to reinforce their own values, flaunt their respectability and discipline themselves. The hops, masquerade balls and "soirees" of the Bachelor Brotherhood attracted the "*elite* and fashion" of the city in a form of entertainment that was at least questionable to some and simply immoral and reprehensible to others. The patronizing donations to the poor in the winter months ironically added a social buttress to an economic distance. Their public exhibitions and parades gave the "best young men of our city," the members of the Sedalia Silver Cornet Band, an opportunity to display their status.[18]

The impulses generating the Empire Fire Company, however, went deeper into the wellsprings of class. Not only did this organization satisfy the gregarious proclivities of people with common goals, but it supplied a mechanism of cooperation and mutual protection for the volunteers to ward off the phenomenon which posed a constant challenge to their welfare. The structure of the organization also served to enforce a sense of discipline on its members as punctuality and efficiency became watchwords. They even went so far as to establish a system of fines and punishments as discipline for various forms of "vulgar" behavior such as the use of profanity.[19]

The active exercise of class leadership in the direction of social and economic development was but a matter of time. The spirit of bitterness toward the bungling excesses of the earlier efforts at growth smoldered with the awareness of the potential threat demonstrated by the citizens' revolt. It was obvious that a more thorough and positive approach was essential for growth to come. The foreboding statewide election of 1870 which restored the franchise to potential adversaries encouraged the development of greater cohesiveness, discipline, and a self-consciousness of purpose. That fall, J. West Goodwin, editor of the Sedalia *Bazoo* openly decried the lack of harmony among the businessmen which inhibited economic growth and worked against the interests of Sedalia in competition with other cities. He called upon them to unite in some kind of board of trade.

The following summer the Sedalia Library Association organized. It was an innocuous enough appearing body. As a literary, philanthropic, and cultural institution, the association was not unusual. But the library occupied only a slight amount of the energies of the new organization. It assumed a larger realm of activity, "having at heart not only the literary and educational interests of this city and vicinity, but financial, commercial, and all other interests affecting the growth and prosperity of Sedalia." As if to underscore the urgency of their mission, the members of the association wasted no time working for "growth and prosperity." Within the first few months of the body's existence, they had developed a proposal for a city water works system and had secured its adoption by the Board of Aldermen. They also began negotiations and quickly concluded a bargain that brought the shops of the Missouri Pacific to Sedalia. They donated a large sum of money and a wide acreage for the shops with the understanding that all the shops between Kansas City and St. Louis on the system would be moved there permanently. Industrial growth, of course, was a crucial goal for the Library Association. Besides the shops for the railroads, their efforts in this direction proved successful when they persuaded the Board of Aldermen to donate three lots and loan five thousand dollars for two years without interest to J. R. Hancock to start a woolen factory. And so the activity continued until early 1872, less than eight months after the formation of the Library Association, when the same people organized the Sedalia Board of Trade, leaving simply a skeleton body to administer the library. And the efforts of the Board of Trade were even more ambitious and disciplined. The board began its work with a careful assessment of the city's economic needs and began long range planning for the cooperation of all businesses in Sedalia's competition with other cities. As the Board of Trade did so, it provided real evidence of the strides the city was making.[20]

Besides engineering the economic growth of the city, this new class gave direction to social development. The use of law was a particularly keen instrument of social change. In Sedalia, the persistent and never quite successful effort to rid the town of the "roughest and most violent element," all strongly identified with the Lost Cause of the Confederacy, was not just an effort to bring order to the city, but a particular kind of order. And when Deputy U.S. Assessor T. W. Moses of Sedalia was murdered while trying to arrest the operator of an unlicensed distillery, local businessmen and city officials, the governor and U.S. officials together, recognizing the incident as a key test for authority, offered a reward amounting to several thousand dollars for the apprehension of the murderer—the man who originally had simply failed to license the still he operated.[21]

It was not just in terms of law and order that social discipline came. The same goals extended to the children of Sedalia. The sudden mass-ing of people into Sedalia at a time when enormous pressures worked against family integrity and against the functions the family had traditionally served in child rearing, and when the social functions of apprenticeship could no longer be counted on (as opposed to the economic functions that Sedalia's printers sought to keep alive), gangs of youths would terrorize the city. The corruption of these kids represented to many a shocking problem that could be treated effectively only with public schools. The YMCA could only do so much. Of course the public schools had a broader mission and the gangs roaming the city were the most flagrant examples of the need for discipline. As one advocate summarized the argument for tax supported schools, "it is the duty due to the civilization of the age that property should educate the ignorant to decrease crime and better fit the generation to become useful and practical citizens." With a system of public education initiated the city began efforts to attract a normal school, an agricultural college, and the state university, all of which failed.

Part of the opposition to these efforts lay within the county. James G. Magann, a local Radical leader, observed that the same people opposed to roads, railroads, "and other public improvements brought by Yankee enterprise," were also opposed to teachers' institutes and public schools. These institutions were, the conservatives charged, "engines of oppression." Sponsored by the state government to provide a professional training mechanism for teachers, the teachers' institutes conducted in Sedalia did not escape the opprobrium. The Radical *Times* enthusiastically endorsed a policy of hiring teachers who attended the institutes over those who did not, since "No one can be fit to teach who is so lacking in the spirit of progress." To the opponents, the institutes were simply "Radical organizations expressly designed and conducted in the political interests of the dominant party of the state."[22]

The limits to the efforts to secure a new society notwithstanding, by the mid-1870s the framework for the future growth of the city had been permanently established. This framework was a comprehensive one insofar as it extended to many areas of life, not just politics and economics. But it was a narrow framework in the sense that it was capable of dealing with only certain kinds of questions. These were issues of maximizing growth, planning, discipline, and the coordination of productive effort for greater prosperity. These categories of concern had attained a certain normative value and only within them could social and economic concerns hold claim to legitimacy, the legitimacy patently absent at the end of the war. The circumstances of Sedalia's position as a market center, its heavy dependence on commerce and industry, and the necessity for growth simply to stay alive in the competition of a vast market society made this materialist orientation seem only natural. It was, however, not completely isolated from sources of fundamental criticism. The persistence of older attitudes became apparent as they continued to surface in different forms and in the most unlikely places. They too needed discipline.

ii. The Juggernaut

The wheels of commerce, the wheels of industry turned inexorably in the creation of a new society of material productivity. And the technology of the wheels of industry pervaded the entire economy of the city and symbolized the changes underway. In 1873 the Sedalia Board of Trade toured the manufacturing establishments in the city and then, quite proud and satisfied with what they had seen, the members resolved that "the mechanical industries of our city are growing and expanding, [and] we contemplate their extent with pride and pleasure."[23] Then they continued their activities to bring other industries to town and to encourage the growth of those already there. While the state of the industrial development of the city may seem limited in retrospect, it held exactly the opposite prospect and meaning to witnesses at that time. It represented nothing less than a revolution. By virtue of the changes in technology and the development and introduction of a machine process that seemed to power itself, the system of making goods bore little resemblance to what it had been. It operated at a faster speed. It enabled fewer people to produce more. It eliminated the ancient dependence on nature for basic motive power as steam replaced water. It assumed, even, a life of its own. The limits of nature, and thereby of individuals as well, it appeared, had finally been overcome.

Just how much of a revolution these changes signified can be glimpsed by noting the state of the economy in the county a decade before the Civil War. The 1850 industrial census required less than a single sheet to enumerate all products of industry, their producers, and their productive systems. The county had two blacksmiths, two woolcarders, a hatter, two wagonmakers, one potter, four grist mills and four saw mills (two being the same), and two tanners. The woolcarders, the potter, and one wagonmaker used horsepower but water prevailed as the source of power in the mills. Handpower ran everything else.[24] The scale, the speed, the sounds, the local source of materials and markets all suggest the archaic nature of the system. They also suggest the limits of the system.

The ultimate symbol, and indeed, the substantive core of the system was the water driven mill. In early Pettis County the watermill nourished the substance of life in its functions; it also nourished the spirit, the larger purpose—something akin to the soul—of that existence. From the very first considerations of locating the mill, not an easy task given the physical requirements for a pond and sufficient drop for the water to run the wheel efficiently, to the considerations of the proper material to be used in the mill, with wet elm working best because of its resistance to rot, the construction and operation of the mill was the task of a craftsman. The mill would, obviously, have to be individually crafted to fit the particular stream. The huge stones that did the grinding, or more accurately the cutting, of the grain were themselves the products of time-honored crafts. To get the ten spokes radiating tangentially from the eye of the stone, as those surviving stones in the county were dressed, required an uncommon skill. So too did it require that same skill to redress or regroove the wheels after wear. The itinerant wheel dresser had a simple way to prove his experience and the talent and skill that implied. He would just "show his metal." The high carbon steel cutting tools he used to chip away the stone at precise intervals themselves chipped away with the minute bits of metal lodging permanently in the skin of the hands. His experience as a craftsman was readily visible. He wore the badge of his calling. The emphasis on quality and experience and craft pervaded the construction and care of these great wooden engines. The dependence on craft and the dependence on nature defined the watermill, and, in turn defined the society that depended upon it.[25]

The definition is made more precise and revealing by attention to the minor elements of the process. Behold the sounds of the watermill: the sound of running water in this area of gradual drainage was probably little more than a babble and with a race the sound would be a little more of a gush with the water never falling a great distance. Inside the mill, the miller would listen to the "singing of the stones," keeping grain between the powerful stones to prevent their actual contact and the consequent rapid wear of the stones and the likelihood of even knocking one off the spindle and sending it through the floor. A careful attention to that "singing" would prevent such a calamity. The miller would also listen to the sound of the "damsel," a long device attached to the rind or gimbal barbar of the runner stone, which would vibrate against the hopper jiggling grain into the wheels. The sounds were the sounds of nature, at the pace and intensity of nature. The watermill fit into this society and symbolized it. It had its limits, but so too did the people and their society. It would never dominate humanity.

That was the system of 1850. By a decade later, on the eve of the Civil War, the only fundamental change of this system involved the introduction of several steam engines to run mills. But by 1870 steam had completely replaced all the water power mills and there were nine such engines in operation.[26] The importance of this change was obvious and was probably what led to its eventual triumph: the steam engine liberated the economy from its traditional dependence on nature, its vulnerability to weather cycles, and, for that matter, its dependence on ancient and specialized skills. With a short period of training, far removed from that associated with the craft system, anybody could operate the steam engine. It could operate at any time. It could stand above and even spite the humble limits of the watermill. And it would not need to fit in to, to be subordinate to, life's cycles; it could generate changes of its own.

The basic contours of the revolution are obvious. The machinery itself was different and required a different appreciation. One business report examined, in 1880, the machinery in operation at Jacob Zimmerman's Farmer's Mill. The output of that mill was tremendous as a fifty horsepower engine ran the mill while four runs of burrs turned out seventy barrels of flour daily. The report went on: "The entire machinery has been put together by a master hand and runs as smoothly and regularly as clock work."[27] This could not have been said of the watermill. Put together as it had been by a master hand, it lacked the automaton regularity of the clock. The engines were huge. When the members of the Board of Trade visited William Hoberecht & Company's Sedalia Mills, they found an establishment "literally stuffed with machinery from ground to garret" and eight men employed. The engine was a fifty horsepower model that had a boiler twenty-eight feet long and four feet in diameter. It had two fourteen inch flues and two twelve inch flues.[28] (Unlike the watermill, it seems to have emitted something other than fresh water.) That machine could produce a hundred barrels of flour every twelve hours.

Everywhere the machine was at work. Everywhere it revolutionized the system of production. In 1872 when the Board of Trade made one of its tours, it found twelve people employed at J. R. Hancock's woolen mill, a forty horsepower engine operating the mechanism, and a productive capacity of one hundred-fifty yards of cloth a day. The horse collar factory produced twenty-thousand collars a year and employed ten men. The soap factory could produce thirteen thousand pounds of soap a week. John Nauman's flour mill, with six operatives, could produce sixty barrels of flour a day.[29] There was no comparison with the watermill.

The symbolic nature of the steam engine reached into other areas as well. In its very operation the contrast was vast. Behold the workings of the steam engine: a business report marvelled at the machinery of the Smith Manufacturing Co., a foundry and machine shop: "A monster engine drives all the machinery and the hum of countless wheels and revolving shafts makes one unaccustomed to it both dizzy and careful."[30] Even those accustomed to the machinery had to be careful. In 1877 Jacob Zimmerman's hand was mangled in the cogs of his machinery at the Farmer's Mill.[31] This would be the new showing of metal. The wheels of industry ground on.

Just as the new technology made venerable skills and crafts obsolete, it also created new opportunities for workers, especially as operatives on the machines themselves. They did this in Sedalia. The manufacturing census records of 1860 indicate that twenty-four people were hired in

THE ENGINES OF ECONOMIC GROWTH

industry. Ten years later one hundred ninety-four hands were employed in sixty businesses. But by 1890, as the town's population stabilized at around fifteen thousand, the city would have 1,328 operatives.[32] The new system was abroad throughout the community.

There was one special place, however, where the factory system, the steam engine, and the labor force operatives converged to turn the wheels of commerce and industry with special force. The jewel in the economic crown of the Queen City was the railroad shops for both the Missouri, Kansas, and Texas Railroad and the Missouri Pacific Railroad. These shops, in important ways, provided the basis for Sedalia's existence and growth. They were the only shops on those lines between Kansas City and St. Louis. They accounted for substantial employment with the M. K. & T. shops employing forty-seven men in 1881 and the Missouri Pacific shops hiring three hundred fifty-four men at the same time. The shops occupied twenty acres of land and included multiple brick buildings and a huge round house.[33] Locally, at least, it was not the steam engine that gave birth to the railroad but the opposite. The commerce provided by the railroads nurtured the steam engines in the factories. The census reports and the Board of Trade reports repeatedly noted that most of the manufacturing in town was not done for local consumption but for shipment to other places via the railroad. The factory owners invariably tied their fates to the railroad. So too did the community.

It is at this point that the symbolism of the railroad starts to run deeply and powerfully. The railroad itself was but an enormous steam engine that could move itself and move other things with it. And that engine came out of the factory, came out of the shops powered by steam engines too. And those factories and engines were located in Sedalia. The shops made freight, passenger, and sleeping cars. They also made the locomotives. Except for a few casting operations, their parts were produced there and the locomotives were assembled there. In 1881 seventy-six engines operated out of the Sedalia shops; that year forty locomotives were repaired or rebuilt there (not counting repairs in the round house).[34] It would be technically accurate to say that the steam turned the wheels in the factories in town. But it would be more revealing to note that the steam in the train engine turned the wheels of the railroad which then, in turn, turned the wheels in the factories which their own operatives tended in the din and the smoke and the clash of metal on metal. And it was the same system of factory operatives that produced that locomotive.

What had happened is clear: the machine had assumed a life of its own, with abilities and rhythms that far outdistanced its nature-bound counterpart of earlier years and with demands and force and priorities that also exceeded traditional standards. The dependence on nature had been sundered. Nature had been conquered. But now, the dependence was on technology and devices of human design, a dependence ultimately on the market. And, indeed, instead of liberating individuals and removing the limits placed on them by nature and then leaving them free, the new system replaced those limits with others that called for different disciplines and sacrifices. The sacrifices and personal restraints that had earlier been imposed had been born in resignation and justified by nature and the good of the community. Now the sacrifices and limits were not those of material gain and ambition alone; they involved each person's relationships with others. Discipline and sacrifice would not be for the good of the community or for the greater happiness of the individual either, for that matter, but for the greater productivity and profitability of the economy. Where earlier the economy had been subordinated to other purposes and goals in life, the market and the machine now ruled supreme and dominated those other elements. The spirit of life, the larger purpose, the soul of humanity's collective existence was being sacrificed under the wheels of progress.

Behold the juggernaut.

V

God and Mammon:
The Birth of East Sedalia

In a very humble cot,
In a rather quiet spot,
  In the suds and in the soap,
  Worked a woman full of hope;
Working, singing, all alone
In a sort of under tone:
  "With a Savior for a friend,
  He will keep me to the end."

Sometimes happening along,
I had heard the semi–song,
  And I often used to smile,
  More in sympathy than guile;
But I never said a word
In regard to what I heard,
  As she sang about her friend
  Who would keep her to the end.

Not in sorrow nor in glee
Working all day long was she,
  As her children, three or four,
  Played around her on the floor;
But in monotones the song
She was humming all day long:
  "With a Savior for a friend
  He will keep me to the end."

It's a song I do not sing,
For I scarce believe a thing
  Of the stories that are told
  Of the miracles of old;
But I know that her belief
Is the anodyne of grief,
  And will always be a friend
  That will keep her to the end.

> Just a trifle lonesome she,
> Just as poor as poor could be;
>   But her spirits always rose,
>   Like the bubbles in the clothes,
> And, though widowed and alone,
> Cheered her with the monotone,
>   Of a Savior and a friend
>   Who would keep her to the end.
>
> I have seen her rub and rub
> On the washboard in the tub.
>   While the baby, sopped in suds
>   Rolled and tumbled in the duds;
> Or was paddling in the pools,
> With old scissors stuck in spools;
>   She still humming of her friend
>   Who would keep her to the end.
>
> Human hopes and human creeds
> Have their roots in human needs;
>   And I should not wish to strip
>   From that washerwoman's lip
> Any song that she can sing,
> Any hope that songs can bring
>   For the woman has a friend
>   That will keep her to the end.[1]
>
> Ironquill

The convergence of particular forms of political behavior, applications of law, economic activities, urban growth patterns, and condescension into a single pattern helped to mark off the emerging ruling class of Sedalia. Of course, the opposite was equally true: being excluded from political participation, resisting certain forms of economic expansion, being labeled an outlaw not for a change in behavior but because of a change in law, and living apart from the "elite and fashion," all worked to draw those same lines by those excluded, if still with the mark of deference and subordination. This much was done. But the same process of separation and class formation at another level was not simply the passive consequence of the establishment of such a social structure. The active impulse in the generation of this other class found its earliest expression in deeply moral and even religious terms.

One distinctive quality which encompassed much that was transpiring in the development of the city was the secularization of society. The values implicit in the pattern the city was forming reflected a definite materialist bias. The goal of the city was economic growth and the institutions and behavior appropriate to that goal received official sanction.

The activity of the Board of Trade, which came to be the quintessential expression of this effort, provides an obvious example. The railroads, factories, and communication advances the board promoted held explicit economic functions. The disciplining functions of the public school system (even rewarding punctuality and obedience with "honor rolls" published monthly in the local press) as well as the inculcation of values with a success theme patently oriented around work illustrated in a slightly less direct fashion the larger material social orientation the city assumed. This comprehensive alteration focused not just on individuals, but on the relationships between people. The enforcement of contractual relationships with an inherent bargaining posture encountered a strong tradition with different priorities. The defense of these priorities that valued social obligations over social rights emerged in conflicts fought on the grounds of moral compulsion.[2]

When people are aroused to spontaneous collective action they can present vivid glimpses into the assumptions they hold concerning the proper social organization. One such incident erupted in Sedalia in 1867. Joseph Wood was known locally as a hard drinker. Still young, he had lost a good reputation curried by his parents just because of his drinking. On one of his frequent trips to a saloon, Wood began drinking, and he continued drinking. This was not unusual. But this time he carried a revolver. The more he drank the more reckless he became and before the afternoon ended he had pulled the revolver and shot and killed a man innocently standing by. The reaction was swift. The marshall arrested him and put him in the small, airy, log jail for a future trial. But his trial and execution came during the night as a band of unknown parties stormed the cell, mercilessly beat him, and then hanged him.

Like the mutilation of the slave Sam in the previous decade, this lynching conveys important insights into the social context that legitimized that course of action. The regard for law and order as defined by its midnight administrators was obvious. Neither in contemplation nor in reflection did it appear that such a course was anything but natural. Moreover, Wood had not just crossed the legal boundary set by civil society; he posed a threat to the stability of the Christian community. He had not just committed an inexcusable crime. He had sinned. In keeping with this pre-modern conception of criminology, the incident served as a warning: one local newspaper offered a full description of the events with a casual endorsement of the lynching and then observed: "Let the above suffice as a fearful example to others in our midst who are plunging along the same reckless course."[3] But the most telling feature of the episode came in the identification of alcohol as the seed of destruction of the community.

The drive against alcohol formed a prominent theme in the thrust to retain the moral qualities of society. Ironically and significantly, this effort could be mounted with the assistance of one contribution of the new social order—the right of free association. This legitimizing and protective feature itself was based in a longstanding conflict between spiritual and secular authority. Now it assumed institutional expression in the form of the proliferation of secret societies everywhere the market reached.

In Sedalia the establishment of the Independent Order of Good Templars in 1867 provides a poignant example. "An agency for carrying on the work of reform . . .," its local organizers proclaimed, the Olive Leaf Lodge #91, IOGT held as its objectives to form "a 'Fraternal Union' of every friend to moral reform; to establish order in more perfect tranquility; and to provide for and promote the general welfare of all connected with the institution." The functions and structure of the order reinforced the qualities embodied in its goals. The strong emphasis placed on fraternity in function and ritual endowed their brotherhood with a sacred mission. The secrecy of the order, including secret signs and passwords, placed a special quality of separateness from society on the brotherhood and made recognition of their fellows certain. The elaborate, convoluted ritual also served as a means of instruction less by rote than by active participation in an experience with the initiation being but one example. And the instruction extended into the realm of entertainment where recreation, besides providing a healthy alternative to debauchery, also provided moral lessons. Their activities reached the public arena if not the government when the order drew a sharp focus on temperance. When the murder perpetrated by Wood raised the issue, the Good Templars called upon Sedalians, not to enact more laws, but to refrain from drinking and selling alcohol "which is the source of so much crime, poverty, and sorrow in our community." The real culprit in the tragic event was alcohol, "the greatest criminal of our age."[4]

The IOGT did not monopolize the field in moral reform. Other organizations ranging from the Freemasons and Odd Fellows to the more exotic sounding but similarly constituted orders shared common purposes, and forms, and held similar social significance. The Sedalia Amateur Dramatic Association overcame a strong skepticism concerning vices associated with the theater by its presentation of plays with strident moralization such as the popular "Ten Nights in a Bar Room." The Sedalia Lyceum, a debating society, produced active and heated discussions by focusing repeatedly on the question of the applicability of the Fourth Commandment to Sabbath observance in modern society, a topic generally carried by the Sabbatarians.

The common element in these forms of experience lay in a reverence for the moral duties of neighbor to fellow neighbor and to society. As these obligations were interpreted as having sacred origins, they were not taken lightly and the passionate intensity that fulfilled them—a lynching, a moralistic melodrama, a secret initiation into the brother-hood—suggests that a large conflict between alternate conceptions of the social order was being staged. The moralistic—even pietistic—side of that conflict represented an effort to preserve and sometimes even to change society by venerating the moral qualities being removed. That their goals could be realized outside the structure of legal compulsions suggests even more that they sought the internalization of a moral code.[5]

This moral code, however, contained a striking ambivalence and duality of function. In one of the supreme ironies of the nineteenth century it stood quite capable of fulfilling needs generated from two opposite poles: the demands of community and the demands of industrial discipline. The same internalized moral compunctions that repressed destructive energies in the moral community also provided industrial capitalism a necessary tool in the conditioning of a labor force. But the goals of each were quite different and in a way irreconcilable. The productive orientation of the one conflicted sharply with the nonmaterialist fulfillment implicit in the other. Of course the acceptance of nonmaterialist ends could also work to the advantage of a system that provided the grossest partiality in the distribution of its material benefits. But the key to its ambivalence was that this code bestowed not just contentment in the face of despair and discipline for industrial growth but a sense of moral dignity—even righteousness—and of self respect on a basis vastly different from the success orientation of the work ethic. Perhaps the most representative symbol of the ambivalence rested in the difference in how the moral code was transmitted and how it was received.

Organized religion in Sedalia furnished important channels for the transmission of this moral code. It also was an explicitly elitist endeavor. Normal church services attracted, as the First Congregational Church boasted, "a fair share of the financial standing and business enterprise of the city" for membership, or, as the Christian Church proclaimed, its congregation represented "some of the best and most influential citizens." And those churches possessed a distinctly sterile quality that reflected their notions of proper social organization. The hierarchical, top down flow of authority within the churches militated against spontaneity within the congregation. A doctrinal opposition to voluntary moral action groups outside the structure of the church reflected this tendency as it also indicated the larger stance of the church before temporal issues. A form of worship that stressed ceremonial rites and liturgical cant could not be expected to extend to secular society the tone of moral passion denied the spiritual services. "Going to church" on Sunday was less a spiritual experience than a status function. As religious involvement dwindled to a series of forms and ceremonies the characteristic activities became infant baptism, church socials, and fund raising benefits. The grandeur of the church edifices themselves reflected their faith that salvation came through good works rather than through the experience of grace.[6]

The more active side of the social role of the churches came when they attempted to fulfill what they interpreted as a Biblical injunction: ". . . and the poor have the gospel preached to them." Each winter, coinciding with seasonal unemployment and increased burglaries and thefts, the prominent ministers of the community made a regular practice of conducting revivals. One of the most effective revivalists was the Reverend J. M. Van Wagner of the Congregational Church whose reputed "influence over the masses was very great and salutary." Van Wagner indicated his position on social issues when he brought Henry Ward Beecher to Sedalia and when he filled Beecher's pulpit while the Brooklyn divine was on vacation. But in his own words, what Van Wagner told his revival audiences came close to being a classic summary of the tenets of a Calvinist work ethic as a mechanism of social control: "the man who will not sweat and labor, earn his own living and provide for those dependent on him, whoever he may be, a son of the rich or poor, breaks heaven's most beneficent law and disgraces himself. Labor now becomes an important factor in man's redemption." And indeed an encouraging number were redeemed through the acceptance of this doctrine. This acceptance, however, was colored with the shades of submission that distinguished the religion as a disciplining force. For it was not simply a submission to God but acceptance of the system of social relations that valued work and productivity most of all.[7]

The revivals were but the most obvious signs of the work the churches conducted more regularly with less fanfare. Equally significant was a focus on children in the inculcation of habits of frugality, industry and competition through the Sunday Schools. Augmenting this routine function were the organizations to spread the gospel by the children themselves to others, organizations such as the Children's Heathen Mission Society, the Little Helpers, and the Missionary Society. The relationship of the churches to what they called "the masses" took these forms and others as they worked to establish lines of communication for spreading the code of morality conducive to the new social order.[8]

The most energetic, the most devoted, and the most enterprising preacher to the masses was the Reverend Edwin T. Brown. By the time he came to Sedalia in 1865, the Reverend Brown had established a wide reputation as a revivalist and was one of the most active representatives of the American Baptist Home Mission Society. His work in Sedalia testified to his ability. In very short order he established the First Baptist Church of Sedalia, saw it to a permanent building with a substantial congregation and moved on to Henry County to build new churches and reorganize others that had scattered during the war. But after he left Sedalia the city began to emerge as an important commercial center. Of sig-

nal importance to Brown was the location, in this growth, of the shops for
the Missouri Pacific in Sedalia in 1872 and 1873. This rapidly attracted
large numbers of men and their families seeking employment. And this
new field for spreading the gospel brought the Reverend Brown back to
Sedalia.

Although he had preached his first sermon in 1841 from Matthew
6:24, "Ye cannot serve God and Mammon," it was never quite clear
which one Brown chose to serve. While in Sedalia in 1865, he purchased
a large section of land on the outskirts of town. He returned to this land
to build himself a large commodious home and to begin again new religious initiatives. He built a church on this land. He rented rooms in his
house to railroad men. He sold lots on his land to the railroad men. He
loaned the workers the money to buy the land. In every way the Reverend Brown completely dominated the community that quickly emerged
as East Sedalia. When he died in 1879, he was a wealthy man. But he
measured his own success in terms of the souls he saved.[9]

And East Sedalia was founded as much on the Reverend Brown's
theology as on his land. Physically apart from the city, the different qualities that Brown's religion possessed marked an even greater separation
from Sedalia. As a Baptist, Brown's commitments belonged to a pietistic
tradition which stood at an opposite pole from the more liturgical forms of
worship characteristic of the churches in downtown Sedalia. Where those
sects relied on elaborate hierarchial forms of church government and administration with the theology being passed from the central offices
through the chain down to the parishioners, the Baptists held a strongly
decentralized conception of church government that kept the relationship
between believers and beliefs close. Instead of the ceremonial observance
of key parts of the liturgy, the pietistic worshippers in East Sedalia found
religious expression in the most intense religious experiences filled with
the passionate commitment of deep emotionalism. And in contrast to
awarding social merit according to secular activity, these pietists nurtured
an abiding egalitarianism that emanated from equal suffering in the eyes
of God.

The most telling differences came in the nature and achievement of
salvation. Redemption for the liturgical sects came as a fairly simple process involving the acceptance of a creed and form of behavior. For the
congregations in East Sedalia conversion meant much more. It came as
an intense experience that separated two different ways of life. Most of
all it was salvation from a sinful society, a society made that way by Adam's fall. The Baptists bemoaned this fall while the downtown liturgicals
accepted it. The Reverend Van Wagner had the pietists in mind when
he told a public meeting about Adam's curse, to have to labor for his
bread: "This is only a command to meet our changed condition. Labor,
now, after man's sad fall, becomes man's natural, normal condition, and

in our present state is a blessing instead of a curse." For the pietists the curse remained a curse. And salvation meant a washing away of the sins inherited from Adam. And it meant recapturing God's favor. Salvation was then, not the acceptance of secular morality, but admission into a religious moral community which involved the acceptance of duties, discipline, and civic virtue similar to that of a new citizenship.

Moreover, as important as the different conceptions of salvation were the different roads to it. As opposed to the rational arguments presented by the liturgical ministers, in the Baptist church of East Sedalia no amount of preaching could bring conversion. It had to come from within. This extremely personal grappling with the guilt and sinfulness of society and the transfer of loyalties from that society to a righteous community, was, as the congregation affirmed, "perfectly consistent with the free agency of man." Before Reverend Brown died he had baptized nearly nineteen hundred people and had seen six hundred twenty "added to the Redeemer's Kingdom."[10]

Physically, East Sedalia was on the outskirts of town. Culturally, it was in another world. The steady growth of its institutions with the East Sedalia Baptist Church as the center of social life brought an inward direction to the definition of their society as opposed to simply being defined in terms of the relationship with the parent city. The sheer absence of public services available to Sedalians accented this separation. The unpaved streets, the tenement houses, the ubiquitous animals (pigs for scavengers; cows for milk), were everyday reminders of the different experiences of the two communities. The common experience of working for the railroad provided an important bond within East Sedalia and a division with the society on the other side of the tracks. It was in fact difficult to see what the two communities had in common.

The policy makers of Sedalia as much as recognized this chasm when they inaugurated comprehensive programs designed to integrate the workers' community into the mainstream of the life of the city. The extension of the city limits to include East Sedalia in 1874 meant not just the increase in education facilities, lines of communication and transportation, and other services (although some, such as a water system, did not reach the East Sedalians until the mid-1880s); it also meant the extension of the tax structure to include more people. The education system was only a beginning in the effort to break down the cultural barriers separating the two societies.

The Library Association, and then the Board of Trade, inaugurated a popular speaker program with just this intent. Although they seem to have done little more than the bidding of the railroad companies when they invited speakers, they were actually reinforcing the separation. The Library Association invited the popular political orator, author, and Wisconsin newspaper editor, Marcus M. "Brick" Pomeroy to Smith's Opera

House. Pomeroy, a Copperhead during the war, had a far reaching reputation for his paternalistic concern for workers, his attacks on the national banking structure, and his persistent expostulations on the virtues of the self-made man—a strange combination. His efforts, however, were explicitly patronizing both in intent and execution. Colonel Robert S. Stevens of Sedalia had spent a hundred dollars to provide his workers on the rails copies of Pomeroy's *Our Saturday Nights*. He wrote Pomeroy of this, explaining "I have many brave, true, noble, workingmen in my employ whose hearts will be made glad as they read" the volume. The author's response was even more to the point: "May the present you so generously make them bind their hearts still closer to you, and add to the happiness of each recipient and family." And the doctrine Pomeroy preached was one of utter quietism and submission. "No matter what our burdens," he reminded the workers, "there are heavier ones borne by others . . . and *here* is cause for thankful happiness." He stressed over and over again, both in his writings and in his address in Sedalia, simultaneously the value of self help as a means of uplift and the important compensations available in a life without economic advantages. As he developed the latter part, to which *Our Saturday Nights* was largely devoted, he was forced onto grounds that affirmed the values separating the East Sedalians from the structure of the city. He made this antimaterialistic theme explicit at many points, and in so doing brought together several threads of the East Sedalia culture:

> Thank God the rich, who hold our notes as bonds which we must pay, cannot keep us from loving each other, nor from paying tribute to trusting hearts. Nor can they keep the ones who labor from loving each other truly, if their hands be hard, homes poor, and raiment scant. And if the rich do not care for us when we, too, are called to that rest which awaits us, not only here, where those who are but laborers are unnamed and unhonored, but in that better land where the rich are not our masters, and where there is no Saturday Night.[11]

Here was the dignity in nonmaterialist relationships, the promise of a future reward to compensate for the lack of reward on earth (but it too is a promise of honor and final triumph), and even a latent antagonism to the masters who worked against fulfillment on earth.

But Pomeroy was still Pomeroy. The views he expressed did not attack capitalism or offer much hope this side of the grave of escaping that system. Those attitudes only indicated that values not determined by the market could still exist. That they should find expression in rank paternalism suggest, however, that they belonged to an earlier day, the day when Pomeroy was a Copperhead defending a deferential society of inherited obligations. Nevertheless, they did affirm an essentially different kind of human relationship, one that was being subjected to the abrasion of an increasingly secular, materialist oriented set of relationships. And as such these values remained mainly as a solace and a standard of judgment of the life experience itself. In a sense they comprised a moral vision. The transformation of that moral vision into a conscious effort by people to secure its promise in this world, and thereby trying to alter the basis of society, would be the story of the development of new institutions, values, disciplines, and theories through their own agency. This would be the achievement of a consciousness of class—itself an expression of the agency of people.

VI

A Vale of Tears:
The Experiences of Change

The pains arising from industrialization have often been defined in terms of the measurable quantities of economic benefit and suffering. There is merit to this approach since the advantages of industry were seldom distributed in an equitable manner and since society itself was assuming an increasingly economic form or organization. But such an approach contains definite limitations that create a bias before the investigation proceeds. Basically, it carries the assumptions of market society back to a debate in which those very assumptions were under attack. To see exploitation only in terms of economic benefit reduces the experience of a transformation in social relationships to fluctuations within an unchanging set of market relationships. The institutions and values of the market society being erected in Sedalia, like those elsewhere, were growth oriented and hence contained a dynamic quality obscured by the static analysis of economics. What was involved, as both employers and workers, not to mention the rest of society, were acutely aware, was not just making more or less money, but the changing quality of life. This included alterations in the work experience but it also extended to larger social issues: the roles of family and sex, the nature of authority, and even the very tempo of life. These qualities came under serious strain in the process of change, a strain that the focus on the cash nexus can but skirt. Indeed, what was at issue in Sedalia in the 1870s and the 1880s was the ascending dominance of the cash nexus king and its retinue of quantitatively derived priorities.[1]

i. More Than a Machine

When master mechanic Walshe retired from the Missouri Pacific shops in Sedalia in 1883 he spoke with pride of the good discipline of the men who had worked under him "men moulded in our own garden school." As a foreman, he had been aware of the problems involved in the adjustment of a preindustrial labor force to a different pattern of work and he appreciated the proportions of the change. The dimensions of the transformation to a disciplined industrial workforce are deceptive. A fundamental aspect in that change was an alteration in the apprehension of time, a perception which held important social implications. In the prewar years of Pettis County, the fundamental unit of time measurement was the year. Geared to an agricultural pattern of life, the entire social and economic organization conformed to the calendar year. With a work day that varied according to weather and to available hours of daylight, generally conforming to the needs of farm animals, with weeks punctuated only by the Sabbath, with months that served even less as a guide to economic activity, the season assumed paramount importance and the yearly cycle stood as the only meaningful calendar of productive effort. Because of the very nature of the agricultural oriented activities, including the craftsmen in Georgetown, the entire system of credit and ultimate settling of accounts was based on a yearly schedule. (This system had presented an enormous obstacle to General Smith when in his rush to buy land for the future Sedalia, he discovered that money simply was not available no matter how meritorious the project because his neighbors had standing commitments for the year.) And beneath this system of reckoning time lay the notion that the requirements of the task determined the time expended, instead of the time being the determinant of the labor expended. This way of viewing time stood sharply opposed to that introduced by the railroad.[2]

The railroad brought two major innovations to Pettis County in the respect of time discipline. The most immediate thrust was that of an industrial form of work organization itself. The workers recruited from the countryside and brought into the shops or cars were rewarded not on the basis of the performance of individual tasks, a traditional and essentially individualistic scale of operation, but on the basis of the amount of time actually worked. This system of wage labor broke with tradition at a number of points. In the first place, it called forth the separation of work from the rest of life's activities, a separation which had been by no means obvious in a myriad of activities that combined work and leisure such as in shucking and quilting bees, hunting, cooperative barn raising affairs and all the joint efforts that caused neighbors to come together for work and play as well as the more individualized activities permitting each to work at a personal pace, by a personal rhythm, often marked to the tune of a traditional work song. And instead of the undisciplined habit of exerting a great deal of energy for a period followed by a period of revelry or an intense relaxation, which could be practiced in this preindustrial setting, industrial production demanded an even, regular, sustained work exertion, with the leisure warrened into increasingly artificial after-hours entertainment. Secondly, the preindustrial apprehension of time could persist only so long as it remained locally centered. The railroads forever destroyed this isolation. Just as they took the initiative in establishing a system of standard time in the 1880s to facilitate the operation of their lines, so too did the railroads impose their own system of time on the points of their traffic even earlier. When the railroad changed time, Sedalia changed time. The project undertaken by leading businessmen to provide the court house with a clock defensively proclaimed, it "is no one's special scheme, but is for the benefit of everyone, from the boy who goes to school to the laborer." Sedalia ran by the tick of the clock, the device Lewis Mumford aptly termed "the paragon of automatons."[3]

The actual work experience with massive machinery and an enormous productive system also generated a new form of work discipline. The tools quite literally became not creative objects guided by workers but in fact instruments to which the workers had to conform. On one level, that of the relationship between the worker and the system of work, this involved following a schedule determined by the running of trains. Those actually working on or with the moving locomotive experienced this change quite visibly as switch tenders, brakemen, and others had to operate with mechanical precision and synchronization of effort with each other and with the machines. The key to the different nature of the work lay in the large scale synchronized effort, for one part, and in the impersonalization attendant to the division of labor, for another part. Both of these factors became active disciplining agents in the physical relationship between workers and machinery. The pains were most visible here. In 1867 a worker in the Sedalia yards was trying to couple two cars. He slipped, fell between them and was crushed to death. He was the first victim in Sedalia. In the next quarter century countless others would follow him. Many more suffered permanent disfigurement by a loss of limbs, a fate common in work with the heavy machinery. It was here that the conflict between man and machinery was most obvious and that the discipline necessary to work in harmony with the machinery was at an almost inhuman level. Discipline was not just a matter of coming to work on time. It was a matter of survival.[4]

In his speech to the workers, foreman Walshe also suggested another form of discipline that was worthy of comment: ". . . I found you respectful and obedient," he told them, "whenever you were called to perform any duty, night or day, cold or hot, rain or shine." The respect and obedience was by no means natural in an area that had gone to war to resist the imposition of the authority associated with the railroad. And the existence of that obedience at any depth should have been doubted more by the retiring foreman; within the next few years two strikes by the same employees shut down the entire Gould Southwestern System. But the day-to-day following of orders was sufficient discipline to be noteworthy. For though the new corporate managers and executives attempted to graft themselves onto an earlier conception of deference, they held power by virtue of physical control of what had come to be the central institution in the market city and by the enforced dependency that made it central. And though the ideology of industry and self-help endeavored to buttress this distribution of power, the importance it attached to work as a positive virtue also brought the legitimacy of the power of the owners and managers into serious question.[5]

The total effect of this system of discipline can never be computed precisely. The costs and pains were not translated into dollars and cents. Nor can we really determine to what extent this system was in fact internalized instead of simply surfacing at particular moments of need. But inasmuch as the entire work experience had become an ongoing crisis situation it can be seen that an essential part of the lives of workers involved a submission to a form of authority, to a process of production, to a conception of time even, that "moulded" them to fit the needs of industry and in turn of the market. It involved nothing less than the denial of spontaneity, a crippling of the human spirit as real, if less visible, as that of the body.

ii. Visible Destruction

As constant as the hazards of railroad work were the reminders of unemployment: the new phenomenon of vast armies of tramps moving from city to city seeking food and shelter. Sedalia, because of its central location as a major junction of railroad lines, became a common target for tramps who rode on, under, and in the cars, and even on the cow catcher. With a life that included the perils of moving cars, they also suffered active oppression while on the trains—including the use of clubs to force them off—as well as the intensified law enforcement efforts in the city. "They are hungry, desperate, idle and vicious," was the common view within the city's establishment. They brought to Sedalia "a regular saturnalia of crime" and they "pretend to be seeking work, but are really looking for opportunities to ply their vocations as burglars, pickpockets and robbers." The contrast was as much one of priorities and values as an issue of law. When one reporter used an opportunity to talk with a tramp to learn his experiences, his frame of reference was not adequate to capture the essence of the life of a tramp. When he asked the man if he had "managed to get by all this time without doing an honest day's work," the tramp could only reply, "Well, that's perhaps what you fellows would call it." Hounded around town by the police, thrown into jail on the slightest pretext, chased from the doors of affluent Sedalians the "knights of the road" found a better reception and a more familiar culture in East Sedalia.[6]

The quality of life in the East Sedalia workers' community demonstrated other effects of the new social order. In fact, the roaming bands of unemployed were added to by the workings of the market locally. Although the businesses that responded to seasonal demand were able to build a cushion for the lean months, the workers, with neither property nor savings to provide an alternate income, had to seek other forms of employment. When the railroad reduced its work force for the winter, when the brewery closed its door in the fall, and when other businesses slowed down for the winter, large numbers of unemployed men hit the rails in search of work elsewhere, enough to drastically alter the population statistics with a regular seasonal variation. Young men vacated the boarding houses and married men would often leave their families while they went on the long hopeful search. At another level it meant an ever increasing number of desertions with the concomitant effect of forcing the wife and mother to find another source of income.[7]

But it was not just in work and out of work that the experiences were felt. The new conditions pervaded the entire environment of East Sedalia life. Unlike the main part of the city which had a public water system, East Sedalia depended on private wells for a water supply. After 1880 when the city required (ironically, for the purposes of sanitation) the enclosure of the pigs that had run wild through East Sedalia as scavengers, the pigs were penned next to the wells and cisterns with the consequence being epidemics of typhus. The wells also provided a constant threat to children playing near them. And if the area around the home was unsafe for children, the alternative playground, the railroad yards, claimed more lives. Compounding the high incidence of disease and accidents was a lack of adequate medical treatment. Even with a number of physicians in the city, and although the railroad moved its hospital to the city, professional medical treatment remained a luxury. The high incidence of infant mortality, the prevalence of patent medicines, and the strong reliance on superstition and faintly magical treatments (such as the madstone for the treatment of hydrophobia) all bespoke the contrast of physical conditions between people who benefited from this system and those who suffered from it.[8]

In this context, the ever present bands of tramps appear to have been the victims of a particular process not far removed from the system at work on those who remained at home. And hitting the road was but one way of coping with the physical problem of deprivation. The alternatives were not much better. One possibility was to seek charity from the city officials or other well-to-do people by begging. Although the image of the hapless beggar dominates much of modern compassion for the pains inflicted by industrialism, the actual practice of seeking charity was mitigated by two factors. The city was most reluctant to provide poor relief. Since poverty was a useful stimulus to get people to work, the provision of alms was seen as an encouragement for laziness. But besides being extremely difficult to receive anyway, there was a more important reason for not seeking charity. To go to the city for a hand-out came only as a last resort and often not even then. The social pressures against applying for relief were enormous. The convergence of a market system which placed a premium on the free, mobile individual as part of a labor force with a tradition that conceived the male as the head and breadwinner of the family fostered a notion of self respect that was inseparable from the amount of independence he was able to provide his family. It was more honorable to suffer, more honorable even to die than to lose one's dignity and pride by seeking aid while still able-bodied. The uncommon but bleak testimony of this in Sedalia took the shape of families starving to death before asking for charity. The family of James Nesbitt, out of work because of the winter reduction, was on the verge of death when one of his five sons was found gnawing a bone in an alley downtown. Others were found too late. The entire family of Nels Ficks, a Swedish tenant farmer on the Gentry farm, weakened by hunger, and without medicine, died after the family quit receiving help from Ficks' brother-in-law, a worker on the Missouri Pacific. The number of deaths of this sort were reduced considerably by the suicides. In 1871 the Sedalia *Bazoo* observed that suicides in the city were "alarmingly frequent." By 1889 they had become accepted as almost a regular part of the life of the city. It was, in these cases, better to die free than to live a life of dependence.[9]

It was not in poverty or even in death that the new experiences of industrial market society came; poverty was not new and death remained as the always available escape from a life considered in religious terms "a vale of tears" in contrast to the afterlife. Instead the agony of the new society came in the effort to stay alive and to live a life of honor, according to tradition, in a social structure that worked actively against the preservation of traditional roles and obligations, bringing people to compete with each other instead of working together, forcing families to separate to stay alive. It was within this systematic reduction of the human qualities of life that the fluctuations of the market operated to heap moral degradation on physical despair, adding insult to injury.

iii. The Corruption of Eve

Perhaps nowhere else were the pains of change so dramatically portrayed as they were in the transformation of the role of women in society. The pains were those of people caught between the opposing demands of tradition and social realities, whether in the family or in society. On the one hand the secularization of social relationships, the removal of moral restraints on economic activity and the release of productive energy could provide a new world of opportunity for woman since she was offered the promise of reward on the basis of merit, not on the basis of sex. On the other hand, the actual workings of that process intensified the family's task of providing moral inculcation and fulfilling relationships. The wife

and mother's responsibility in this latter function had the weight of ancient tradition behind it, albeit a weight that would crush the spirit and
hopes of countless souls, an entire gender. Just as the male, as breadwinner, held the responsibility of head of the household, the female was the
acknowledged head of the home. The origins of the two were the same.
Both came as punishment for the fall of Adam. As with the wrenching
demands on the breadwinner so too with the homemaker: the new order
came as a loss of a way of life.

The conception of the proper role for woman was in important respects the projection of Edenic purity into femininity. "The sweetest,
purest thing in all the world is a pure girl, when she is just emerging
from the daisy and violet field of youth and blushing into all the beauty
of womanhood. Standing thus in her purity, she moves more a thing of
heaven than of earth, and all heaven contains nothing more sacred from
the touch of the spoiler." So said the Sedalia *Bazoo*. In so proclaiming
the supreme distinction of the female sex it echoed a larger national set
of values that put women into a separate category, that made them con-
stitutionally and morally different from men. The qualities associated
with women were the virtues of purity, chastity, obedience, and fulfillment of obligations, and all the other virtues of the home. As such
woman could hardly have stood in sharper contrast to the aggressive,
competitive, materialist values honored by the market society.[10]

That contrast penetrated to every aspect of woman's relationship with
the world. Most obvious were the kinds of work incumbent on women as
mothers and wives. Her tasks represented in profound ways the persistence of the preindustrial work habits as they were regulated not by the
clock but by the task at hand, whether the crying of the baby, the boiling
of the water, or even the seasonal variants of canning and spring house-
cleaning. Emphasizing the distinctive qualities of this time orientation
was the existence within the same family of a disciplined worker who
came and went at regular times to a completely different form of work. It
was in such a situation that clearly "a woman's work was never done."

In the matter of motivations, purposes, and rewards, the chasm between the expected orientation of men and of women grew immense.
Love, devotion, submission, and the fulfillment of time honored obligations to the other members of the family combined to mark the woman's
role as one that focused on duties. Much of that duty was the duty of
serving as a restraining moral force. "The refining influence of woman is
the most delicate and potent factor in the social, moral and even the
political world. Unto her is instructed a holy mission," a Sedalia minister
reminded his congregation. Most immediately that mission was the moral
guidance of the home. To the children, this was a process of socialization, the nurturing of values and priorities. The same minister attributed
Charles Guiteau's assassination of President Garfield to the murderer's

lack of moral guidance in his early home life. He had been, he said, given unrestrained liberty, and the assassination was the consequence. For young women the consequences of ignoring the advice of their parents or the failure of their parents (namely, the mother) to provide the guidance would be even greater.[11]

The forces that sharpened the definition of women's role paradoxically worked against the fulfillment of that role. She was, after all, when performing her duty, supporting a social unit that responded in its larger orientation to the demands of the market, whether it be in the work of the husband, the education (in the broad sense of rearing) of the child, or even in the relationships of the household to the market as a consuming unit. The existence of the conflict between the two opposing forces within the family worked its greatest pains on the wife and mother. As the submissive party, hers was the final internalization of the tension. The choice that she could exercise doomed her to agony. In even such a literal encounter involving sexual relations, she could follow her duty of submissiveness and yield to passions incapable of release elsewhere, indeed passions that could no longer find expression in less physical relationships with the larger social unit, or she could resist, in the name of virtue entrusted to her, and violate her duty of submission. She could not win. And just as the loss of her children, itself related to the market, was probably the greatest injury she could bear, almost tantamount to it was the daily effort of providing training in moral behavior and inculcating virtuous social attitudes for her children when followed persistently by those same children confronting the very forces of the market she was striving against.

It is not difficult to find the incredible anxiety this maze of blocked passageways produced. In Sedalia the tension generated produced two prominent and related forms of release; suicide and drugs. When Mary Barlow told her neighbor that her life had become "nothing but a hell on earth," she was not expressing an uncommon sentiment. Her heart was broken, she said, since her husband had been drinking again. The despair this produced was unbearable for her; she drowned herself in the well. It was a similar despair which led Mary Hammond to commit suicide because her reputation had been slurred, and which caused two young women in 1888 to kill themselves after being seduced with false promises of marriage. A common death for women came in an overdose of laudanum, a tincture of morphine, or chloroform. Whether such deaths were intentional or not would be impossible to verify. Indeed, some few like Lizzie Cook, who was revived from a near fatal drug induced coma, claimed that they had not attempted suicide but had simply taken an overdose. The picture is blurred further when the victim had been accustomed to taking the drugs on a regular basis to settle her nerves, as some had been. That it was a matter of course, an acceptable explanation, to admit to the normal taking of drugs in a manner every bit as free as taking an aspirin the 1980s, suggests less about the personal problems of the people involved than about the nature of the society which recognized the need and found the escape justifiable. It suggests that the personal problems were social problems.[12]

Outside the home, where the woman had even less room for expression, she encountered similar tensions. One solution, according to J. West Goodwin, was to stay home: "Your lives are so circumscribed and set about by certain metes and bounds, that it is impossible for you to learn of the wicked wiles and cruel ways by which men entrap and ruin their victims." The restrictions on her were already abundant though. The outward badge of this restriction was the binding nature of their fashions. For encouraging and just discussing the abandonment of corsets with girls in their physiology classes, two female teachers in neighboring towns were dismissed from their positions. Besides the teaching job (itself an extension of home duties) few opportunities for work were open to women. And these normally consisted of mending, cooking, washing and other household associated chores. But the circumstances for the performance of these tasks had been sharply revised. What had once been done out of love or a sense of duty to the family now came as a commodity with a price. And this form of alienation precipitated still others: when a woman from Houstonia appeared in Sedalia wearing a man's clothes so that she could secure a job as a cook at a dollar a day instead of the customary three dollars a week for woman, she was arrested for impersonating a male and being seen in public in long pants. Even the leap year concession allowing women a more forward role in initiating relationships served to mark the distinctiveness of her situation and to reinforce the norm of a male dominated, male initiated society.[13]

It was this tension that was woman's reward in the development of market society. That tension intensified in an oscillation between the two poles of respect and independence, the valued ends of two opposing cultures. In the process of changing from one world to another she received the worst of both. In this she was not too far from the experience of her male counterpart although the manifestation and tensions came at different points and in different ways. But the challenge for both was the same. It was not to accept either world but to create a new one.

iv. Of Faith and Fear

Considered for their fullest meaning, the experiences of several people around Sedalia late one night in February, 1885, offer a special commentary on the pattern of social change generated in the rise of industrial market society. What these individuals saw was of little actual consequence: a stunning display of the aurora borealis. What they perceived it to be held great social meaning: an apocalyptic vision that personified and dramatized fundamental hopes and fears.

The night air was crisp, sharp, and clear around 3:15 in the morning of February 14, 1885, when a newspaper reporter began to walk home after a late night at work. He stopped when he saw something unusual. At first he thought it was the first light of dawn—a dull, lurid oval of light that seemed to stretch for nearly a mile on the horizon. Figuring the hour, though, he changed his mind and began to regard it as a distant fire. Even this proved wrong when the light grew brighter, became a brilliant red, and lit up the earth so brightly that chickens began to squawk. Then he saw

> a vapory cloud as white as snow rise upon the crimson field [and] gradually unfurl itself into the form of a beautiful female, in flowing robes and hair, with outstretched arms, bare to the elbow, and across her brow [was] what bore the resemblance of a flaming crown. Her left hand was extended with the index finger pointing downward and in her right hand was a sword whose point was raised at an easy angle, the tip of the blade being tinged with red, resembling blood, which gradually ran down the hilt.

The reporter stared at the apparition for several minutes, until the figure blurred and dissolved and the light faded, leaving only the stars twinkling in the cold night. He ended his written account of this extraordinary phenomenon, in hopes that others had seen the spectacle, with the natural questions: "What was it, and what does it portend?"[14]

Indeed, the anonymous reporter was not the only person to have been awed by heavenly lights early that morning. Jay Elder, a worker for the railroad in Sedalia, replied to the reporter's questions that he too had seen an apparition. It was not quite the same, though. Elder saw the skies turn red a little later, around 4:30 in the morning. The light grew brighter and turned the color of blood, formed the shape of a circle, and then quickly changed to a black hue. That dark specter remained for a minute until the image suddenly

> assumed a red color again, and seemed to be filled with men as thick as they could stand, with weapons of war and while I was gazing at the strange movements it was making, the men all seemed to engage in a hand to hand struggle, for life as soldiers do in a charge fight, and beneath all this, but in close proximity was a streamer, like a rainbow, on which was written, "All nations shall become engaged in war and confusion, wo! wo! to the inhabitants of the earth." And suddenly the whole of the phenomenon passed away, in great confusion.

Elder ended his story with an assertion that he knew the meaning of "these strange things," and he promised to write shortly what he believed "is to follow."[15] He never wrote further, but the general meaning was clear from his account. A dramatic struggle had been foretold in this vision.

A half-dozen people in the area wrote the newspaper with a variety of impressions. Some laughingly discounted the whole experience as being the result of too much "bug juice." Correspondents from Jefferson City used the incident to suggest that the red sky represented only the shame and embarrassment Sedalians should feel for trying to remove the state capital to their town. But others were more serious. "P. J.," an engineer on the railroad, declared that he too had seen something that morning as he brought his train into Sedalia from the west, and he assumed it to be a big fire in town. As he came around a curve, though, the light disappeared. While he saw a cloud of light, it never formed any definite shape. Thus: "My opinion is it was a reflection of a northern light from an iceberg and some kind of mirage. I don't take much stock in superstitions if I am an engineer and never carried a rabbit's foot in my life."[16]

It would be easy to discount these premonitions as fantasies whose significance, like the apparitions themselves, dissolved into the cold night. The engineer probably grasped the germ of physical truth in the matter; while it was rare for the northern lights to extend to this area with such brilliance and intensity, other sightings of ethereal hues with less vivid forms testify to the possibility. But the discovery of the physical source of these spectacles does not explain the meanings imparted to them. For as long as mortals have watched the lights and attempted to divine the future in their movement and color, the aurora borealis has been a source of elaborate visions. Those people who witnessed the dazzling sky around Sedalia believed that what they saw held an insight into their own society. The two most precise observers were willing, after all, to risk public ridicule because they believed so firmly what their senses told them or because they knew from their understanding of their community that no real risk was involved. They were confident that they should and would be taken seriously by others. Even the skeptical engineer betrayed the exceptional nature of his hard realism. When he declared that he did not take stock in such premonitions, even "if I am an engineer," and that he "never carried a rabbit's foot" he suggested that his cohorts would be much more amenable to finding a larger meaning in the cluster of lights and figures they saw. And both of the lengthy accounts, despite the diversity of the observers and their sightings, seemed to suggest the same meaning for the visions. In their descriptions both implied the specter of social conflict; indeed it was the imagery of cataclysm.

The insight into that society suggested by this incident is not restricted to a test of the predictive ability of the visions. If it is true, as

Keith Thomas has suggested, that "in hallucinations, no less than in ordinary vision, human perception is governed by stereotypes inherited from the particular society in which men live,"[17] then the insight raised by this experience centers on the social origins of the particular shapes the lights assumed. The source of these visions and these shapes lay in an enormous feat of projection, the projection by different individuals of different images with incredible precision and detail—including even in one case the letters and words inscribed on a banner—onto the dancing and shifting lights of the aurora borealis with the same essential meaning—the apprehension of social conflict. The historical function of the visions was not to predict social struggle, as the witnesses believed; the function was to reflect the tensions and conflict that already pervaded their society.

This was not the only metaphysical apparition to visit Sedalians, although the others were characteristically more personal and less collective in purpose. Ghosts or phantoms appeared to people on a number of occasions. It was uncommon for a complete and full account of such sightings to be published and recorded and most of these encounters probably remained the knowledge of only small groups of intimates. Yet sometimes they did surface. Conductor Jones, for example, in 1887 announced that he was quitting his position with the railroad. He feared he was going mad. Some three or four months earlier Reverend Pierce was killed when, on the train, he fell onto the tracks and under the wheels. Ever since then Jones saw the minister's ghost every time he passed that fatal point.[18] Or, in the village of Beaman, a ghost, presumably the spirit of a worker who had lived there but was killed, repeatedly visited the house of J. D. Earheart where several railroad workers boarded.[19] The possibility of a phantom presence even became subject to careful, skeptical scrutiny as when the *Bazoo* sent an unbelieving reporter to expose a local seance. While remaining unconvinced, he reported that "things happened for which he does not pretend to account and no accomplice could have been present. . . ."[20] And perhaps it was another seance of sorts that caused some commotion when the *Bazoo* referred to a "ghost show" in town.[21] What especially stands out in all of the reportings of such sightings and the apparent market in spiritual communication is the apparent assumption of the validity, or at the least the possibility, of such spiritual existence and presence. They were, at a minimum, taken seriously. This should not be surprising given the reference by sociologists and psychologists to "the almost universal belief in ghosts in preindustrial societies."[22] This society was not that far removed from its preindustrial origins. For that matter, even the skeptics guarded themselves. The local newspaper *The Truth* once quoted Madame de Stael's answer when queried if she believed in ghosts. Her answer was a diplomatic, "No, but I am afraid of them."[23]

To explain these phenomena, and their significance, without assert-
ing either the positive truth of their existence or the denial of such a
possibility can begin by a consideration of the circumstances under which
the personal spirits commonly apear. As Robert Blauner has observed, the
death of those still in the prime of life creates the social discord conducive to the appearance of ghosts. "Dying before they have done their full
complement of work and before they have seen their children off toward
adulthood and their own parenthood, they die with *unfinished
business*. . . . Ghosts are reifications of this unfinished business."[24] Max
Gluckman similarly pointed to the individual's "social personality," the
total set of relationships with the rest of the community, that survives
after death, that attempts to fill the vacuum left by the deceased.[25] The
relevance of these theories in understanding the phenomena of the individual ghost sightings is obvious. But there also seems to be a relevance
to the larger collective vision witnessed. The apparition in the colors of
the aurora borealis bore no individual's "social personality," nor did it
speak to any particular individual. The message was to the community, a
warning to the society. If the soul of the individual wandered loose during the period of adjustment to new social relationships, so too does it
seem that now the soul of the community wandered in the wake of the
annihilation of earlier social relationships and the ascendancy of new
ones. Haunted by both the past and the future, what these people saw in
the sky that cold February night in 1885 was the vision of their community's tormented soul.

The spirit world could strike ghastly fear into the hearts of mortals.
So too, however, could it generate supreme faith and hope. This function
emerged especially, but not exclusively, among the diseased, the infirm,
and the afflicted—and those around them. For as long as people have
suffered, so have they sought recovery in ways that required faith in one
healing process or another. The faith healing normally identified in religious circles appeared in several instances in this area. The laying on of
hands, as used to cure a man from Moberly who suffered an unidentified
but apparently critical ailment, possessed both traditional magical sanction and the scriptural approbation from Mark 16:18: "they shall lay
hands on the sick, and they shall recover."[26] The new denomination of
Christian Science also entered the area and vigorously defended its tenets. Drawing a stark line between the spiritual and the material worlds,
and the association of redemption from sin with redemption from mortal
maladies, this approach to healing—and indeed to life—possibly made
most explicit the rejection of worldly materialism.[27] But there were other,
similar, agencies to be consulted as well in the treatment of sickness.
Eliza McLaughlin, the wife of a carpenter on the M. K. & T., was well
known as a clairvoyant, a future teller, a mind reader and a healer. By the
utilization of electricity—although never clearly defined as something in-

volving raw electrical current with a generator or something closer to common theories of animal magnetism—she could cure rheumatism, headache, neuralgia, and other ailments.[28] To rely on any of these healing agencies required faith, a faith in the mysteries of life unfathomed by most people and controlled only by supernal or miraculous phenomena. Some of this was no doubt written off by contemporaries as so much superstition. Other of it would be labeled heresy. In either case, though, the point of significance of these processes likely has little to do with the relationship of this healing to orthodox Christianity. Instead it reflected hope, not in the material world but in forces that transcend material existence. It reflected hope not in science but in a transcendent spirit. And it reflected a dependence not on licensed physical therapists in their clinics and laboratories but on agents higher than mortal humans.

In terms of effectiveness, indeed, such faith-healing practices may well have been as satisfactory as the treatment offered by the clinical physicans. Certainly some elements of the process were identical, elements which have been demonstrated to be of critical significance in producing recovery. The faith in an expected result, obvious in the practitioners of the occult and religious healing, was every bit as evident in the modern clinic. In either case, as Keith Thomas has noted, all medical prescriptions beyond the immediate comprehension of the patient have the appearance of magic and stimulate the same confidence and hope—and faith—in the results of such treatment.[29] Indeed, the placebo effect whereby the patient's recovery is stimulated by a bolstering of that confidence remains an important element of any treatment of nonorganic maladies. And whether manifest in the ritual and hocus pocus of gazing into Mrs. McLaughlin's crystal ball or in the ritual of paying the physician and the corollary that the more paid the better the treatment, the ritual, the faith, and the mystery bears a striking resemblance. For that matter, the "science" of the medical practitioner sometimes seemed less than confidence inspiring. In 1884, a Dr. Lee went to Warrensburg to revive an executed murderer by means of electricity. This man of science went upon the principle, "that in the human body there are hundreds of small animals which he denominates life builders, and which carry little secretions in their mouths to build up the waste places in the system. The diminutive animals never make a mistake but do their work with the precision of an engineer." Thus, with shades of Mary Wollstonecraft Shelley, he sought to revive the little animals by inducing electrical current between the feet and the tongue of the cadaver.[30] By contrast the faith healers and their injunctions to the divine and the occult appear timid. They knew their limits. They may have tried to communicate with the spirits of the departed and they may have tried to prevent the death of those who were approaching their end. But they stopped far short of the blasphemy or arrogance of attempting the resurrection of the mortal remains of the dead.

Respectful of those limits or not, the material world of mortal existence was gaining ascendancy. In terms of markets, commodities, and the structure of life itself, the exchange of goods between individuals and the institutions and technologies facilitating that exchange, the material world ruled and gave life its purpose. Yet the nonmaterial world, the world of supernatural visions, ghosts, and troubling fears, and the world of deeper meanings and sources of comfort and well-being, that world held on. After all, whether as a source of fear and faith or a broader sense of fulfillment and satisfaction, that was the soul of existence. And the soul would live on.

PART THREE

The Agency of the People

VII

The Businessmen and the Market

The depression of the 1870s rudely challenged the course of Sedalia's development and set new forces in action. The depression affected businessmen most directly as it intruded on both the values of the market and its material operation. The impulse toward thrift and away from active speculation received considerable force from the shortage of money and from the reduced level of economic activity. Indeed, the fulfillment of routine financial obligations to the local government was actively impaired as sources of income dwindled. In this crisis, the businessmen, the class directing the growth of the city, fell back on basic assumptions concerning the proper functioning of society. Most explicitly from the view of the businessmen, the issue focused on the contract as the axiomatic basis of social relationships.

i. The Social Contract

In 1873 the Missouri Pacific Railroad secured an injunction against Pettis County along with other Missouri counties to prevent the collection of property taxes levied on its land. By the standards of the assessments on the railroad by other counties, the rate of assessment used by Pettis County was not exorbitant. At a time when the assessment by other counties ranged between eight thousand dollars and twenty thousand dollars per mile, the Pettis County officials taxed the road at fifteen thousand dollars per mile. The variation among the counties normally followed a pattern of high assessments where the rail lines were sparse and lower tax requirements where more miles of track existed to be taxed. The local origins of the assessments reflected the particular needs of each county rather than the physical value of the lines themselves. It was this variation that the railroad sought to eliminate in its suit as it hoped to secure a standardized basis of tax assessment. Involving a number of counties, the case followed a complex path through the courts that lasted for years with a final compromise settlement restoring part of the back taxes for those years to the counties. But the denial of the funds in the midst of the depression meant that the county would be unable to meet its own obligations.[1]

One of the expenses the county faced was the payment of bonds on railroads that had been issued in the previous decade but that were now coming due. Since the tax revolt of 1869, opposition to payment of the bonds had persisted in an unorganized but widespread and persistent effort to refuse payment of those taxes. Now in the 1870s as the availability of public funds dwindled and the need for them increased and as the Missouri Pacific refused to pay its taxes to the county, the movement for resistance gained a new impetus. The crucial catalyst for action came in a United States Supreme Court decision in 1876 which responded directly to the same issues raised in Pettis County for the past seven years. The decision finally determined that the county courts did in fact have the obligation to secure public approval for the issue of railroad bonds after 1865—something the Pettis County Court had failed to do.

In a much less confident spirit than when the bonds were issued, the county court called a mass meeting of the citizens of the county to determine explicit sentiment on the disposition of the bonds. Even this action registered negatively with some businessmen. R. T. Lindsay in Dresden considered the proper course plain and this action superfluous:

> Whose agents are the County Court Judges? Are they the agents of the bond holders or of the tax-payers? The calling of the meeting by the Judges is senseless, if they are so trammeled by their oaths of office as not to be able to carry that expression.

The point was obvious: the court should simply refuse to pay the bonds now declared illegitimate. The public meeting bore out this feeling. Against the urgings of one judge and a few of the original promoters who called for a more generous policy of paying some of the funds to retain the good credit of the county, one reporter found that "there seemed to be but one expression and feeling . . . and that was to throw off the heavy bonded debt which hangs over the county."[2]

The court ultimately chose to bring the bonds to a test in court instead of directly applying the higher court's decision. But the significance of the meeting's resolution that payment on the bonds and collection of taxes for that payment be ceased immediately was lost on no one. One account of the behavior of the insurgents suggests a crucial point in this regard: "They do not seem to regard such an action as one of repudiation, but one of duty to themselves claiming that they had nothing to do with the contracting of the debt, and that it would never have existed if they had." The seeds of this rebellion, like that of the continued resistance to the railroad bond payment lay in assumptions of the primacy of the contract as a social bond. The railroad had not filled its obligation of the contract when it refused to pay the taxes society demanded. At the same time, however, the railroad demanded payment from Pettis Countians on a contract to which they had never consented. The conception of the contract, the system that enabled marketable relationships, also provided a measure of protection. And the protection loomed large not only in economic affairs, but in the responsibility of public officials to their constituents.[3]

If the rights of citizens were heightened by the depression, though, so also were the obligations entailed in the social contract. These too relied on a market conception of social relations in which reward came according to productive effort. In 1876, following retrenchment programs reminiscent of the earliest years in the city, including another fiasco with the fire department, the city elected a new mayor. That mayor, David Blocher, an agricultural implement dealer, promised to bring the principles of sound business practice to the city government. In his inaugural speech Blocher made his reform explicit. Admitting of few ways to cut further the expenditures of the city, when quite visibly the sorry condition of the streets testified to the need for more attention, Blocher proposed a new source of revenue. There was a very large element in the city, Blocher declared, who enjoyed all the benefits of citizenship without contributing their share. In particular, this element paid no taxes. They would henceforth have to pay their way. These tax evaders, it turned out, were those who did not own enough property to be taxed. His solution was to impose an annual improvement tax of two dollars on every person regardless of wealth, income, or property. If a person could not afford to pay this tax he could, instead, donate two days' labor to the city.[4]

The design of the program had two explicit goals. First, it would add money to the city treasury. Second, it would get some work out of the hordes of tramps and unemployed inhabiting the depression ridden city. But the measure held importance and far ranging implications that reflected the expansion of market relationships throughout society. In its intended function of bringing everybody into the workings of society, the measure provided a literal example of the extension of the productive orientation. What Willard Hurst has described as "the release of energy" came in this instance as an enforced policy exacting productivity. In its large thrust it affirmed the tenets of the work ethic as the basis for social organization, but in its particular enforcement, the acceptance of work in place of money, it went even further. By allowing such payment, the city affirmed that even those who had no money still had a property they could part with: work was a transferable commodity. All this held converse implications as well that were less clear. By equating work with the means to full citizenship, the new mayor suggested that society held obligations to workers, obligations that were by no means evident in 1876 beyond the provision of routine services.

The enforcement of the gospel of work found support in a less advanced form when J. West Goodwin, editor of the Sedalia *Bazoo*, initiated a campaign to reintroduce the whipping post as a punitive measure for dealing with the petty crimes that came with the burden of unemployment: "The *Bazoo* unhesitatingly advocates THE WHIPPING POST!" Though harking back to a primitive conception of criminology this campaign justified the whip in the same terms of the work ethic that Mayor Blocher used: "There is no evading the curse (if it can be called a curse) that has fallen upon the human race—that it shall live by the sweat of its brow." Speaking both of idle blacks and white tramps, Goodwin noted that:

> Liberated from the restraints which held them in wholesome subjection and which made them producers instead of consumers, a very large proportion of them became consumers instead of producers and threw an additional burden upon society. They must live—if they eat not the fruits of their own labor, they certainly do those of others.

Whether as vengeance or enforced opportunity the gospel of work extended from the businessmen and from the city to those parts of society where they felt it most lacking.[5]

ii. Competition: The Lifeblood of Freedom

But it was not just the problems of a preindustrial, precapitalist orientation that the promoters of enterprise and the work ethic faced. On the one hand they sought to spread the doctrine of work, of success, of the release and fulfillment of Promethean capacities; on the other hand they encountered very real barriers to such fulfillment not only in tenacious forms of primitive organization, but also in new obstacles that derived from the enforced acquisitiveness of the market society itself. The barriers were centralized concentrations of power with demands that ran counter to the needs of the local market since both operated from a scarcity consciousness. The perception of this problem, whether as a monopoly, a process of loss of control over home institutions, or an effort even to counterbalance large corporate power with equally powerful opposing institutions, reflected a decisive reorientation in the culture of the businessmen, although one that proceeded from the same assumptions as the efforts to transform a precapitalist society. Although in one sense this change involved an about-face from Promethean ambition to a defense of local independence, the two impulses remained closely related in their origins.

The first confrontation over the issue of the exercise of control over local society came in the arena that held a potential in the eyes of Sedalia's commercial class as a sanctuary for the gospel of work: the public schools. The spirit in which education was conceived in Sedalia was the spirit of freedom, and that was the spirit of the marketplace. "In the schools and churches and Sunday Schools, the poor and illiterate man has a chance for hope," one student proudly proclaimed at the Franklin School Thanksgiving entertainment. "His children have a chance, and those of us who are poor ought to rest with no little sense of security behind the bulwark of our free institutions." The common school system, he continued, was the basis of a free society. One teacher described the goal of education as the creation of "an aristocracy of talent," a society that rewarded merit, itself a goal that fell clearly within the structure of market society. The inculcation of habits of discipline was important in this framework. A visitor to the kindergarten observed what he called "a combination of work and play," and then noted of the experience, "it will be profitable to the children, because it learns them early in life the value of discipline and an easy, graceful use of the body as well as a drill of the mind." Of far more importance, at least to some of the teachers, was the inculcation of a free, untrammeled spirit. At a meeting of the public school teachers, Mrs. M. E. Wood defended this function of education from the criticism of her colleagues and then turned her attention to the excesses of discipline they sometimes demonstrated:

> The most perfect quietness, mechanical movements and clock work precision does not always indicate the best managed school. It rather shows that nature has been crushed out and dull machinery substituted.

That Mrs. Wood could equate nature with creative energy, that the student in the Thanksgiving presentation could identify the school with opportunity, and that the kindergarten should attempt to channel the energies of five-year-old children into a productive direction all suggest the market assumptions of the education system of Sedalia.[6]

Because of this important role, Sedalia's businessmen proved reluctant to restrict the operations of the public schools. The opportunity certainly was there. Throughout the period the board of education was dominated by the city's commercial class that sought to infuse education "with a thoroughly practical cast." The constant shortage of funds did force some retrenchment, however. In 1871, a lack of money forced a reduction of the school year from its normal thirty-six weeks to thirty weeks. The board would go no further though. The following year when two proponents of further retrenchment called for the abolition of one school and the elimination of teachers at others, and then sought election to the school board to enact their proposals, they failed miserably. But the force of the depression ultimately gave them a belated victory. After cutting corners to save money for three years, in 1876 the board of education finally restricted school activity further by reducing the school year now to twenty-four weeks and suspending the operation of the high school. This came as a last resort and within two years, the board began to take steps to restore the regular education system. It lengthened the school year to the normal thirty-six weeks and began construction of several new rooms in the school buildings. Money was still a problem, but the board met that need, not by maintaining a low level of operation but by initiating a larger school tax levy, reducing teacher salaries by twenty per cent, and by abolishing the office of superintendent of education. The businessmen on the board of education practiced what they preached and preached what they practiced.[7]

Equal to the threat to the schools presented by the limitations of money caused by the depression were the limitations presented by a state imposed system of school book selection. In an effort to secure uniform education within the counties, the Missouri legislature required the county educators to choose the books for the whole county for five years at a time. As early as August, 1879, the issue of schoolbook change began to generate excitement. Some, in the interest of getting rid of outdated books, wanted to proceed with the selection of new books even though the five-year period would not expire until December. The school board, however, despite the members' own aspirations for a change, decided to wait until the end of the year. At the same time the board delayed the decision, it expressed strong reservations about the operation of the current system. The state law, the board observed, bound only the counties to the fulfillment of a contract—not the publishers. Thus, while counties were forced to buy books from specified companies for five years at a time, the companies would often raise the prices of the volumes; the county was then forced either to pay the higher price or violate the state law. It was a one-sided contract. The source of the law was evident to the members of the board of education: the schoolbook trust had exerted power over the state legislature.[8]

The meeting to choose the new schoolbooks in January, 1880, attracted widespread attention and participation. For months Appleton's and McGuffey's had been running huge advertisements in the local press in an attempt to secure adoption of their own texts. The chief executive of each school in the county was to have a single vote in the decision of future books. As the meeting convened in the city council chambers, the assembly swelled with teachers, publishers' agents, and interested citizens. To allow more room, the meeting moved to the courthouse. There, in a long process, the educators forced the publishers' agents to debate the relative merits of their texts. In this highly competitive atmosphere, reflective of values instilled in the classroom, the county schools chose the readers, spellers, arithmetics, grammars, and other books to be used, as provided by law, for the next five years. Most of the books chosen were from Appleton's.[9]

The meeting seemed to settle the issue. But slightly more than a year later Appleton's brought suit against the Sedalia Board of Education. The city schools, it seemed, were using McGuffey's texts. In the January, 1880, meeting the Sedalia board quietly sat out the decision process declining participation on the basis that the members of the board wanted to be completely free in their own selections for the city schools. Former mayor, now president of the Board of Education, David Blocher, explained the situation. After refusing to commit themselves at the meeting, the members of the board had agreed with an Appleton's agent to use the Appleton books on a trial basis only. Not satisfied, Blocher said, they had changed to McGuffey's. The suit continued in the court for a while, but the law was clearly on the side of Appleton's. Finally, the schools of Sedalia had to return to the Appleton texts until January, 1885. The pride of Sedalia's market spirit, the opportunity-creating public school system, had been whipped into line by the state in an alliance with a publishing company whose wares the board of education had rejected.[10]

iii. The Curse of Consolidation

In the schoolbook fight, Sedalia's educators attached considerable importance to the competitive nature that was supposed to prevail between the two suppliers of textbooks. The five-year law drastically limited the gains that could come from constant competition, even erasing them. It was only natural then that Sedalia's commercial class should be equally sensitive to competition and local control in the city's relationships with the railroads. But the larger tendency was away from competition and decentralization. After the original efforts to build the three railroads serving the city, the actual control of the lines became increasingly distant and less responsive to local needs. For example, in 1868, the city refused to issue the bonds voted for the Tebo and Neosho Railroad until the other counties on the line had paid their shares. With three local bankers, Asa C. Marvin, Cyrus Newkirk, and J. R. Barrett, on the railroad board of directors, they pressed their demand effectively, and when the city paid its bonds, Marvin became chief executive of the corporation. But in 1870 it became necessary to secure financing from New York banks in order to complete the road. With this, the management changed hands. The road now became a part of the Missouri, Kansas, and Texas Railroad with Colonel Robert S. Stevens as president. It was not a complete alienation of control, however, since Stevens moved the main offices of the larger line to Sedalia and since he maintained a close personal contact with his fellow townsmen. The buckets of coal he provided the unemployed in the winter, like his donation of Pomeroy's books to his workers, extended that contact to most in the city. But Stevens was an exception, and the process by which Sedalia's businessmen lost control of the central institution of the city was just beginning. The process on other roads came even faster in the wake of expanding spheres of activity. Within five years, the control of the railroads was remote indeed and was following a course taking it constantly further from the needs of Sedalians.[11]

In the absence of locally responsive corporate management of the railroads, the quality of the market that served to perpetuate the interest of the Sedalians was its competitive nature. The city's commercial growth would be insured so long as three separate lines competed for the traffic of Sedalia. Hence, Sedalia's businessmen especially welcomed the occasional rate wars between the competing roads. But in one such war, in 1875, the possibility of the defiance of local interests, once control was lost and competition broke down, became manifest. Competing with the Missouri Pacific, which connected St. Louis and Kansas City through Sedalia, the St. Louis, Kansas City and Northern ran well north of Sedalia to connect the two points. The latter road, in August, 1875, began a series of rate cuts in an effort to capture the commerce between St. Louis and Kansas City from the Missouri Pacific. This was not unusual. However, Superintendent Talmage of the Missouri Pacific refused to meet those reductions as he attempted to force the opposing line to operate at a loss. The conflict generated a strong opposition to the Missouri Pacific in Sedalia as regular customers began holding their freight and others simply refused to travel on such an arrogant line. The Missouri Pacific, a local reporter argued after less than a week of the tension, "will have to come to the cut, despite all that has been said to the contrary, for not only is she losing much of the great prestige enjoyed lo these many years, but the loss of travel is becoming so palpable as to render matters desperate." Although the two railroads persisted in their practices for a few more days, they eventually reached an agreement at rates close to the old, high level. Well before then, however, it was obvious, in the way that the railroad had flaunted the principles of competition and spurned the material interests of the city, that "the Missouri Pacific has made a mistake, one in fact that it will take years to cancel." Actually, it would be more than a decade afterwards when only the perceived presence of an equal countervailing threat could refurbish the alliance between the businessmen and the railroad.[12]

If there were any doubts about the source of the impulse toward centralization and consolidation, they were effectively dispelled at the end of the decade. In 1879, in an effort to provide noncompetitive channels for commerce between Chicago and the West, Jay Gould began a series of bold moves to bring the Missouri railroads under his control. Through secretive stock market purchasing he was able to gain personal control of the Kansas Pacific, the Kansas City, St. Louis and Northern Railroad, the Missouri, Kansas and Texas Railroad, and the Wabash. With appropriate consolidations, the only two lines between Kansas City and St. Louis became the Missouri Pacific and the Wabash. Gould had earlier acquired the Missouri Pacific. Likewise, the only two lines going through Sedalia became the Missouri Pacific and the M. K. & T. since the Sedalia, Lexington, and St. Louis line had merged with the Missouri Pacific. The next year, Gould gained complete control of the M. K. & T. in his ongoing battle with the Burlington and he proceeded to bring that railroad under the management of the Missouri Pacific. Now, in 1880, Jay Gould controlled absolutely without fear of competititon, every line connecting Sedalia to all other points. "You fellows in Sedalia now belong to Jay Gould," an old Georgetown settler who came to the county in the early years chortled. The perception, however had its measure of accuracy in the terms of the Sedalia merchants. No more would be the competitive rate wars that had been as much a real benefit as a symbolic mark of the life of the city; no more would be the opportunity for Sedalia to compete with other cities in the state; no more would would be the close contact between the operators of the railroad and the people who relied on it . As the removal of the M. K. & T. offices from Sedalia to St. Louis, the forced retirement of high officials in the M. K. & T, and the elevation of the arrogant Superintendent Talmage to even more power all testified, Sedalia no longer controlled her own fate.[13]

In 1879 the aging General Smith died. After having founded Sedalia as a market community with three railroads to provide competition and expansion those qualities he valued gave way to the larger forces they spawned; acquisitiveness was no longer competitive but organized and systematic and predacious.

Sedalia needed a new railroad to restore competition, the lifeblood of commerce and freedom. Although several possibilities for new rail lines received consideration, a plan that had already been presented and just recently concluded sapped the resources necessary for the construction of a new road. The discovery of rich mineral deposits in Benton County, just south of Pettis, attracted the attention of the commercially alert in Sedalia and encouraged the development of plans to exploit those resources. The urgency of the situation heightened when it became apparent that interests in Jefferson City and Clinton also wanted to build a road into the region. Jefferson City's efforts particularly aroused the Sedalia businessmen. Sedalia, less than a decade and a half in existence, had initiated a campaign to secure the state capital from Jefferson City. The competition between the two cities now focused on their abilities to command the machinery of the market in respect to the Benton County coal and agricultural resources. For their part, the Benton Countians expressed little enthusiasm for either plan. The minimal financial support offered from the county thrust a clear burden on the competitors for the road.

And so began a gigantic poker game. When the Jefferson City promoters offered to pay most of Benton County's portion of a road connecting the two points, the others had to meet the bid. Clinton left the match. A state requirement severely limiting the amount of public bond obligations forced a much heavier than normal reliance on private subscriptions for the railroad in Sedalia. Still they had been forthcoming. Local merchants stepped forward with small amounts as they hoped to secure the state capital, take advantage of the new market, or simply thought the road a good investment. The need for additional funds changed that. It soon became apparent that it was not Sedalia that was able to play the market but sheer capital. The promoters able to provide the necessary amount to meet the Jefferson City proposal grew to substantial power as they did so. If the road were built, Cyrus Newkirk, Major Gentry and a few others would be able to control it because of their timely investments. And Sedalia did get the road. In 1881 the Sedalia, Warsaw, and Southern Railroad was opened. Shortly afterwards, much to the consternation of the smaller investors, the large stockholders who had been so important in securing the road but who had also been prominent in earlier efforts that wound up in the hands of the large companies sold their shares to the Missouri Pacific. Once again Jay Gould had complete control of the city's rail commerce.[14]

If competition by the early 1880s was valued in the business community as the proper form of relationship between rail lines and between cities, cooperation was the watchword for business affairs within the city. The flight from competition that had been evident in the city's business life since the very beginnings of Sedalia when physicians, realtors and newspaper editors each organized along their own professional lines to eliminate competition and control standards and prices became an exodus. Such was the mark of the new industrial order which the same people were quick to decry in the national market.

The subtleties of the process were evident at every level, however. In 1877, John Morrison, who carried the largest volume of local business in firewood, pressed for a standardization of the measurement of wood for sale. He called upon the city council to set standards for measurement and to enforce those standards. Although his argument stressed the hardships the lack of standardization worked on people who bought only small quantities, it also reflected a serious concern with the competitive advantage small dealers held in those transactions. It was at any rate an effort to impose uniformity and central control over a competitive and chaotic market. This was equally evident in the 1882 formation of the Retail Grocers Association of Sedalia. The immediate actions to set standard operating hours for the grocers so that none would be open at a time when the others were not, to coordinate the prices of their goods, and to forbid business by credit reflected the purposes of the organization: "to the end that extortion and unbusinesslike competition may be discouraged and eventually prohibited."[15]

Sooner or later many of the efforts to curtail competition found their way into law, a factor that suggests perhaps the transitional nature of the 1880s in this regard. The impulse for competition was still sufficiently strong to require consolidation to become enmeshed in the law. A symptom of the tension this impulse generated was the Market House Ordinance. The city market house contained stalls for a number of different merchants of perishables. The city offered these stalls periodically to the highest bidders. Along with the butcher's stall went an important attraction: other butchers were forbidden to conduct their business within six blocks of the market, or for practical purposes, within the heart of the downtown commercial district. The law met frequent challenges as, for example, in November of 1884, when two butchers, Henry Kruse and Charles Snedaker attempted to penetrate the forbidden territory. Like earlier efforts, this also failed. The protected market house, potentially the archetypal embodiment of the operations of free flowing, unimpaired market transactions, suggested in reality the ever increasing limits being placed on economic activity from within the business community.[16]

iv. The Imperative of Autonomy

The same thrust towards centralized control, however, when outside Sedalia, brought the merchants into vehement antagonism, enough, in fact, to forge an alliance between the businessmen of Sedalia and the railroad workers. The strike of 1885 demonstrated this. When the Sedalia workers at the shops of both the Missouri Pacific and the M. K. & T. went out on strike on March 7, 1885, few Sedalians were surprised. The winter had been notoriously difficult for the workers. The two companies, both parts of the Gould Southwestern System, cut wages drastically, lengthened work hours, and discharged long time employees without explanation. The workers on the Wabash at Moberly, also part of the Gould system but now in receivership, had gone out on strike a week earlier, but the Sedalia workers stayed on the job. Their patience loomed large in the eyes of many observers. But more important in securing the broad support of the city's businessmen were the reasons the strikers gave for walking out. They were not asking for much, they declared—just the wages and hours they had received six months earlier. While the companies persistently claimed that a general economic downturn forced the retrenchment, the strikers countered that the same companies released reports demonstrating substantial profit increases over the last year. The workers, it appeared, stood in the same relationship with the railroad that was so familiar to the merchants, a position in which the railroad flagrantly abused those who depended on it for the sake of higher profits.[17]

The railroad's swift and aggressive response to the walkout underscored the defensive posture of the striking workers, a factor which helped bring the support of the businessmen of Sedalia to the strikers. Even before a hand had been raised to stop an outgoing freight train, Superintendent A. M. Hager, under instructions from his St. Louis supervisors, demanded immediate law enforcement to move the trains as scheduled. Mayor John B. Rickman complied by hiring some ninety extra policemen, sending all but a few to the railroad yards. But contrary to the expectations of the company, most of the new police were brakemen, conductors, and others idled by the strike—and even included some strikers themselves. The practical effect of this action quickly became visible. Repeatedly, the superintendent called upon witnessing police to make an arrest or at least prevent what he thought were clear infractions. Each time the officers, including the marshall himself, told the superintendent that he had seen no violation of the law. In his frustration, Hager attempted to debate the matter with one of the officers, except this was not an extra but a policeman of some years' standing, and Hager found himself charged with disturbing the peace and using loud and profane language. Irate at this clear favoritism toward the strikers, the superintendent sought to have twenty Pinkerton agents deputized. This the mayor refused. State law demanded, he explained, that all public officials, including police officers, meet a one-year residence requirement. If additional police were needed, he added, citizens of Sedalia would be appointed. Moreover, Rickman told a citizens' meeting, bloodshed would have been the almost certain result had he sworn in the Pinkertons. Even when Superintendent Hager warned that the railroad would hold the city responsible for any loss in property or commerce, the mayor and city attorney shrugged off the threat saying that no case could be made for such action in Sedalia. The city officials appeared openly in support of the strikers.[18]

Further cause for support came when the railroad escalated the conflict. Vice President Hoxie in St. Louis wired the governor, John S. Marmaduke, requesting the dispatch of the state militia to Sedalia to get the trains moving again. It was not enough that the railroad should try to tell city officials what needed to be done: the company even wanted the state to intervene to do what the city refused. Pettis County Sheriff L. S. Murray countered this by immediately sending the governor a telegram explaining that the situation in Sedalia was calm and peaceful, that no troops were needed. The governor, caught in a crossfire of conflicting pressures and reports responded by calling up a unit of the state militia with tentative orders to proceed to Sedalia, "the fountainhead of the uprising" that had halted commerce on the entire Gould Southwestern System from Missouri to Texas. He also ordered state Adjutant General Jamison to Sedalia to make recommendations. The city's businessmen, called together by Mayor Rickman, urged the adjutant general to attempt to persuade Marmaduke not to send the troops. And indeed Jamison's investigation proved to him that the citizens were not only in favor of law and order but that they were prepared to enforce it themselves. Although the governor, impatient, had ordered the troops on to Sedalia, Jamison wired him to stop the troops and returned to Jefferson City immediately to dissuade the governor from his move. Expressing a lack of full confidence in the efficacy and sincerity of the adjutant general's efforts, the businessmen's meetings selected a delegation of their own to travel to Jefferson City with a group of striking workers to present the city's plea that the troops be kept out.[19]

For their part, the strikers made it easier for the city to support them actively. By focusing purely on the relationship with outside forces, the workers did not alienate their local support. Equally important, however, the strikers remained throughout a paragon of self-discipline and restraint. Pledging themselves to temperance for duration of the strike, guarding the railroad's property to prevent any damage that could be attributed to them, and conducting their picketing with utmost caution as they limited themselves to requesting the engineers not to take out trains instead of issuing demands or warnings, all brought considerable respectability and approval to their cause from the Sedalia business community.

But the same exercise of discipline meant to General Jamison the existence of covert intimidation, a perception not unreasonable considering the nature of discipline. When he returned from Jefferson City with the state labor commissioner he had obviously been impressed with the governor's determination to get the freight trains moving again. The two officials repeatedly mounted the engines of the trains and issued orders to the engineers to proceed past the crowds of strikers who requested the trains to stop. Each time, with a firm denial of any explicit or implicit intimidation, the engineers refused to obey the state officials and returned the trains to the shops. So thoroughly did the officers rankle the engineers that finally, after less than a week's duration, even Superintendent Hager pleaded with Jamison to desist from putting his good engineers in a position where they were to obey the decree of the state as opposed to the clear sentiment of their own community. With that Jamison now directed his efforts at pushing the governor to secure assurances from the railroad officials that they would accept the demands of the strikers. He admitted, and Hager concurred in what amounted to a concession of defeat, that troops in the situation would be both futile and dangerous. A meeting of the governors of Missouri and Kansas with the officials of the Southwestern System was then arranged for three days later in St. Louis. When that meeting adjourned, the Gould system had submitted to the demands of the strikers. But it was more than a victory for the strikers. It was viewed in the eyes of Sedalians as a victory for the city against forces seeking to deprive Sedalia of its own power of self-determination.[20]

To a considerable extent the incident involved an immense expression of local pride that merged with the untrammeled spirit of the competitive market. And when combined they reeled at the prospect of being regimented into the pattern imposed by a giant monopoly with the aid of state troops. As the prospect became more ominous, the more the city's leaders turned their attention to ways of preventing the intervention of outside forces. In another way, the support of the strikers also stemmed from sentiments which resembled the argument Mayor Blocher had used in pressing his tax reform a decade earlier, sentiments that stressed the importance of work and workers in society. One local editor approached this during the stike when he declared that "If this city retains its present prestige it is to our interest to have these men to *not* go somewhere else, but to stay here and be paid enough to enable them to pay their grocery bill, keep their homes in decent repair and pay their taxes." On that basis, the premium of work, the businessmen could cross the barriers of class. The incident finally was sealed with a benefit celebration sponsored by the wives of Sedalia merchants to provide assistance for the workers.[21]

The issues themselves, however, lived on. So intently, in fact, did the feelings of local independence and freedom from outside control come to be felt that almost exactly one year after the 1885 strike the same forces surfaced in a different shape. This time, in the strike of 1886 on the same rail system, those forces worked against the strikers they had supported a year earlier.

In distinct contrast to the first strike, the origins of the walkout were confused and obscure. Although general work grievances formed an important backdrop to the strike, the immediate precipitating issue was the discharge of a member of the Knights of Labor district assembly executive board in Texas, by the Texas Pacific, part of the Gould system then in receivership. Sedalia worker and executive board chairman Martin Irons then called out all the Knights of Labor on the entire Gould Southwestern System. When the Sedalia workers received the strike order, they walked out. But they were never quite clear as to why they were striking. Indeed, when, after several days, the state labor commissioner arrived in Sedalia to investigate the causes of the strike no one on the local executive committee could provide him an answer. After debating their own conjectures, the committee finally settled on the vague consensus that the railroad had broken the contract. All the evidence, however, pointed to deeper issues. The workers had gone on strike at that particular moment, not because of their own local grievances, but because they were fulfilling their loyalties to a distant centralized organization. The spontaneity and the immediateness of the problems were not visible, particularly in remembrance of the origins of the previous strike. As such the issue that brought the workers and the businessmen together a year before now divided them.[22]

The progress of the strike deepened the division. The railroad had emerged from the 1885 experience wiser. After refusing to take any action, to make any statement for nearly a week, Vice President Hoxie in St. Louis issued a statement describing the Gould system's position as essentially one of innocence since the Texas Pacific, where the trouble began, was no longer under Gould control. There were no efforts this time to force local officials into line. Instead, the company simply announced that the unprovoked strike terminated the employment of the participants. This conveniently removed the legal technicality of who belonged on railroad property. Then the railroad, sensing the power of its approach, began to wait, making only a few testing attempts to move freight trains.[23]

The behavior of the strikers themselves operated to their own detriment. When the company did try to take out freight trains, it met the same response it had a year before. But this time the actions were more vigorous. The strikers generally boarded the trains, ran them a short way out of town and then killed the engines. The minor acts of nuisance sabotage—the stealing of hitch pins, tampering with the engines, and removing vital parts of the mechanism—all of which had been conscpicuously absent in 1885, began to increase in frequency. The railroad had little trouble securing injunctions against the strikers forcing them off company property and also received official and voluntary armed protection. By the end of the month, nearly three weeks after the beginning of the strike, the railroad officials were able to move a freight train outside the city limits. Fearing that the tracks on a grade several miles outside the city had been soaped by strikers, the engineer began to build up speed. At that point, however, the tracks had not been soaped; instead the bolts and fishplates securing a joint in the tracks had been removed and one of the rails moved several inches to the side completely severing the track. When the train hit the dislocation, it bounded off the rails destroying three cars and derailing five more. Four people suffered injuries and one of them was the superintendent of the M. K. & T. It was obvious where the blame was to be laid: the strikers.[24]

The immediate tangible response to this was the formation of the Law and Order League. This league, a semisecret organization composed of Sedalia merchants, vowed to protect the railroad property from further damage and to protect the strikers who wished to return to work. In keeping with the spirit of the community that produced it, the league did not present an uncritical defense of the Gould system. Gould, their leaders contended, was not being hurt at all by the strike; the increased profits from his pool receipts on competing lines more than compensated for the current loss on the Southwestern System. The person who benefited from the strike, they argued, was the man who ordered it. Martin Irons was exercising an enormous amount of power from his position as executive of a centralized body, power that could be broken only by an assertion of the independence of the workers. In his position of power in the Knights of Labor he appeared to be a counterpart of Gould. Both seemed to have little regard for the people of Sedalia and both seemed beyond control by those they supposedly served.[25]

The issues defining the Law and Order league grew as the municipal election approached. The league allied itself with the Citizens' Movement, a group of businessmen that had been pressing for reform in the city government since the fall of 1885. The issues raised by the Citizens' Movement at that time stemmed from the same set of values that the Law and Order League sought to enforce. The city government had lost its mandate in the eyes of these reformers after the mayor apparently accepted a bribe in his re-election campaign, the city officials became implicated in a scheme to collect back taxes from people who had not originally been informed of their assessments, the city council attempted to evade a court order challenging the grant of a butcher monopoly in the market house, and most of all, the city council offered no help in the effort of businessmen to break the Gould monopoly by building a line to the north to connect with a non-Gould railroad. Captain E. W. Stevens, superintendent of the Fair Association, an organizer of the Law and Order League, and Citizens' Movement candidate for mayor, spoke clearly from within the tradition of the market in his campaign. Just as Stevens had helped mobilize his fellow businessmen against the Gould monopoly in the fall, he now urged workers to repudiate the one-man power of Martin Irons. He promised that under his administration, workers would "not only stay here and be able to find jobs on the railroad, but that foreign capital will be drawn here and industries will emerge in which laborers will be able to work and not be dependent upon Gould or anybody else."[26]

The easy victory of Stevens marked a triumph for the merchants. Although the strike lingered for nearly another month, the businessmen had their way. The armed protection they furnished strikers who wished to return to work allowed sufficient encouragement for some to return. By the end of March, railroad agents had been instructed to begin receiving freight again and by April 9, the trains were running close to a normal schedule. While the strikers had nothing to show for their efforts, and many were leaving town to seek employment elsewhere, the Law and Order League announced in April that it had secured a promise from

Vice President Hoxie for the construction of new shops in Sedalia. The shops to be built, they noted, appeared to be shops being removed from cities that had not resisted the strike.[27]

In the waning of the strike, however, the principles involved were not forgotten. The intrusion of centralized control into the fate of Sedalia, from whatever source, was not welcome. Two months after the strike began, May 3, 1886, Grand Master Terence V. Powderly of the Knights of Labor, ordered the strike ended. He did so at the behest of a Congressional committee that had been created to study the issues surrounding the strike. As this committee made preparations to tour the strike area conducting a thorough investigation, one Sedalia businessman expressed his concern over the move: "It is probable," he said of the members of the committee, "they will merely usurp the duties of the legally established courts."[28]

It was altogether appropriate that the significance of the strike, at least so far as the businessmen were concerned, should hinge on the issue of their freedom of action. This quality, basic to the market tradition, had been evident in the activities of the businessmen since the conflict that gave birth to the city. In the early years of Sedalia, this premium on independence had surfaced mainly in contrast to the relationships of duties and obligations characterizing the society the market sought to replace. The forms of expression this quality assumed suggested a tone emphasizing the release from bonds. Whether as emancipation and access to a national market in the context of an isolated slave society, or as an active inculcation of the habits of productivity and competition in the context of an emerging society still struggling for dominance against a long tradition of customary restraints on activity in the young city of Sedalia, the tone was unmistakable: it held the promise of the future by releasing promethean energies. Even with the maturation of Sedalia, the same quality of independence or repudiation of uncontracted obligations provided a measure of consistency to the course of the business community's involvement in controversies that on the surface were riddled with contradictions. From one perspective indeed there was little continuity in the behavior of those who carried the market tradition beyond the crudest perceptions of self-interest. The businessmen, after all, had supported the strikers one year and opposed them the next; they had encouraged the growth of railroads and then condemned particular forms of that growth; they frequently called for obedience to the law, but they had consciously moved to subvert the law in the schoolbook crisis and then in the defiance of the will of the governor and state officials in the 1885 strike, not to mention the repudiation of railroad bonds in 1876. In each instance, however, the particular context proved to be the variant, not their position. Each time, Sedalia's businessmen extended the logic of their own values to the crisis they faced and emerged consistently on the side of contractually determined obligations and rights, on the side of the independence they thought should prevail in market relationships. This quality was consistent. But the tone it carried had altered. Instead of actively working to shape a premodern society and culture to fit the pattern of the market in an aggressive fashion, the efforts of the businessmen now betrayed a defensive tone. Those who had introduced the powerful changes and promises of a new society into the region in the active propagation of a market way of life now found themselves and the city they had created on the defensive. The pattern of their response suggests the presence of deeper issues than the material crisis they faced. What was involved, to them, was nothing less than the defense of a way of life.

VIII

The Community of Workers

The development of class consciousness in East Sedalia came as no automatic consequence of being wage earners. It came, rather, as a result of a slow process of cultural change to meet the demands of a society that responded mainly to the demands of power. In this change the workers of East Sedalia developed a sense of collective self consciousness, a social consciousness that found expression in community values and institutions, eventually emerging in articulate behavior as a disciplined movement. The road to this new consciousness was never clear. The effort that Sedalia's workers embarked upon was in many respects a pathfinding effort—an effort to find meaningful ways to deal with problems created by industrial market society.

i. The Wellsprings of Vigilance

Religion, as ever, provided an important means of coping with problems in East Sedalia. The revivalistic enthusiasm of the Reverend Brown fit a larger pattern of religious behavior that brought the dream of future redemption to troubled people as a solace for present ills. The old hymn made this much evident:

> When I can read my title clear
> To mansions in the skies,
> I will bid farewell to every fear
> And wipe my weeping eyes.[1]

How preponderant was this function of religion as a solace—if a solace that bestowed dignity upon values outside the material realm—of course is impossible to say. But religion as a solace fit a larger social pattern in East Sedalia which sought other avenues of comfort and sometimes even a restoration of values that were in conflict with larger tendencies of social change.

The other expressions of solace often appear in sharp contrast to that provided by religion. The saloon was one. Occupying an important position in the realm of leisure activity, the saloon provided a central gathering point for the workers in East Sedalia. The building of a new saloon on Ohio Street or closer to East Sedalia was usually an event surrounded by great excitement and anticipation. Whether just getting drunk or coming into close, friendly contact with neighbors who shared the work experience, the saloon provided a haven for preindustrial habits. There was not room for time discipline, efficiency—or sobriety. The fiddles and guitars set a much different tempo for the workers than did the time clock. Occasionally, these alternate values would even take a more explicit form as at the opening Saturday night of John Taylor's Kentucky Gaieties in February 1877 when Bessie Dunham's rendition of "Jim Fisk," attacking the courts as a system that protected the rich while plundering the poor, "brought forth tumultuous applause." The saloon did not merely provide social cohesion; it provided a value laden form of social cohesion.[2]

But the saloon was only the tip of a substantial iceberg of alternate forms of escape and release from everyday constraints. Indeed, the forms of behavior frequently associated with saloons often tended to assume an independent existence. The "new nervousness," which attracted the attention of a new school of medicine focusing on neurasthenia in the late nineteenth century across the nation and in Europe, found its cure for many in Sedalia in the bottle; for some the cure was located in the whorehouse. Lizzie Cook's Junction House provided a frequent resort for railroad workers while madam Cook herself maintained a steady relationship with one of the switchmen. The distinction between the fulfillment of biological and social needs was never too precise in such a situation, whether in the Junction House or any of the several other brothels in and around the city catering to the workers; at any odds, however, the man who left one, left after a passionate release of tension, whether external or internal in origin.[3]

Other forms of leisure activity also reflected qualities at odds with the dominant pattern of industrial market society. In June, 1877, an argument broke out between two workers playing cards in the Erie Saloon. The witnessing crowd arranged for the final settlement of the dispute— not by a compromise of interests but by a fight to the finish. The two men, after the fashion of recent popular professional wrestling matches, were to engage in hand-to-hand combat, but, unlike some professional matches, without extraneous rules. What was more significant than the actual fighters in this bout was the behavior of the witnesses, the crowd who egged the two into physical combat. Less concerned with which party emerged victorious than with the fight itself, the crowd seemed to revel in the bloodletting. It is tempting, under these circumstances, to view the exhibition as others have viewed similar performances, whether religious, theatrical, or even subconscious, as a vicarious working out of deeply-felt emotions, and in this case of antagonism. It is especially tempting since these same workers turned out in force a month earlier to watch—under official discountenance—another such match; six weeks later the same workers were rampaging Ohio street in a riot that brought the force of Sedalia's establishment vigorously down on them.[4]

The East Sedalians, however, were moving toward a social awareness that produced actions with a more explicit social content. One such indication came in the spring of 1876. Following a winter in which the hog cholera had a particularly devastating effect, Louis Kumm, a prominent land owner and merchant of Sedalia, started a new industry designed to reap a profit from the dead swine. After an initial experience that proved to be unsatisfactory to Sedalians, Kumm moved his soap factory to a point just west of the cemetery where the public would not be bothered by the odor of the decaying carcasses as the fat was rendered. The stench from the new location of the factory, however, infused the air of East Sedalia. After sentiments opposed to this nuisance were voiced and no action resulted, late one night in May the factory received a surprise visit from eight men wearing strips of black cloth over the upper part of their heads with holes cut for their eyes. The vigilantes entered the building, quickly commandeered it and drove off the watchmen and closed down the operation. There was no doubt about their origin and intent: they declared that the factory could continue operation only when the wind was from the south, not when it blew in the direction of East Sedalia.[5] The midnight raid had its limits, obviously. It did not bring an important challenge to the system that fostered institutions like the soap factory. Nor did it even, in the narrow sense, impose general restrictions on the operation of the factory. They were simply concerned with the immediate effect of the stench on their own daily lives. But that concern did, and in this lies the significance of the event, generate a spontaneous collective action to take care of a common problem. That it was successful and that it came without the legitimacy of legal approval perhaps provided further importance to the raid as an element in the growth of a culture equipped to deal with the problems of market society.

But this was only one instance in which the issues were clear and the remedy patent. And it was in the more subtle, the more pervasive, and less narrowly defined experiences that the workers responded to the larger issues of market society. In the Missouri hills that Frank and Jesse James roamed there was always the possibility of such experiences. These two brothers, along with the Younger brothers, had begun their careers as outlaws during the Civil War. Joining the band of Confederate guerrillas led by William Quantrill, the Jameses became associated with a vicious hostility to the Union and with acts of outlawry that followed from that antagonism. After the war, they persisted in their unlawful behavior even though no longer with implied sanction of the Confederacy as a legitimate resistance. If, however, the Confederacy no longer existed, the support for the Lost Cause lived on; so did support for the James brothers. They operated in such circumspect fashion that they and their gang were able to move virtually unhindered in a large area of Missouri and adjoining country. Careful not to alienate support, the Jameses selectively chose their victims, and in so doing made war on the same institutions that had been identified with Yankee penetration into the region: railroads and banks. Jesse James, after all, had never surrendered after the war. Not only did he keep his support, but before his death, his activities had become enshrouded with an aura of dignity and a mete of justice, qualities denied his antagonists. When he was assassinated in 1882—shot in the back by a trusted cohort—Major John N. Edwards' editorial revered the memory of Jesse James in his Sedalia *Democrat* as he declared that Jesse James "refused to be banished from his birthright, and when he was hunted he turned savagely about and hunted his hunters." And Sedalians took up a collection of several hundred dollars to send the widow of the dead bandit. The legend of Jesse James as a man who avenged past injustices and set right new ones lived in Sedalia.[6]

It is not difficult to see how this legend came into being and grew. If nothing else, the contrast with his opponents set the ground for considerable embellishment. Early in July, 1876, a Missouri Pacific train was robbed as it reached the crossing of the Lamine River, a place known as Rocky Cut, near Otterville, less than twenty miles from Sedalia. It was robbed by a gang that was widely identified as the Jameses and the Youngers. The robbery was both daring and highly successful. The haul from the safes of the Adams and United States express companies amounted to more than fifteen thousand dollars. As the Boonville *Daily Advertiser* reported, "No one was hurt, and no one loses anything save the express companies."[7] But those who were hurt were quick to seek the bandits. Captain Thatcher, agent for the Adams express in Sedalia, and Mr. Nichols, agent of the Missouri Pacific, organized a posse of Sedalia men to catch the thieves. With the promise of liberal wages for their efforts, many workers turned out to join the pursuit. For miles and miles and days on end the posse searched for the robbers. Finally, after more than a month the posse returned to Sedalia and disbanded. But the wages that had been promised were not forthcoming. The bandits had not been captured. As men who had lost considerable time from their regular jobs in what had initially appeared to be a short venture began to rankle with bitterness toward the agents who promised them remuneration, the spirit spread to the rest of the city. Even J. West Goodwin, whose friendship for corporations was equalled only by his hatred for the James gang, declared that:

if they [the same companies] should be robbed in broad daylight within the limits of Sedalia it is doubtful if any of these same men would respond to a call to attempt a capture. And as long as everyone knows the manner in which these men have been treated, it is doubtful if anybody would turn out, although our people are as law abiding as any upon the face of the globe. The facts are that they consider the acts of the Jameses and Youngers just about as reputable as that of the men who have had charge of this pursuit.

Private individuals, continued Goodwin, "do not feel like donating thirty or forty days hard service to wealthy corporations who are amply able to pay their just debts."[8]

It was not an infatuation with the daring exploits of the James gang that generated the support for Jesse James; it was the issues associated with those exploits, issues that had been well established as worthy of fighting for in this area since the Civil War. Two years after the Otterville robbery, the Missouri Pacific put some detectives on the trail of workers who had been systematically robbing the company. Significantly, a detective was able to enter the group perpetrating the crime only by voicing sentiments against the railroads—"grinding monopolies"—as opposed to expressing desires to get rich. The issues once again found a similar form of expression.[9]

On the one hand, the effort to come to grips with the social problems the workers encountered reflected a considerable breadth of experience and intensity of involvement. On the other hand, however, this effort knew very real limits. As much as anything, the variety of means of fulfillment of social needs reflected contradictory and still not completely satisfactory conceptions of what the proper alternative to the emerging market society should be. The workers were still groping for alternatives. Sometimes these alternatives came in efforts to recreate previous relationships and sometimes simply in efforts not to change, but to escape the pervasive social forces of market society. And even when attempting to change those relations, the limits were patent. Partly reflecting the absence of a systematic cultural awareness, that is, failing to view the various aspects of their social relationships as connected in a system, their efforts at change could at best be only immediate and short range in duration. The redress of grievances—whether the closing of the soap factory or the abetting of social bandits—could only be temporary. Moreover, only on one occasion had the capacity for initiative in social action as well as for disciplined execution been at all evident. Aside from the raid on the soap factory, the workers were following the leadership of others, like John N. Edwards who represented a strong tradition of paternalism. In both these areas—a comprehensive social vision and the development of independent leadership and discipline—the Sedalia workers soon made a breakthrough, if a meager one.

ii. Responsibility: Moral Vision and Social Need

Early in July, 1877, two representatives of the Pittsburgh based Murphy Temperance Movement, the Reverends Page and Dunlap, came to Sedalia to begin a crusade for the cause of abstinence. It began much like any other revival but quickly emerged as an unusual phenomenon. With a large, circus-like tent erected on the courthouse lawn, the crusade held nightly meetings and soon brought existing local churches into the movement. The goal was to bring as many people as possible to sign a pledge of abstinence. The meetings spread to all parts of the city and quickly achieved what one newspaper described as "astonishing success." Within the first two weeks of the campaign the movement boasted more than 1700 converts, most of them working men.[10]

The movement focused on two important aspects of the problem of temperance. First, the ministers made open pleas to the sense of guilt felt by drinkers. The saloon keeper was not in the wrong; he simply filled a demand. It was the source of this demand, the man who wanted alcohol, who bore the burden of guilt. "The man who drinks whiskey is alone responsible for it." His responsibility extended from a sacrifice of his own dignity, the speakers urged, to actively bringing shame and poverty to his family. The money he spent came from the much needed everyday expenses of the average worker's family. The man who drank was no better than a thief since he as much as stole food from his family and the crime compounded since his drinking kept him from being an effective breadwinner. As guilt provided the wellsprings of conversion, workers came, according to the crusaders, to seek assistance and moral support in following principles that they believed right but had difficulty maintaining. The temperance advocates urged women and girls "to refuse the attentions of young men who chewed cloves and cardamon seeds" to reinforce the tendency toward temperance. Those women took the admonition seriously. The wife of John Myers, a man who often drank very hard in his times of unemployment, threatened to poison her husband (and indeed tried several times) if he did not sign his temperance pledge.[11]

Once signed, the pledge became a binding commitment. This was the second point the advocates emphasized. With such enormous statistical success—gaining between fifty and a hundred fifty new converts each night—the fears circulated that for some the pledge was taken lightly. It was not to be taken on a temporary or trial basis, the crusaders urged; it was a permanent and an overriding commitment. They "should take it with a determination to keep it or *die* in the attempt!" one proponent of temperance declared. The backsliding which "is true of most converts of all revolutionary movements" was to be carefully guarded against in Sedalia, he further stated. And repeatedly the speakers, not limited to the two Pennsylvania divines, emphasized the seriousness of the commitments and called upon the Sedalians to take the permanent step. Even the saloon keepers who kept a wary eye on the entire proceedings refused to serve the wearers of the blue ribbon who broke their vows. Each evening when the crowd sang "Hold the Fort" the commitment assumed social dimensions as they pledged to resist the forces leading to departure.[12]

On these points the crusade continued day after day, then week after week. Bringing in speakers from a wide region and offering testimonials as a main course in the evening, the level of local participation was unprecedented. The proceedings of the crusade throughout July overshadowed all other news, local or national. The spreading national railway strike, of vital concern to this railroad town, held second place in deference to the local temperance movement. The speeches became more vehement, the audience reaction more vocal, and the numbers of converts daily growing as the movement seemed to develop a dynamic that became the reference point of the life of the city.

The frenzy of the movement reached a climax in riot. Extending the logic of his frequent argument that people who drank were guilty of robbing their families, the Reverend Page took an ominous step. He declared that saloon keepers and other dealers in spirits were no better than thieves since they took the money that properly belonged elsewhere in a family's budget and returned only sorrow and disrespect. The reaction of the city's saloon keepers and druggists (who sold whiskey) was swift. Herman Schmidt, of the Wine Hall, and James Kelley, of the Second Street Saloon, trailed Page around town trying to get to talk with him but Page kept evading the pair. Finally, the two confronted the reverend and demanded that he take back his words. Only the arrival of police prevented a fight. Then several similar confrontations developed and crowds gathered on Ohio Street as temperance advocates and drinkers engaged each other in small fights. The city suddenly grew quite tense and crowds began to line the sidewalks. Several fracases erupted but for the afternoon, anyway, a general fight did not materialize. The Reverend Van Wagner, as a personal friend of the crusaders and an ardent temperance advocate himself, took to the streets to persuade the challengers to avoid violence and the destruction of property. With the prodding of ten extra policemen summoned for the task, the crowd began to disperse. The tension, however, lasted throughout the evening, and at midnight a group of men gathered outside the hotel where the Reverend Page was staying. They had a rope with them. Despite the dispersion of the crowd and then the placement of twenty armed guards in the hotel, by 1:00 a.m. more than fifty men had gathered outside the hotel seeking the temperance advocate. Again Van Wagner appeared to urge the men to return to their homes as he declared that they were honest men, not thieves, but that if they persisted, they would be criminals indeed. As the men tendered their revolvers to the marshall and began to go their separate ways, the excitement that some perceived as threatening the city subsided, and the incident came to an end. The few men who had been arrested at various points in the day were not prosecuted.[13]

The meaning of the episode, locally termed a riot, for the growth of an independent worker culture is blurred by the way in which the experience cut through the ranks of workers. The main thrust of the temperance movement and its main claims to success came in its relationship with workers. At the same time, however, the social composition of the disruptive element responding to the aggressive claims of the crusade is unclear. That workers were involved in the taunting and attempt, whether serious or not, to lynch the Reverend Page is evident since the three men arrested and a few others mentioned in altercations were wage earners and residents of East Sedalia. But the issue as perceived by both sides does offer some clues to the significance of the experience. For those who joined the Murphy Movement, the experience was twofold. Coming first of all to a realization of social obligations and responsibility, the converted workers pledged themselves with a binding commitment to fulfilling those obligations through temperance—indeed, abstinence. Even with the limited terms of this commitment, the process held potentially important social implications since the pledge came only after an enormous social importance had been attributed to alcohol. And for those who became involved in the explicit resistance to the movement a similar experience came. If alcohol was important to them, important enough in fact for them to take active steps to protect it, then the change represented in the experience bears a certain irony. In moving actively to preserve alcohol for its social importance, they were taking active steps to preserve a way of escape. The very way in which they affirmed the importance of alcohol suggests that a new way of coping with social realities was emerging in the sense that it was becoming more conscious and focused. In the end, however, the alcohol was probably as effective as the explicit action. The action would remain ineffective so long as it remained undisciplined. But in all this, it should not be forgotten that the dimensions of social conflict were still there inside the workers' community. Before effective social action could be possible, this, like a social vision that focused on whiskey, a commitment that pledged abstinence, and an idea of social action that ranged from escape to riot, would have to change.

Change was in the air, though. On the Monday following the "riot" the workers made new initiatives in other directions. After holding two meetings at White's Hall, the Missouri Pacific workers demanded of Superintendent Talmage a restoration of wages to the scale paid two years previous with a twelve hour ultimatum. There is little evidence that any effective coordination with the other workers on that system existed, but when the workers at St. Louis received from Talmage a restoration back only to the scale before January 1, 1877, the Sedalians followed the other workers in accepting the lesser concession. The Missouri Pacific workers stayed at work.[14]

The workers on the M. K. & T., however, initiated a more comprehensive action. These workers met and issued a series of specific demands: instead of calling for restoration of wages to an earlier rate (though often this was a guiding factor) they set the scale that the company should pay in each department; they demanded the payment of all back wages due, since they had received no pay since the first of April; they demanded that the strikers not be discharged without good and sufficient reason unrelated to strike activity; and they pledged themselves to abstain from the use of liquors and the destruction of property. As soon as their strike went into effect, they set up their own discipline force complete with a boxcar sweatbox for violators of strike rules and began methodically to prevent the movement of freight by spiking down cars and draining the water from the engines. At the same time, however, they remained sensitive to local needs as they permitted and assisted in the unloading of a shipment of farm machinery that had recently arrived and they permitted passenger service to continue unobstructed.[15]

From the first, the strike carried an overarching local flavor. In the end, it would be this stress upon the local origins of the strike and the local responsibility of the railroad that would bring results. Colonel A. D. Jaynes of Sedalia, the Treasurer of the company, met with the workers at the beginning of the rumors to plead with them not to go out until Superintendent A. B. Garner could return to Sedalia to meet with the workers. Although they did not heed the request, the workers maintained communications with both Jaynes and Garner as local representatives of the company. And within their own number the strikers daily emphasized the local, spontaneous, nature of the strike as they called upon each striker to state his position regarding the fate of the strike. Repeatedly, they stressed the solidarity of the effort by this process. But there were also calls for organization, for taking the effective machinery of the strike onto a larger basis by coordinating with other striking points. Compared with later instances, the organization brought about was indeed primitive, and amounted mainly to an exchange of delegations from other points in an effort simply to find out what was happening. But the local emphasis had a substantive as well as a procedural importance. After presenting the demands to Treasurer Jaynes and Superintendent Garner, who then transmitted them to William Bond, General Manager of the railroad, the workers finally received a reply stating that they would receive pay increases in most instances, but the rate would not be the scale formulated by the strikers, but the going rate on other railroads. In a blunt and vociferous statement the strikers rejected this proposal for the implications it held within a context of increasing centralization. Acceptance of this proposal meant, they declared, their own abdication of any voice in the determination of wages while on the other side, "the roads will combine together and fix our wages to suit themselves."[16]

As if to underscore the importance of the immediate context of their actions, the workers met the following day, the fourth day of the strike, not at White's Hall where they had been meeting, but in the Murphy tent. It was truly difficult to distinguish the meeting of the strikers from the normal temperance revival. But the difference was there. The audience that had called upon the mayor the day before to close all saloons and forbid the sale of liquors in drug stores and was now assembled in the temperance tent was still the body of strikers. The speakers concerned themselves with a different cause as once again the strikers presented their own testimonials, their own calls for solidarity. And when this time they sang "Hold the Fort," the causes of the strike and temperance became inextricably meshed. But they heard other speakers as well. Reverend Page, of course, commended the strikers on the sober manner in which the strike had been conducted. Reverend Van Wagner laid the chances for their ultimate success to the self discipline of the movement, emphasizing temperance.

Others were there as well. Jaynes and Garner, representing the railroad, both spoke to the workers encouraging them to return to work. They would receive immediately back pay for the months of April and May but would have to accept the wages paid on other roads at other points. This, they argued, was only fair since the railroad had to compete with these other roads. But the workers presented pointed rebuttals to these arguments, questioning how competitive the M. K. & T. actually was and speculating once again on the future course of wage determination once the railroad's policy was accepted. If the railroad really held good intentions and if the road maintained that the wages paid by other companies would even in some instances provide more than the workers were demanding, why could not the company simply accept the scale offered by the strikers? The question remained unanswered during the meeting.

But immediately after the meeting adjourned, Colonel Jaynes announced that he and Garner were assuming responsibility, on their own, to reach a settlement with their workers. Following this move, which involved in large measure an affirmation of the same sense of local responsibility, at least when contrasted with the alternative course, that the workers themselves valued, a committee began meeting with the two officials. Within a day the two parties had come to agreement on wages that generally followed the lines of the scale presented by the strikers which had been based on a restoration of wages to the level preceding January 1, 1877. Only a few departments received less than they demanded as the earlier rate took precedence over recent demands.[17]

Many of the experiences of the strike resembled and even seemed to reinforce the closely related experiences of the temperance crusade. The intensity of commitment to a cause, the self discipline, and the focus on local issues all emerged for the second time within a very brief period to form an active social movement. The demand for immediate social action surpassed all but the tense day of conflict between the temperance advocates and their opponents, and this time the obvious restraint underlying their behavior contrasted sharply with the spontaneous outbreaks the previous week. But the signal development of the strike was the solidarity which characterized every aspect of it. Divided a week earlier on the temperance issue the workers now united solidly on a more commonly felt issue. And the issue this time was unambiguous; it involved the position the workers held in a market society.

But if the growth was clear so too were the limits the strike represented. Although the strike had definite local origins the actual initiative for the walkout came from St. Louis and other points. Had not two ranking officers of the company been located fortuitously in Sedalia, the Sedalia workers would have been obliged, in the absence of a comprehensive organization, to follow the bidding of the St. Louis workers. The success that they reaped derived partly from an element of luck but more importantly from a limited stage of social development that meant that the tendency toward large scale centralized organizations was not yet dominant; local obligations were still honored, if only as a last resort. In the future that resort would not always be available or necessary.

iii. Amity and Equity

At the final meeting of the strikers among the speeches lauding their success, the chairman, James Morton, reminded the workers that they were unprepared for the time ahead. He called upon them to form a more lasting organization. It is unclear what sort of response this call produced. Quite possibly in the wake of the strike's success a permanent organization appeared unnecessary even if desirable. And the nature of such an organization was another question. Whether it would be a structure that performed essentially the same functions as the strike unit— bargaining with the company—or whether it would serve other, broader purposes were questions that would have to be raised once a new organization was considered. Whatever the difficulties, its attractiveness, its functions, or even its potential failure to meet the needs of the workers, the Sedalia railroad workers seem not to have formed a new organization immediately following the strike.

When a new organization was formed a few months later, its relationship to the strike was obscure and perhaps even remote. That it would be so indicates in a way the new course the workers' culture was taking. The formation of local Equity Lodge (and soon afterwards also Amity Lodge) of the Ancient Order of United Workmen in the fall of 1877 signaled the beginning of more than a decade of fraternal activity among the Sedalia workers. The needs filled by this activity were in some respect obvious, particularly material needs. In the spring of 1878, J. H. Kehn, himself a worker on the railroad, wrote a public letter to the *Bazoo* describing the experience of his son George who had been killed under the cars a few months earlier. About three months before he died the younger Kehn and a group of his coworkers organized a lodge of the AOUW. One of the benefits of membership was access to a life insurance program for a class of workers that could receive life insurance only at exorbitant rates if at all. Thus, it was noteworthy, according to the father, that his son held a two thousand dollar policy and when he died the order had paid promptly and freely. The importance of this indemnity was one that the writer dwelled upon as he urged others to join the order:

> All true and honorable workingmen, of whatever class, can avail themselves of these benefits. And their duty to themselves, and [to] their wives and children should urge them to a serious consideration of the matter. By so doing they may save their family from poverty, misery and possibly crime.

Following the depression of the 1870s, not yet past, this emphasis upon the material benefits of membership quite possibly found a certain resonance in the community of workers.[18]

The needs filled by the order, however, were not limited to those that could be met with financial assistance. Indeed, even this material assistance had its roots in deeply felt cultural priorities. In his letter Kehn stressed the duty of the breadwinner to his family, a duty that did not end with death and in fact a duty that became particularly evident at that point. This intersection of cultural needs and economic aid provided only a glimpse of the larger social function of the AOUW. The cultural demands that produced a life insurance policy were equally at work in the routine activities of the order; life insurance was but the byproduct of an organization formed to bring workers into fraternal contact. One local reporter noted that the order, "while maintaining its distinctive social character, united the members in one common bond of sympathy and fraternal allegiance." The watchwords uniting the order, according to its founder, J. J. Upchurch, were Faith, Hope, and Charity. Deriving obviously from Christian teachings of brotherhood, these words provided the core of the ritual and direction of the organization. Operating in secret so as to provide a certain basis of recognition of members, the order followed a ritual at the biweekly meetings that brought all members into participation in scenes of the active demonstration of brotherhood by David and Jonathan, Damon and Pythias, Joseph, and other celebrated and sacred instances of devotion. One student of these ritual proceedings commenting on the effects of this camaraderie noted that it was virtually impossible for a person to go through the same ritual repeatedly and to "participate in the same unpretentious charitable work . . . without being affected in his inmost soul. The very fiber of his being must show all this in its structure." To this inculcation of brotherhood the order added its "distinctive social character": membership was open to "all mechanics, artisans, engineers, firemen, train conductors, blacksmith's helpers and all white male persons in any branch of the mechanical and scientific arts and sciences, twenty-one years of age, of a good moral character." Based on the values of the work ethic, the AOUW was able to achieve an egalitarianism that set it markedly apart from fraternal efforts with elitist constituencies. A brotherhood of workers was taking institutional form.[19]

The major strength of the fraternal orders like the AOUW, however, also proved to be their greatest weakness. The potential for social change within the ideology and structure of the order was clear. But the functions of these orders in many ways simply buttressed the existing system of power. The successes in the realm of mutual assistance removed any obligations from society at large by vesting them more narrowly, even regressively, in those being injured. Responsibility for taking care of workers who needed help, when accepted by the workers themselves, chipped at one of the foundations of paternalism—that of dependence on those for whom they labored—in such a way as to separate further the two poles. Moreover, the enforcement of the work ethic in such areas as temperance and general notions of "good character" served directly the ends of market society.

And the kinds of problems the beneficial society could effectively deal with indicated further limits. The orders proposed to unite whole bodies of people in mutual assistance not for collective defense but for the protection of the injured individual. This suggests two things. First, the fraternal order saw the problems of industrial society in terms of injustices to individuals although it recognized and drew its constituency from a distinct group of people prone to experience those problems. It remained outside the realm of the fraternal society to protest grievances felt by all its members collectively. Secondly, the problems recognized and acted upon by the fraternal order all came after the fact. When workers suffered injury or death the AOUW was quick to provide the appropriate assistance to alleviate the suffering. But the *sources* of injury eluded them. The irony once again emerged as a firm distance between ideology and social action: the success of relief and benevolence in immediate terms contradicted the implications of the values of community revered by the fraternal society.

The limits of the AOUW, however, were not necessarily the limits of the worker culture. This became particularly evident in 1880—a brief two years after the formation of the second chapter of the AOUW—when the workers on the Missouri Pacific confronted the railroad they worked for. The wages that had been won by workers on both railroads in 1877 took them back to wage scales approximating those applicable before 1877. If this represented an increase in wages, it also meant returning to a wage scale that still bore the marks of depression. This was acceptable, the workers explained, because all business was faring poorly. Just as wages were low so also were prices on the necessities of life. But with the subsequent upturn of the economy commerce picked up; business was better on the railroad and the cost of living itself rose. The workers on the M. K. & T. received gradual wage hikes to compensate for the higher cost of living. While prices increased, however, the wages of the Missouri Pacific workers remained at their depression level. When the shop workers on the St. Louis branch walked out on strike the workers in Sedalia gathered at the East Sedalia market house and voted to join the strike, demanding a ten percent wage hike.[20]

The significance of the strike became clear from the very beginning. The railroad and the workers embarked on a course of conflict that indicated the disruption of the remaining vestiges of paternalist relationships. The transformation was not without pain, however. Both sides indicated in some way a sense of reluctance about the step. Master Workman Walshe pleaded with the workers not to strike but rather to allow him to take up their cause with his superiors.

> Your case will be safer in my hands than anybody else's. You are about to take a step now that will dissolve your social relations and our friendship. You are making your friendship a matter of dollars and cents and forget what the company has done for you. The company may be led to take the same view of the matter.

The workers rejected this and proceeded with the walkout, declaring those members of the committee who had met with Walshe and seemed to support Walshe's paternalism to be "weak-kneed." After pleading with the strikers as a group and being rejected, Walshe announced that if anybody went back to work at the old rates within a day, he would be accepted. After that, applicants for work would be treated as strangers and at that only as individuals: "I will never treat with them collectively," the Sedalia supervisor explained.[21]

The rumors that spread through the city suggesting the possible presence of imported strike breakers (which never materialized) confirmed in the minds of the workers the actual market relationship that existed between themselves and their erstwhile employer. They also found the city's officials pronouncing a similar relationship as mayor G. L. Faulhaber, a Radical Republican, appeared at one of the strikers' meetings in the East Sedalia Engine House to read the group the text of the city's riot act as a warning that they not interfere in the normal functions of the city. This largely came as a response to communications between the governor and the mayor in which the governor requested the possible assistance of the city's militia (which had been formed immediately after the strike and temperance activity of 1877) and had sent to Sedalia ample ammunition should a confrontation take place with the strikers. The city and railroad officials both acted in explicit defiance of a petition circulated among many of the older citizens of Sedalia calling upon those in the appropriate positions to consider the value of the shop workers in bringing the present prosperity to the railroad and city and to consider the families of the workers, and their attachment to Sedalia and to meet with the strikers to bring them back to work. Walshe's answer made clear the distance now separating the two parties which he had a few days earlier considered to hold essentially a paternalist relationship. He told the townspeople that none of the strikers would be hired even if they asked for employment.[22]

The disastrous consequences of the strike brought this change into perspective: none of the men who participated in the strike were hired back. The company simply closed the doors of the shops and relied on shops elsewhere for the necessary work. Since the other workers on the road, the firemen, brakemen, engineers, conductors, were not on strike, the road could run as usual. The Missouri Pacific could wait for new workers to take the place of its former mechanics in the shops of Sedalia. And these workers themselves placed their hopes not in the company but in themselves. The loyalties of both the company and the workers after the strike had been in force for only a short period represented a far different set of obligations than the earlier paternalism implies.

The independent course opted for by the Missouri Pacific's Sedalia mechanics depended on two important qualities: solidarity within their own ranks and an effective organization to direct their effort. Throughout the period of active resistance the strikers put on an impressive show of unity and solidarity. At each meeting—often twice daily—the strikers repeatedly affirmed their unanimous commitment to the cause of the strike. Frequently each mechanic present was required to stand and declare his own feelings concerning the strike to the rest of the group assembled. As a body they would visit the shops to see what was happening, if anybody was at work. The few to be found at work promptly left their jobs and took up cause with the strikers. When it became known that a few men were being forced to return to work because of extreme poverty, the other strikers offered to take up a collection to provide for the more vulnerable of their number, though this charity was never accepted and the poor stayed away from work. The workers on the M. K. & T. promised more help if money was needed. The meetings seemed even to have solidarity as the main goal. One speaker urged "that the men stand by their demands and one another until they fell by hunger or the bullets of soldiers. But if any man now showed the white feather to hang him like a dog. [Cheers]" The latter part of this call reflected the other side of the buoyant confidence displayed by the workers: an obsessive fear of betrayal from within their own ranks. The motto adopted by the strikers made this explicit since it concerned not the issues involved in the strike but the central issue within the strikers: it was simply, "Death to Traitors." One morning the officials found posted on the door of the shops a blunt warning:

HE WHO ENTERS HERE BEFORE
the Strike Ends
Will be Hung by the Neck[23]

The threats, of course, could be taken to indicate the weak commitment and division within the ranks of the workers. This was the view taken by the city officials. But every other indication suggests that this was not the case. Certainly none was hurt, and there is no evidence of the slightest conflict within the mechanics. None returned to work. And the way in which the strikers responded to the possibility of men returning to work under pressing financial circumstances suggests that intimidation did not play a significant role in the conduct of the strike. What the use of this sort of rhetoric does suggest, on the other hand, is something larger than a threat for noncompliant workers. The enmity toward the traitor, that was so evident in the strike, performed an important function. In the transition from paternalist relationships to class relationships the focus on the person whose actions violated obligations to his fellows helped define new categories of social identity. When the person who appeared to be an antagonist claimed to be a friend, as Walshe did, then what criteria could be used to separate friend from foe? For the strikers, a person either supported the strike or opposed it. The commitment to a cause loomed as large as the wage relationship. That it was part of a process of coming to a sense of collective identity is reinforced by Walshe's angry statement that he would refuse to deal with the workers collectively. He, of all people, was perhaps most aware of the significance of what was happening.

The course of independence was partly sought by workers and partly thrust on them. In 1881 following the merger of the M. K. & T. and Missouri Pacific roads, the railroad decided to move its company hospital

from Washington, Missouri to Sedalia. Sedalia provided a central point
for all the railroad's activity and the junction of the two important lines
made the location of the hospital in Sedalia a logical choice. But the key
point about the hospital was that it was an experiment in the words of a
Sedalia newspaper, "of a railroad hospital supported by and for the benefit of the employees." By deducting portions of the pay of workers for
the hospital, the railroad company denied the responsibility for medical
assistance and pushed it onto the workers themselves. The workers accepted this responsibility and in the next few years even made occasional
supplementary contributions to provide additional comforts such as the
collections made for a piano and for a library for the hospital.[24]

iv. The Sources of Discipline

The hospital was but one instance of collective independence in the
form of assumption of responsibility for the workers in the early 1880s
and this was not a product of internal growth. The mainstream of the
cultural growth of the workers in these years seems to have been concealed, whether deliberately or not, from the eyes of the rest of Sedalia.
That this should be the case, of course, suggests further the amount of
self consciousness the workers were attaining. Toward the end of the
1880 strike one paper noted that "What the workmen are doing is known
only to themselves."[25] That silence did not end with the strike. Early in
1885, however, it became quite apparent that such growth was under way.
The strike of 1885 came as the culmination of many of these tendencies.

The outstanding quality of the 1885 strike was its enormous success.
Without a prior system of organization, the strikers in less than a week
managed to bring a complete stoppage of freight traffic to the entire
Gould Southwestern System and to secure their demands. In Sedalia,
which Governor Marmaduke referred to as "the fountainhead of the uprising," the contrast with previous efforts by workers made the success of
the strike that much more salient.

Of all the factors leading to the success of the strike, the most important was the highly developed self discipline so evident throughout.
This even appeared as a new quality for previous efforts in Sedalia exhibited nothing comparable. The strikers of 1880 had not even formed
any kind of organization; each time the workers met they elected a new
chairman and set a time for the next meeting. The direction of effort
from such a loose structure obviously was minimal. The abysmal failure
reflected poor organization. By contrast the organization formed in 1885
was extremely tight and closely directed. At their first meeting, a highly
secretive affair, the strikers chose a chairman, a secretary, a yard manager,
and a few other purely functional positions to comprise an executive committee. Although the strikers reserved to themselves the power of final

decisions to be arrived at in mass meetings (generally held daily and sometimes several times in a day) the committee was important for its interim functions. The young chairman, James Fitzsimmons, only twenty-three years old, remained both the voice of the strikers in their dealing with the public and the responsible official within the strike organization.[26]

The behavior of the strikers themselves, however, provided the most pervasive demonstration of discipline as they exercised extreme caution in all matters to avoid alienating the necessary support from other sectors. The strikers moved in all areas to prevent anything from happening which could break down their ranks by creating new issues and to guard against any activity that could be attributed to the strikers with a debilitating affect. On the Saturday that they called the strike, the workers pledged themselves to temperance for the duration of the strike and seemed to follow that pledge as none of the normal crowds filled the saloons during the week. On Sunday the strikers declined to hold a meeting but instead appeared en masse at their various churches in East Sedalia. The proclamation urging support for law and order repeatedly received unanimous approval at the strike meetings.[27]

This much was easy. The sensitive points of potential conflict that could assume large proportions were the real test of the strikers' discipline. To avoid any sort of pretext by which the railroad could justify the use of force, the strikers established their own guard force to protect railroad property. When a band of tramps came through following the tracks on their way west the strikers halted them, put them on a box car and escorted them through Sedalia under heavy guard, setting them on their way at the opposite end of town. But even this form of protection raised the possibility of strikers' being blamed for anything that took place on railroad grounds. When Superintendent Hager ordered the men off railroad property, the executive committee immediately issued the same order to the men, and the next mass meeting confirmed the rule.[28]

Probably the most delicate matter for the strikers came with the stoppage of freight traffic. They did nothing to stop passenger traffic and the delivery of U.S. mail. At one point a section foreman reported an unsafe track, and the strikers quickly furnished a crew to make the necessary repairs so that the trains could pass safely. But the freight trains were another matter. The process of halting the trains proved an exemplary model of restraint and discipline. When the company officials or state government officials attempted to order a train loaded with freight out of the Sedalia yards, they were always met by a crowd of strikers. After the company ordered the men off railroad property they moved the confrontation to public crossings. Under the firm leadership of twenty-eight year old Fred Page, the strikers' yard manager, the crowd would stop the trains. After Page raised his right hand to signal the train to stop the engineer always complied. At that point Page carefully told the engineer: "We request you not take that engine out. If you insist on doing so we will not prevent you, but as a favor to your striking co-laborers we request you not to do so." Each time the engineer returned his train to the yards. The main source of friction in the stoppings came not from the strikers but rather from the ordering officials. Irritated after the engineer repeatedly refused to obey his order to proceed past the strikers, Adjutant General Jamison suspected intimidation and asked the engineer if he were afraid of the strikers. The burly engineer, equally perturbed, turned to the general and told him bluntly, "I'm not afraid of anybody." From there the controversy escalated into a shouting match. Finally, the engineer brought a halt to the argument by telling Jamison after insistent demands to know why he would not take out the train, "Because I just don't want to!" The strikers themselves emerged from the blockade unscathed. The strikers seemed more disciplined, more able to restrain themselves than did the state officials.[29]

By the end of the week the strike's presence had been felt everywhere. The bars were empty. The churches had not collected the customary nickel contributions from children of strikers in Sunday school. The police noted fewer disturbances of the peace during the strike period than had been the case for months. Now the city moved from soberness to celebration. On the Saturday before the St. Louis meeting, some sixty Sedalia women, "among them many of the most prominent ladies of the city," began to chart plans for a benefit celebration to aid the strikers. On that night jubilant Sedalians converged on the county court house to mark the practical end of the episode. Businessmen, strikers, and city officials addressed the crowd in a generally congratulatory way. Each speaker urged his own point, but the newspapers noted a common thread giving meaning to the meeting. The speakers repeatedly told the gathered citizens, "that unless they stood up for their rights as free men of a free land . . . they would never be able to secure justice from monopolies, and that they should take a lesson from the present experience."[30]

But what, exactly, was the lesson? The workers supported the strike with a solidarity that grew day by day. Such solidarity could be achieved because of the immediately visible origins of the strike, because the goal of the strike was essentially defensive, and because the issue rested not alone on economic gains and losses, but on the notion of antimonopoly. This last feature, the antimonopoly sentiment, also motivated the businessmen of Sedalia to give support to the strike, support that in other frameworks would appear to be a violation of self-interest. The railroad failed to receive local support because it violated traditional conceptions of freedom and independence by attempting to trample local sentiment with outside force. The prospect of being regimented into the pattern imposed by a giant monopoly forged common bonds between workers and businessmen, bonds that were based on a common appreciation of decentralized authority.

In one sense, the strike left an ambivalent legacy. Though brief and defensive, it permanently altered the collective choices available to workers in Sedalia. It made possible new institutions and new opportunities that could both fulfill and undermine the traditions that had made the 1885 strike a success. These conflicting possibilities became evident the following summer and autumn as organized worker activity reached an unprecedented level. In this period, the workers grappled with profound questions about the purpose of their activism and control of their institutions. Should their activities be oriented to political and economic goals or be concerned with perpetuating traditional forms of brotherhood and community assistance? Would control remain local and decentralized, or would it become centralized and possibly less responsive to local needs? The choices were hard. The implications were far-reaching. The period after the strike revealed a fundamental tension between differing purposes and aspirations within the worker community. The force that generated the tension was the emergence of a new system of rationalized and centralized relationships. The purpose and structure of social authority was at issue.

This issue lurked never quite in sight, but always just beneath the surface. Two new phenomena—both by-products of the strike—signaled the larger changes. The first was a communications network linking Sedalia workers with others on the Gould system. Because of the initiative taken by its workers, because of the importance of its shops for the operation of the system, and because the governor had singled it out as the scene of an expected confrontation between strikers and militia, Sedalia became the nerve-center of the strike. Workers from as far away as Denison, Texas, and Parsons, Kansas, sent representatives to Sedalia to confer with the local executive committee. Thereafter, dispatches went out from Sedalia to other points on the system coordinating activity all along the line. After the St. Louis meeting, when the company issued an order to end the strike, the strikers at Atchison, Kansas, even wired Sedalia chairman Fitzsimmons for an order to resume work. This level of coordination came after the strike began spontaneously; it was a completely new development. The effectiveness of this coordination in the immediate situation obscured its implications as a precedent for a permanent institutional network that could undermine local autonomy.[31]

The other product of the strike was more concrete: within four months nearly a thousand workers in Sedalia joined five local assemblies of the Knights of Labor. A small group of nonrailroad workers had organized a local assembly during the winter, but this assembly had not been instrumental in either the initiation or settlement of the strike. When the workers walked off their jobs, the local Knights met and endorsed the actions of the strikers and offered their moral support.[32] In return, a few strikers joined the Knights. More enlisted when Joseph R. Buchanan, an organizer for the Knights, visited Sedalia toward the end of the strike. Although he did not arrive in Sedalia until the focus had shifted to St. Louis, Buchanan and his coagitator managed to organize another assembly. In the coming weeks its membership multiplied, and local affiliation with the Knights of Labor extended throughout the city.[33] The precise sources of the impulse to join the Knights are obscure. It is clear that the fraternal practices of the order touched a familiar chord in the Sedalia workers' community as they strongly resembled those of the AOUW. In emphasizing brotherhood, secrecy, mystical allusions, biblical precedents, and the dignity of work, the Knights even surpassed the AOUW. By midsummer, the Knights' most visible activity in Sedalia was social and fraternal. The Knights of Labor Concert Company, organized in summer 1885, performed often in Sedalia and outlying communities, usually offering a diverse program of music, recitations, stump speaking, and theatrical farces. In other ways the resemblance of the Knights to other fraternal orders was even closer. When the city sponsored memorial services upon the death of Ulysses S. Grant, the Knights marched through the streets, displaying their fraternal badges and ceremonial garments along with other lodges. They conducted funeral obsequies for their members and used their own ritual, much as the AOUW and other lodges saw their members pass from one world to another. In these respects the Knights in Sedalia appeared to be a fraternity devoid of explicit political and economic content.[34]

Nevertheless, the organization had potential leverage in the political and economic affairs of this world. This potential was apparent in the heady and contagious atmosphere created by the success of the strike. Every worker with a grievance called upon the Knights for support, and received it. The barbers organized a union and raised their prices in combination. A new barber shop, not belonging to the union, revived the lower prices and soon found itself boycotted by the Knights. The boycott proved a success. Likewise, the cigar factories in the city began to employ entirely union labor and to use the union label on their products. Their workers, again with the Knights' support, boycotted dealers who sold cigars without the union label. The Knights also joined a boycott of two local newspapers because they did not hire union help. Shortly after the strike a new periodical, *The Labor Union*, began publication in Sedalia; apparently, it coordinated this burst of activity.[35] Before the strike such a level of organized activity would have been unthinkable; in the late spring and summer it was commonplace. This was an important development, first, because it was local and spontaneous and thus in keeping with the spirit that had propelled the strikers to victory earlier.

Second, it showed a clear preference for the boycott over the strike and thus a clear predilection to unite across trade, craft, and skill divisions. But it also showed a propensity for economic action that was at odds with the more narrowly fraternal aspects of the order.

The process of centralization that eventually took place was anything but spontaneous. In August 1885, the General Executive Board of the Knights of Labor ordered a boycott on all cars belonging to the Wabash system in support of a strike of the Wabash workers themselves. In Sedalia, Colonel E. K. Sibley, who replaced Hager as superintendent of the Missouri Pacific and M. K. & T. systems, received conflicting reports concerning the support and tolerance of the boycott at various places. He summoned Richard W. Drew, a carpenter in the Missouri Pacific shops in Sedalia and chairman of a grievance committee in the Knights of Labor, and asked what the workers expected of the company. In a position of only limited authority but now expected to speak from a broad mandate, Drew hesitated and stalled. Finally, he called upon the company simply not to ask workers on the system to repair Wabash cars and engines. Sibley agreed, and Drew continued for the remaining five days of the boycott as spokesman, empowered not by the workers but by the system itself, for all workers on the enormous Gould system. When the Wabash boycott ended, so too did Drew's temporary authority. But a fateful step had been taken. The railroad company had essentially created a centralized worker bargaining agency and imposed it on the workers.[36]

The company had responded to a need created by the decentralized nature of the Knights of Labor. The local assemblies on the Gould system exercised a certain autonomy as assemblies at large in the national organization. The centralized form that the company introduced became permanent shortly after the boycott, when representatives from five local assemblies met and organized District Assembly 101, Knights of Labor.[37] The ease with which the new organization came into being concealed for the moment the demands that centralized authority could place on local workers and the tensions such demands could generate.

The potential conflict that lay hidden beneath this move toward organizational rationality came closer to the surface when Sedalia workers began to incline toward fundamentally different goals. One course, represented by the district assembly, was clear at the outset. Martin Irons, the first chairman of the executive committee of District Assembly 101, shaped the development of that organization out of his own experiences and assumptions. With a worldliness impressive to some, Irons was in his midfifties when he came to Sedalia shortly before the 1885 strike. A native of Scotland who had been roaming the United States since boyhood, Irons had engaged in a wide variety of workers' efforts to organize. By his own account, those efforts were but a prelude to the opportunity and circumstances he found in Sedalia. After participating in the strike and joining the Knights of Labor, he discovered what he thought to be the solution to workers' problems: a "broad and comprehensive union for labor on a basis that would counterbalance the power of aggregated and incorporated wealth." In turning the structure of the Knights of Labor to the purpose of achieving countervailing power, Irons generalized his own goals to that of the organization. After serving as a member of a committee formed to meet with the governor during the strike, he never lost prominence in the Knights. Irons became master workman of one of the new local assemblies. When the Wabash boycott ended, he was instrumental in the formation of District Assembly 101. He then became first chairman of the executive committee—the formal representative of workers all along the southwestern system.[38]

The modernizing spirit was not unanimous in Sedalia. The prevailing mood suggested that contrary values, priorities, and purposes held the loyalties of most workers. One indication was the election of a new master workman in a local assembly that fall. The contrast with Irons could not have been greater. H. B. Wieman had worked for the railroad in Sedalia since his youth, had lost a thumb in its service, and had been corresponding secretary for the strikers' executive committee in the spring. He was the oldest of the strike leaders, though only in his midthirties. Prior to the strike, Wieman had gained a citywide reputation through his activities as Select Commander of the Select Knights of the AOUW. Wieman was known as a person deeply associated with the fraternal traditions of the prestrike worker community. At the moment when the new organization of workers was becoming more centralized, the workers chose him as master workman.[39] The order's intensified activity as an institution promoting fraternity and providing recreation also indicated the mood of Sedalia's workers. The Knights of Labor Concert Company performed more frequently and in more localities in the fall, and began to draw local people with specific talents into their programs. Nellie Ingram, the daughter of a minor county official, graced the stage of the concert company with her recitations, usually of labor-related spoofs and themes. Her renditions of "The Brakeman at Church," "The Blacksmith's Story," and "Asleep at the Switch," were natural favorites; each stressed the dignity and responsibility of workers in society. The concert company's performance were so successful that the Knights in the fall donated $200 out of the proceeds to a campaign to bring a new railroad into town and break the monopolistic hold of the Gould system, a donation that revealed some political and economic implications of fraternal values—antimonopoly, decentralization, and community bonds.[40]

By fall the Knights of Labor in Sedalia had become so polarized between fraternal functions and economic centralization that a third course emerged—political action. The Sedalia Trades and Labor Assembly, organized in fall 1885 with Hugh Fitzgerald its president, assumed the

function of uniting workers on local economic problems. Fitzgerald had
been president of the local typographical union, and had led a successful
boycott against a local newspaper when it refused to hire union men. He
was telegraph editor of another paper until the end of the railroad strike
in the spring, when he began publishing the *Labor Union*. Fitzgerald and
his new organization saw the main need of workers as the formation of a
strong, local political coalition. When the Knights of Labor brought Richard Trevellick to address a crowd packed into Smith's opera house, it
was Fitzgerald, instead of Irons or Wieman, who introduced him. A
former president of the reformist National Labor Union and a founder of
the Greenback Labor Party, Trevellick discussed the political potential of
the Knights of Labor and called upon workers to use that organization to
build a new world. This speech indicated how prepolitical Wieman and
other fraternal-oriented Knights remained, but Trevellick's new world
also differed sharply from that which Irons envisioned. Saying nothing
that hinted at a system of countervailing power, Trevellick proposed specific political reforms: redistribution of land to provide independence for
workers, full political and economic equality of the sexes, and abolition of
child and convict labor. Instead of impressing upon his audience the
need and legitimacy of collective bargaining or any kind of syndicalist
framework, Trevellick urged the development of a disciplined political
movement through the exercise of the right of peaceable assembly, the
active and universal discussion of political issues, and upholding in all
instances the principles of Knighthood. Above all, he said, the Knights
must follow and support only people who support those principles and
must always value their own "self respect and [the] manly assertion of
their just rights."[41]

This unity of practice and principle would have remained just so
much rhetoric had the Sedalia Trades and Labor Assembly not set out to
change the world in its own backyard. It immediately called on local authorities to block the location of a new branch of the penitentiary, and
the possible introduction of convict labor, in Sedalia. In October, the assembly heard reports on the condition of workers throughout the city; it
took special pride that there were few idle men and "no trouble of any
kind between the members of other organizations and their employers."
In November, they organized a boycott of selected Kansas City and St.
Louis newspapers that refused to recognize organized workers. When
factory and mill owners pressed the city council to repeal its boiler inspection law, the assembly mobilized a successful petition campaign to
retain the law as a public safety measure.[42] The significance of these
activities was clear: economic problems could be approached within the
traditions and values of Sedalia's workers.

By midwinter 1885–1886, worker activism was more intense and
more institutionalized than it had been a year earlier. It also rested on a

more precarious balance. Potential conflict loomed daily as three separate impulses motivated Sedalia workers toward different goals. In terms of institutional authority, the most visible impulse was represented by District Assembly 101. Under Irons' leadership the goals of countervailing power and collective bargaining were explicit and, to listen to Irons, within reach. But in spite of its larger regional and national importance, the district assembly had shallow roots in local legitimacy. Stronger popular participation, support, and community legitimacy were evident in the five local assemblies of the Knights of Labor. The assemblies and the concert company served workers in ways that appeared to be devoid of political and economic content. But in their stress on brotherhood, the dignity of labor, local autonomy, and the fulfillment of community responsibilities, these activities reflected a concern for the needs and frustrations of the individual in relation to the larger social structure. This perspective might well conflict with that of the Irons group, which accepted the social assumptions of industrial capitalism while seeking to increase wage-earners' power and rewards within that system. The third impulse, represented by the Sedalia Trades and Labor Assembly, combined elements of the other two; it fused political and economic activism with the values of the Knights of Labor. This fusion came within a local context and a focus on local problems. Traditional values—antimonopoly, the dignity of work, equality, fraternity, and community responsibility—were not just to be celebrated and preserved, but actually constituted a set of political goals. By midwinter conflict among these perspectives had not materialized; the balance held. But a crisis could explode the workers' unity, destroy the institutions of action, and shatter the hopes of working-class solidarity.

The crisis came in the railroad strike of 1886. The origins of this strike set it off from earlier strikes and also forecast its defeat. Unlike earlier stoppages, this one had its source outside the community, far from local problems facing the workers. Under Irons' active leadership, the Knights of Labor on the Gould system had grown from five to thirty local assemblies with more than 5,000 members. In terms of sheer numbers, Irons' dream appeared to be moving closer to reality. In early 1886, Irons asked each local assembly if it would support the executive committee of District Assembly 101 in demanding recognition of the order as the legitimate bargaining agent for the workers and demanding a wage of a $1.50 per day for unskilled workers. In February, a district meeting in Marshall, Texas, was considering the locals' responses when the Texas and Pacific railroad discharged one delegate for being absent without leave. Irons immediately began to pressure the officials for his reinstatement, but since the Knights of Labor were still unrecognized and since the Texas and Pacific, now in receivership, claimed that the provisions of the 1885 settlement no longer applied to their employment practices,

Irons was ignored. He then issued a twenty-four-hour ultimatum to the railroad company claiming that this discharge was but the culmination of a long series of contract violations. Still ignored, Irons ordered a strike on the Texas and Pacific. Then he called upon the officials of other lines in the Gould system to use their influence to bring the railroad to the bargaining table and thus settle grievances for the entire system. They did not comply, and on March 10, 1886, he ordered all the Knights on the entire Gould southwestern system to strike.[43]

The response to the strike order in Sedalia underscored the distant origins and meaning of the experience. When the railroad workers received the order, they walked out. This much was automatic. But they were not quite clear why they were striking. Some felt they walked out as much for the settlement of local grievances as in obedience to Irons' order from Texas. Indeed, to hear some Sedalia strikers, the strike order had coincided with, or hastened, a movement that would have come anyway because of local issues. This was the first time, however, those rumblings reached the surface. The editor of the *Labor Union* proclaimed that the company had violated its obligations, and he presented a general list of grievances to support this charge. Older men who had worked for the Missouri Pacific in years past justified the strike in terms of a vague, but noticeable, deterioration in working conditions. Some workers focused on Jay Gould's greedy arrogance and his monopolistic control of the city's fate to explain their action. The cloudiness of the situation was evident when the state labor commissioner arrived in Sedalia to investigate the cause of the strike. No one on the local executive committee could furnish him a precise reason. After debate and conjecture, the committee members settled on a vague consensus that the railroad had broken the contract.[44] That vagueness and the diverse justifications of the strike pointed to a deeper problem. The workers had gone on strike, not because of their own grievances, not because of a decline in material conditions, and not because of Jay Gould's greed, which, after all, was neither novel nor particularly noticeable at this moment. They went on strike out of loyalty to a distant, centralized organization. The spontaneity and optimism, the immediateness and precision of the issues, and other qualities defining the 1885 strike were not visible. These strikers were honoring a commitment, not to a cause, but to an organization.

The Gould system capitalized on the precarious position of the strikers by showing a degree of caution absent a year earlier. This time the railroad officials did not challenge the independence of the city with uncompromising demands. After refusing to take any action or make any statement for nearly a week, Hoxie issued a statement disclaiming responsibility because the Texas and Pacific was no longer under Gould control. There were no efforts this time to force local public officials into line. Instead, the company simply announced that the unprovoked strike terminated the employment of the participants. This conveniently removed the legal technicality of who belonged on railroad property. Then the railroad, sensing the strength of this defensive approach, began to wait and made only a few testing attempts to move freight trains.[45]

Responsibility for the strike shifted from the company to the strikers. Days turned into a week, and then another, and still the trains did not run. Merchants, eager to resume commercial traffic, grew impatient. As a late winter lingered well into March, fuel shortages and coal rationing became imminent. The inability to import fish at the beginning of Lent aroused local ministers. Perhaps the most frustrating element for the workers was that they were being held responsible for the strike's effects; yet they were powerless to promote a settlement. The authority for that rested in the hands of Irons and the Knights' national leader, Terence Powderly, on one side and Jay Gould and his subordinates, on the other. Powderly called upon Gould to submit the issue to arbitration, a measure that Irons apparently endorsed when a Kansas labor commissioner proposed it, but the railroad titan rejected this solution. There the issue lingered and festered.[46]

The burden began to wear visibly on the workers. Instead of the daily, enthusiastic mass meetings of the 1885 strike, small groups gathered nervously in the streets. Occasional ball games of the idle workers eased the tension and broke the boredom. But the initial discipline, with pledges of temperance and orderly action, and condemnations of violence and destruction, could not be maintained long under such circumstances. When the company managed to assemble a crew to take out a train, the crew had to abandon the effort because coupling links and pins had been removed from the connectors while the Knights had been "guarding" the property. When other trains were formed, the strikers presented the engineers with requests to dismount. Achieving quick cooperation, the strikers boarded the trains, ran them onto spur tracks, and killed the engines. After several arrests, the Knights moved their operation just beyond the city limits. Minor acts of nuisance sabotage, which had been conspicuously absent in 1885, increased in frequency.[47] The railroad thus had little trouble securing injunctions against more than three hundred Sedalia workers to prevent them from interfering in any way with freight traffic. These injunctions were delivered personally by Constable Monte Carnes, master workman of one of the AOUW lodges and new president of the Railway Employees' Benevolent Association. They added to the already growing tension between responsibility for the strike and authority to do something about it.[48]

For three weeks there had been no change. No settlement was in sight. Suddenly, the strike reached its climax. Railroad officials put together a train to test the injunctions. The city knew the meaning of the effort. Traffic might resume permanently if this test were successful. A large crowd gathered in the yards and along the line, but no strikers were visible. As the engineer began to move the train from the yards someone passed him a note without being observed. The note asked him not to proceed and he complied. The company soon found another engineer who agreed to take the train. With increased security on the engine, there were no requests this time and it appeared the freight would go through. It moved out of the yards, through the city, and past the city limits. Several miles outside of town, the train began to increase speed as it approached a grade in case the tracks had been soaped to reduce traction and halt the train. But the tracks had not been slickened. Instead, the bolts and fishplates securing a rail at a point had been removed, and the rail pushed to the side several inches, completely severing the track. When the engine hit this break, the train bounded off the rails. In the wreck, three cars were destroyed and five more derailed. Four persons, including the superintendent, suffered injuries. It was obvious where responsibility for this action would be placed: the strikers.[49]

No strike spokesman endorsed this train wreck or the previous sabotage; many had spoken out in opposition. But the pattern of violence was overwhelming, and it became increasingly difficult to justify local support of the strike. Reports of more violence elsewhere on the line confirmed local suspicions. Irons provided no help. In one of his visits to the city during the strike, he told reporters that "if persuasion will not be effective in gaining the strikers' point, violence will not be used—at least not at present." The subsequent acts became universally associated with Irons' leadership. After the train wreck, sentiment favorable to the strikers all but vanished. A short hike out to the wreckage proved to some that citizen action was necessary to rescue the city from the grips of this pointless strike.[50]

The strike had been kept alive up to the train wreck only with great difficulty. In view of the lack of progress in arriving at a settlement and the frustrations of local workers, it now became utterly hopeless. Members of the railroad brotherhoods—firemen, brakemen, engineers, and conductors—were now being fired if they refused to take out a train when called. Their support for the strike dwindled with each call. The railroad company added enough security guards to the trains to make them resemble moving arsenals. Armed members of the Law and Order League lined the streets each day to protect workers who wished to return to work. In such adverse circumstances the strikers needed firm and unequivocating support from the authorities who had ordered the strike. Instead, they found confusion. Powderly had even issued a "secret circular," shortly after the strike began, which condemned all strikes and urged workers to "submit to injustice at the hands of the employer in patience for a while longer. Bide well your time." Publication of this circular in every newspaper along the railroad undermined the central reason for staying out on strike: loyalty to the organization. On March 29, Powderly, believing he had secured a commitment from Gould to accept arbitration, ordered the strikers back to work. Irons and the district executive committee remanded the order. Powderly soon discovered that, through deceit or misunderstanding, Gould had agreed to arbitration only if Hoxie, the immediately responsible official, consented. Hoxie did not change his position that he would discuss problems only with those presently at work. Powderly withdrew his order, and the strikers had one more reason to question their commitment to the strike.[51]

These doubts, combined with local pressure and encouragement to return to work, produced results. A few strikers had already gone back to work. With the protection of the Law and Order League, more returned. The conversion of Eugene Perry marked the failure of the strike. Perry's credentials as one who valued his commitments to his fellow workers were impressive. He had become a hero in the 1885 strike when he led the effort to keep trains from leaving Sedalia. After the strike he had been active in the Knights of Labor, and he supported the 1886 strike completely. Named in the injunctions the company secured to keep strikers off company property, Perry had been the first arrested and convicted for stealing and disabling a train. A few days after the train wreck, however, Perry made application for work at the Missouri Pacific office. Because of his reputation, he was the most visible of a growing number of workers dissatisfied with the shape the strike had assumed. At the end of March the railroad agents started receiving new freight. By April 9, the trains were running close to a normal schedule. Soon after that, the shops were turning away applicants for employment.[52]

The heavy burden of responsibility that weighed upon those who continued to support the strike explains why many quit the effort. The same burden explains the depth, tenacity, and illegal actions with which others honored their commitment to the strike. The momentum achieved in the workers' collective efforts in the preceding year ensured a united initial walkout despite the distant origins of the order. The workers had remained solid for the first several weeks, until they found themselves in a completely powerless position. Forced off the company's property, opposed by hostile law enforcers, and restricted by the centralized nature of the strike organization, the strikers could do nothing to bring a favorable end to the strike. When the railroad actively prepared to resume traffic without regard to the strikers, anything that the workers did beyond sitting and waiting was illegal. When the railroad attempted to assemble trains, clandestine raids to disable the engines succeeded temporarily. When a train finally moved outside the city, it was wrecked. But as these measures themselves proved counterproductive by stimulating more systematic protection for the company property and the disaffection of their own members, the violence turned inward. The armed force accompanying those who returned to work was unable to provide complete protection. Harassed while under guard, the strike violators were vulnerable to more severe forms of reprisal. Strikers beat men who had left their ranks, ran them out of town, broke windows in their homes, poisoned their dogs, and burned two of their houses.[53] From one perspective this behavior suggests a complete collapse of discipline and restraint; from another, it reflects the circumstances of despair. The perpetrators of the violence were trying to support a commitment to an action that even their victims had agreed upon at one time. In this sense, the strikers were enforcers of discipline. But it was the discipline of institutional loyalty, not the discipline of a cause as it had been a year before. Those two forms of discipline were now in conflict.

The formal conclusion of the strike in Sedalia came almost as an afterthought to the practical end. Although the ostracism of the scabs continued, the atmosphere was increasingly calm, disrupted only by an occasional disturbance when individual tempers flared. When Eugene V. Debs of the Brotherhood of Locomotive Fireman addressed the railroad brotherhoods in Sedalia and suggested that the strike had been "hasty and rash," his audience could only agree.[54] Many strikers, unable to be hired back, left town to look for jobs elsewhere. Finally, on May 3, 1886, two months after the strike began, Powderly ordered the strike ended. He did so, though, only at the behest of a congressional committee that had been created to study the issues surrounding the strike.[55]

The 1886 strike was a failure. Its costs in terms of lost days of work, lost jobs, damaged property, arrests and prosecutions, and divisions in the community of workers were unparalleled in Sedalia's past. To a large extent, the problem lay in the workers' inability to combine the salient qualities of their movement into a coherent whole. The two essential priorities that they voiced at various moments in the strike were a need for practical sovereignty in the form of locally responsive leadership and a felt duty to fulfill the commitments of fraternity and mutual assistance. Because these priorities worked at cross purposes in the second strike, it never had a chance for success.

In the depths of failure the workers began to heal the wounds. Toward the end of the strike, the Sedalia Knights met to assess the damage and chart future actions. Speakers decried the division and violence that had plagued the strike, and they proclaimed the necessity of unity. The meeting passed few resolutions, but those few were significant. Fitzgerald, a leading spokesman for the strikers at the beginning, moved with unanimous support that Irons be called upon to resign as chairman of the district executive committee. The strikers promised to obey the orders of the district assembly, but only "those that do not antagonize with the spirit of true Knighthood," and called for an overhaul of the process by which strikes could be ordered so as to make the decisions more reflective of the represented constituency.[56] The blame for the crisis, the strikers seemed to suggest, rested more with the centralized structure of the organization than with the individual who happened to occupy a position of power.

The problem resulted from more than a structural deficiency and poor leadership. The inability of the strikers to merge effective sovereignty in their organization with their commitments to that body stemmed from a fundamentally flawed social vision. Two crucial elements—the conception of authority within the organization and the defined goals of the strike—bound the strike effort to a modernizing conception of society. But if the strikers demanded anything in the final meeting of the strike, it was sovereignty within the organization of the Knight of Labor. The workers were decrying the same form of relationships within their own organization that prevailed in their relationships with the railroad. As long as sovereignty remained ineffective, whether within the Knights or in their other social relationships, they would feel the threat of abject dependence. Denials of personal agency were more critical and onerous when they occurred in a body that supposedly represented the workers. In its very goals, moreover, the strike upheld the larger pattern of modernization at work in society. The point of the strike was not to alter alienating relationships but to increase the power of the workers within a context that put a premium on institutional power. This goal stood in marked contrast to the gift of $200 by the concert company to help break the power of the railroad monopoly. The strike was an effort, as Irons claimed, to maximize the power of workers through organization—to "counterbalance the power of aggregated and incorporated wealth." The conception of organizational strength that Irons valued and attempted to realize had its roots in the narrow scarcity consciousness that produced the corporations he wished to counterbalance. The flaw in this conception was that it had not been generated from below.

v. Ishmael

The aftermath of the strike could hardly have been less promising for the workers to develop an alternative to the social relationships of the marketplace. In their latest effort at change and resistance, they had been completely subjugated and humiliated. Moreover, with an intense antagonism toward the strikers prevailing already, a few days after the strike officially ended the reports of radical carnage and bloody revolution filled the pages of Sedalia's newspapers as the Haymarket riot seemed to fulfill the fearful expectations of Sedalia's business men concerning their own worker uprising. And the attack on worker institutions and activities seemed to span the whole range of worker culture.

Even the innocuous fraternal societies felt the hostilities, though from a different direction. The Knights of Maccabees of the World, organized by Sedalia workers in February, 1886, received steady opposition from commercial insurance companies. Enlisting the state insurance commissioner in their battle the companies claimed that the insurance contracts could be made only with registered insurance corporations that paid fees to the state commission and reported their transactions. Within two years a number of local fraternal benevolent societies had become involved in this conflict. The local AOUW pressed its argument in court that the insurance was not a commercial transaction but a fulfillment of mutual assistance in a brotherly spirit. These societies were then faced with the choice of giving up their mutual assistance efforts or changing them to a profitable basis.[57]

In these circumstances the workers did not seek publicity and, in fact, turned underground. Only a few scattered reports of secret meetings, the persistence of cryptic chalk marks on the sidewalks around the railroad shops, and never ceasing rumors emerged as indications of renewed worker activity. But as it became clandestine, it also seemed to become more radical. Nicholas T. Romaine had been a Pettis County cobbler since well before the birth of Sedalia. After moving his shop to Sedalia, Romaine became a frequent spokesman, especially in the years following the 1885 strike, for the eight-hour day and for government provided homesteads for industrial workers. In the evenings as the old cobbler pegged and sewed, informal groups of workers began meeting there to discuss social issues and possible courses of action. They met also in the shop of the cigar maker next door, E. T. Behrens, a follower of Henry George. Both of these men had been active in the organization of the Knights of Labor, had been speakers before the meetings and provided a certain continuity when a number of strikers were forced to leave town. The stock room of the cigar maker even became a central gathering point for workers in a sort of collective education movement. Stocking their meeting place with various kinds of labor literature and free thought pamphlets and papers, the meetings became regular, and the attendance grew to require a larger store room. With enough room to seat more than a hundred workers, the meetings increasingly focused on social questions and workers' actions. Behrens himself later recalled that "I lectured nightly on trade-unionism, economics, and social problems with special emphasis on working class political action."[58]

By 1888 it was clear that these workers were in fact moving into explicit political action. The Union Labor Party locally had its origins in the activism and purposes associated with the Knights of Labor in 1885 and 1886 which likewise had grown from earlier experiences. The delegates to their state convention demonstrated the basic continuity: H. B. Wieman, secretary of the 1885 strike organization, leader of the AOUW, and master workman of an assembly of the Knights of Labor; Clement Homkomp, an organizer of and first vice president of the Sedalia Trades and Labor Assembly; E. T. Behrens, an activist in the concert company and after the strike the convener of the meetings for workers in his storeroom; J. D. Meyer, long-time mechanic in the shops who was listed in the injunction issued during the 1886 strike and secretary of the trades and labor assembly; and G. B. DeBernardi, a former lecturer of the Greenback Party and in 1887 a lecturer for the state convention of the Knights of Labor and then editor of the *Sedalia Labor Union and Grange*. [59]

What is so significant about the Union Labor Party, however, is not so much the fact that it was indeed a real political party. Nor is it that it provided a medium for the articulation of the views of those Knights of Labor and other labor activists in Sedalia. It obviously was and did. What is most important in understanding its meaning is the fact that it brought together a wide variety of people for a common expression of identity. Included were Greenbackers, single-taxers, trade-unionists, Grangers, people who had joined the Agricultural Wheel, the Farmers' Alliance, the radical Republicans, fusionists and anti-fusionists, people the *Daily Democrat* simply lumped together and called the "political Ishmaelite."[60] They were not simply workers seeking higher wages, or farmers wanting higher commodity prices, or any other particular segment of society seeking its own separate economic benefit at the expense of the rest of society. The truth is that these people were, in fact, Ishmaelites left out of a decision-making process that responded to organized power instead of public need, that proclaimed the goals of growth instead of preservation, that indeed defined human needs in terms of economic gain rather than the time-honored ways of satisfaction and community, indeed, of amity and equity. The congregation of these people in a novel third party represented the breadth of the opposition to the established order and the potential of unity across trade and factional lines. Their common identity was political, in the broadest sense, not because of its institutionalization in the Union Labor Party, but because their broad critique of the system was political. They had drawn the line and the issue was clear. But that line did not focus on a particular agenda or set of solutions; that would be too narrowly political and contradict their basic assumptions about the human condition. It concerned instead the more fundamental question of self-image and identity. At bottom the issue was, Where would they cast their fate, their identity, their posterity: with the new system of market society that promised specific economic rewards or with a way of life of their own that placed other values ahead of such economic goals? What they considered right and what might be profitable did not coincide. And not only was that the issue and the choice, difficult and agonizing as it was; but they *knew* it. And that is what the issue had been all along. Now it formed the essentials of life in an industrial market society.

IX

The Agrarian Commonweal

The rising order of an industrial market society replaced that of a rural, premarket, preindustrial community in Pettis County. And, by many accounts, this general phenomenon throughout the nation was characterized by progress, growth, and material prosperity. Yet the process does not always appear so benevolent or benign. Whether viewed from the grim portrait of agriculture in the nation in the years from the Civil War to the end of the century in the analysis presented by Fred Shannon,[1] or viewed from the more particular perspective of local farmers, the process entailed more than growth and progress and something substantially different from widespread material prosperity. Indeed, what happened in the city happened also on the farm and what happened on the farm was a process of dispossession of a birthright and of a livelihood, a process in which people who produced food and fiber did without both, and a process in which the tools of production became the masters of the producers. In addition to bearing the burden of this change, however, the farmers also assumed for themselves the burden, increasingly and in ways both subtle and bold, of casting it off and making a new moral order.

i. Arcadia and the Scourge of Nature

The picture of the agrarian past drawn by those who lived in the city, one step removed from their rural origins, and by those who remained in the countryside possessed qualities that emphasize the romance of rural life, especially that rural life that faded and ultimately vanished. For those in the city, the recollection went so:

> There is no place more delightful than the beautiful country home, adorned as it often is with nature's lovely foliage and surrounded by fruits, shade, and flowers. Our longings in a city life are frequently for the quiet home of our childhood; that home where, away from the toil and care of business, surrounded by every comfort that heart could wish, we were wont

149

in early days to spend many idle hours breathing the wholesome, pure and fresh air known only to inhabitants of rural districts. The sky had a brighter hue, the birds had a sweeter song, the cattle had a more mellow low, and the watch-dog a more trusty bark in those halcyon days of yore than at the present time.[2]

So said the booster-dominated official history of Pettis County in 1882. As for those who remained in the country, the remembrance of the past stressed not the physical elements of the olden days but the larger set of social relationships:

In those days existed truth, sociability, and Godly fear. Men trusted God because of his unbounded love for them. They loved their fellows because they had a common interest in them. They that are yet living, with tearful eyes relate the story of their hardships, and continue to call that day a happy time—far more enjoyable than the many luxuries that have crowded about them in their last years.[3]

Significant differences are evident in these accounts of the past by those who, for different reasons, nonetheless recalled fondly a benevolent rural order, a golden age of rural life. The vision from the perspective of those who had left the farm focused more on its pace, physical comforts, and consolations, its pastoral quietude, and its precommercial innocence. By sharp contrast, the memory of those "that are yet living," the enduring yeomen of the past, did not discount the hardships of that life, although they associated them with a happy time, one evidently more satisfying than the life that knew material comfort. And, while it would be possible to discount both romantic visions because of the contradictory implications they hold, one searing, common truth unites them: There was a time, within the memory of some, when the satisfactions of life were greater and the hardships, if not fewer, were certainly different. Moreover, the romanticization of the past offers a significant reverse reflection on the present. That romanticization, if nothing else, served as a measure of decline, not progress.

Yet exactly how much of a romanticization this was is not clear. Times had been hard before the Civil War and money had been scarce. Markets were few and the threat of natural disaster and crop failure had been persistent. Of those hard times 1854 was probably the low point as drought plagued the county and crops suffered miserably. One source indicates that in that year "the majority of farmers did not raise more than a hatful of corn per acre."[4] Yet the same source goes on to comment that "the economy practiced that year was wonderful." Indeed, such was the case. R. M. R. Kemp wrote her brother and sister at the time that "it is the scarcest time you ever saw in Missouri. Some of the neighbors have not raised scarcely an ear of corn." The people in the area, she wrote, had to make do with their wheat and old corn. Moreover, hard times caused want and sacrifice but it did not drive the people from their homes or disintegrate social bonds. Kemp went on to say that "every poor man has got a home even uncle Milton has entered a piece and John's wife has a fine one."[5] They would not suffer too much so long as they had a home of their own. The hardships were obvious and by modern calculation which associates various forms of social calamity with those material hardships and wants they could have been insuperable. But by the contemporary reckoning those hardships were part of the way of life, challenges to be met, faced, and endured with the hope that next year would be better. In keeping with the larger pattern of social arrangements those hardships could well have forced people closer together as they practiced their mutual wonderful economy. That every poor man and even Uncle Milton could have a home suggests some level of security. Thus they could call even that day of suffering a happy time because of the challenges and the social relationships they knew. Thus the romance. The embellishment of the past may, after all, not have been substantial.

If, however, one discounts this as so much myth-making about a past that never existed, another equally telling commentary emerges. If the reality of the past was a reality of grimness, of bleak and harsh existence and privation unrelieved by larger social compensations and relationships, the romanticization of the past as a better time serves mainly to delineate the even harsher realities of the present.

It would not take, however, a vision of a golden age of the past as a reference point to comprehend the grim realities of the tillers of the soil in the final third of the nineteenth century. Those realities were complex, ever-present, and all-consuming. A golden age preceding it or not, farming had changed. Part of the problem derived from the eternal dependence of agriculture on nature. There was nothing new or novel about the windstorms that wreaked havoc on the crops in the field or the shortages or excesses of water that also whimsically exercised tyranny over mortals. The grasshopper plague, as intense and devastating as any natural threat, produced prayer and supplication for Godly assistance. But these were acts of God and nature. They had existed in earlier times as famine and drought and plagues and they would exist at later times. On the other hand the political and economic conditions that organized society had created caused these plagues to work an especially onerous effect in the countryside as farmers became increasingly vulnerable. In a society where an individual family owned the land it tilled, where the crops were diversified, where the debts and obligations assumed minor importance, where barter and mutual assistance dominated relationships between individuals, an ill wind could be survived. Without those protections, however, the ill wind could be fatal. Those protections fell, one by one, in the wake of the rise of the new order.

The market transformed virtually every aspect of agriculture as the agricultural revolution of the midcentury meant above all a system of production for profit replacing a system of production for use. The precise elements of that transformation took a number of shapes. The farms of the 1840s and the 1850s produced a variety of goods. Corn, wheat, oats, cattle, sheep, and swine could be found on almost every farm in the county.[6] It was especially in the 1870s that Pettis County farmers turned increasingly to a single cash crop for their production. That crop was corn. Between 1870 and 1880 the production of corn in the county increased by 418 percent while other crops either increased by much smaller amounts or, as in the case of the nearest competitor to corn, wheat, actually declined. In 1880, 43 percent of all tillable land in the county was planted in corn; since that figure includes land that was in grass rotation and land that was fallow, it seems more than likely that an absolute majority of all the improved land in the county was planted in corn.[7] The significance of this shift could be seen in the enormous dependence of these farmers on a successful corn crop and the dependence of that success on the forces of the market. The vulnerability of the yeoman increased and became that much more susceptible to fluctuations of economics and nature that previously could have been weathered. It would no longer be possible to rely on the wheat when the corn crop failed or when the corn crop of other competing farmers, throughout a nation where markets were made and linked by railroad transportation, also yielded bountiful results. There is no mistaking that these farms were now, by intention or force of circumstances, commercial enterprises.

The change in machinery used on the farm both required and made possible such commercial operations. Between 1860 and 1870 the valuation of farm implements in the county increased 40 percent and increased another 78 percent by 1880.[8] Yet that probably understates the actual increased use of implements since the role of depreciation and the valuation of older equipment is unclear. Since older equipment, that figured in the previous census, or that equipment that was still usable but possessed a lower market value, would not be accurately reflected insofar as its contribution to greater production was concerned, these figures are low. More reflective would be the enumeration of horses and mules and oxen—the motivepower for drawn farm implements. The modern implements—the reapers, the planters, the cultivators, the threshers, and so on—used horses and mules instead of the old, slower oxen. Between 1860 and 1880 the number of horses, asses, and mules increased by 102 percent. In the same period the number of work oxen declined by 99.7 percent. Where there had been more than two thousand of the beasts in 1860, only six remained in 1880.[9] Farm production was becoming more mechanized, becoming quicker, and it was becoming more commercial. Indeed, as George F. Lemmer observed, "Commercial farming could not develop without efficient machinery."[10]

The mechanization of agriculture also had other implications. It meant an expansion in the size of the farms since additional acreages were necessary to justify the expense of the implements. Again, the 1870s proved to be the crucial transition point. During that decade the average farm (counting improved land only) moved from 107 acres to 130 acres; or more pointedly, while the number of farms in the county increased by 32 percent the number of acres of improved land increased by 61 percent.[11] And while the land to be tilled increased, the tillers declined. The new machinery simply replaced many of the laborers on the farm. The state Bureau of Labor Statistics quantified the equation: "The barshare plow, requiring three to four men per acre a day of plowing, has given place to the sulky plow, asking for but one man per day for three acres of plowing. The corn planter has replaced ten men; the mower, four to five; the reaper, ten men; and so on for other field operation."[12] The new machinery could make life easier on the farm, if it also made it more difficult to stay on the farm.

To stay on the farm at all, much less to live the life of independence that had been traditionally associated with that agrarian existence became increasingly a doubtful possibility. The Civil War locally marked the great turning point for the increase of immigration and the expanded cultivation of the Pettis County soil. Indeed, between the censuses of 1860 and 1870 the number of farms in the county increased by 140 percent, with nearly all of this increase taking place after the war. Likewise, the amount of land cultivated doubled in the same period.[13] Part of a much larger picture of agricultural settlement and immigration in the nation, this proved fateful as land prices increased dramatically (25 percent in one four month period in 1868 alone), and the average value of an acre of land (a distorted figure itself, however) moved from seventeen dollars in 1860 to twenty-four dollars in 1870.[14] Even the *Bazoo* complained that land prices were extortionate, that it was necessary to reduce the prices to attract more people, and that the higher prices were due to the "avaricious interests" of the landholders who took advantage of their fellow countians.[15] Whereas the lower land prices of the immediate postwar period had meant an increase in farm owners and the felt necessity of attracting farm-laborers rather than owners, the greater need became in the early 1870s to lower prices for the potential free-holder. What the higher prices meant, moreover, was the need to borrow money to acquire land, and to borrow more money to acquire more land, and to borrow yet more money to acquire the machinery that could only be efficiently utilized if sufficient land were available to be exploited. Thus began the cycle that started off as progress, increased production, increased farms, and better equipment but that culminated in dispossession.

The backdrop to this cycle of ruination was neither local in origin nor any the less intense thereby. Credit, debts, and the value of money worked together to place the farmer in an increasingly precarious livelihood. With the inflation of the Civil War and the consequent dwindling in value of paper money, debts could easily and confidently be contracted. Money was cheap and prices were high. And debts were contracted plentifully. And while the new machinery also bore high prices, the necessity of increasing production to compete with others and the necessity of paying off loans made on the newly acquired land, made such debts both justifiable and essential. Yet the common pattern intensified the debt relationship as the farmer who needed to borrow money had limited sources; the short-term loans available were inappropriate for equipment purchases. The implement dealer, however, could borrow that money, pay interest to the banks, and then loan the same money, at additional interest, to the farmer who needed those implements to stay on the farm. But as the payments for land and equipment mounted, they drained from the revenues the farmer generated from his crops. If he but rented the land, this was an obviously exasperating situation as the rents climbed dramatically. But the cost of production climbed in a less obvious way for the owner of the land who had borrowed the money. The inflationary situation of the war was shortlived and came to an abrupt end as the finite amount of money in circulation in the North soon had to suffice for the whole nation as Confederate money evaporated. Then, Congress began a process of withdrawing the amount of paper money in circulation, thereby tightening the money supply and increasing its value that much more. Thus the farmers found themselves paying fixed debts with increasingly scarce dollars and contracting for more to produce more and at the same time depending increasingly on a single-cash crop, along with everybody else, and a cash crop market that was becoming increasingly glutted at that. So the cycle turned. So the farmers found themselves increasingly at the end of a long and involved chain of events and impersonal forces. The farmers themselves were being harvested.

The harvest of horrors came in the 1870s. The "panic of 1873," a financial panic that generated a depression in the nation, created also a shortage of money. So debts were called in and mortgages foreclosed. Locally, the county history, written less than a decade later explained the impact cogently: ". . . very many persons became bankrupt, and property of all kinds decreased in value, in many instances more than *fifty per cent*. Mortgaged farms were sold, and numbers of families who lived in opulence only a few years previous were now homeless, and to make the picture still darker, no avenue of business was open for them to make a livelihood."[16] As if the forces of the market were not enough to dispossess the yeomanry, the forces of nature compounded the misery. The grasshopper plague of 1875, something that occurred periodically in nature, came at a time of already great suffering. One farmer wrote of his despair: "Times here are the hardest that I ever saw. In fact there is no money at all . . . . The bugs nearly all starved to death [but] in the fall the grasshoppers came and ate up all the wheat that was sowed." Then, he lamented, the following spring, because of the eggs laid the previous fall, the grasshoppers consumed the entire corn crop. So he summarized the whole episode's devastation: "The financial crash with two years failure in crops have about 'busted' me up. If it were not for that you might look for me in Oregon soon. If I can close out, pay debts and have enough to bring me to that country I shall come sure."[17] Thus the dispossession worked a curious turn. The farmer was being forced from his land. Yet because that land was worth less (down to around $12.50 an acre by 1880) and the debts worth more and the prospects of successful crops grim, he could not leave the land. To be caught between such incredible forces is to be truly subjugated. As the Bureau of Labor Statistics concluded in 1879, it required at least $150 to start a farm, and "this is certainly a small sum to many, but how are the unemployed poor, for whom farming is prescribed as a remedy, to obtain it."[18] How indeed was the farmer to obtain it?

The way the farmer would stay on the land when its possession was being forced from him was to stay as a tenant, to work the land for somebody else. And that course became the course of more and more farmers. In assessing just how many farmers entered this pattern of peonage the statistics are of little help. Although the census figures indicate that during the 1880s rentals of farms, for both money and shares of crops, increased while farms cultivated by their owners declined slightly, those figures only hint at the larger problem.[19] They count farms as single whole units rather than counting farmers working the land. Thus in 1890 seventeen farms contained more than 1000 acres. Of these thirteen were reportedly cultivated by their owners, three rented for fixed money, and one was share-cropped.[20] It seems more than a slight possibility—given the size of the operations—that in each instance these farms were worked by more than one individual. Moreover, the fine line between renting the land with payment to the owner in a share of the crop and working the land for payment from the owner in a share of the crop, relations which amount to the same thing, is obscured by this enumeration. Indeed those other share croppers, who received crop shares in the place of money wages, an altogether common phenomenon in a money scarce economy, are totally absent from the calculation. Even so, by 1890 the census reported that a third of the farm families in the county were tenants.[21]

On the other hand, those others who were enumerated among the owners who cultivated their soil were not always the proud yeomen the image might initially suggest. The truth of the situation was that they were often, by virtue of a growing indebtedness, beholden to other masters. Their farms, far from being the soil of freedom, were increasingly so much real estate. The Missouri Trust Company, a Sedalia organization that specialized in farm loans advertised broadly for investors to place their money in their organization (or in their eastern account in the Chemical National Bank of New York) which they would then loan to farmers. Farm loans, the company said, have been proven *"the safest and most profitable* investment ever offered to the public." The farm loan, after all, was "as stable as the earth upon which it rests." The mortgage business was secure. Aside from the endowment of nature with something so secure, the laws of the state helped the mortgage business. As the Missouri Trust Company said, the collection laws of Missouri "are more favorable to the creditor than in most other States." Indeed, the company boasted, it was possible by this legal power to exercise the right which they reserved, "to foreclose the loan at any time before maturity . . . ." Court proceedings in such cases were unnecessary impediments and obstacles; thus the law allowed foreclosures without court proceedings. The importance of this constant threat of foreclosure had, as the company expressed it, "a tendency to make borrowers prompt in the payment of interest and taxes, while it gives a speedy remedy should occasion require. To those familiar with its use, it is at once recognized as being far superior to the mortgages and long and tedious foreclosures used in most of the Western States."[22] The position of the farmer in this, whose debt increased, whose income decreased, and whose dependence on the market grew with each season, was obvious. His foreclosure would be prompt and sure, unimpeded by the "long and tedious" mechanisms that elsewhere protected his counterparts. So went the life of the tiller of the soil, the free yeoman who did not rent his land. He was as beholden, or more, as the others. Gone were the days of trust, truth, sociability, common interest, and happy times.

In all this it is easy to mistake the problem for the symptoms. And if there is a conceptual flaw in the analysis presented by Fred Shannon of the growing suffering of the farmer in this period in the nation's history that flaw would be the tendency to focus on the fluctuations of the economy, the fluctuations of income, the pattern of indebtedness, the displacement generated by mechanization, the rise of new patterns of tenancy and dependence, and other direct, raw and brutal economic developments. This is not to deny the force of those conditions or the power of their beneficiaries but rather to suggest another more fundamental dimension. Shannon himself hinted at that dimension when he said that "as on all preceding agricultural frontiers, the Western farmers of the late decades of the nineteenth century were generally poor, but in this era of commercialized farming they were all the worse because of this fact."[23] Yet there was more even. The chronicle of dispossession of those poor emerged because of and on top of an additional dispossession, the dispossession of a birthright of freedom and independence, of a moral economy and society by a system of market relationships. If Shannon neglected this aspect as he focused on the more immediate material concerns of the agricultural population, though, it is all too understandable. Fred A. Shannon, after all, was born the son of a sharecropper outside Sedalia, Missouri in 1893.

ii. Sowing the Wind

Aside from the social and economic realities decimating the countryside and ravaging the lives of those who remained as farmers, yet another problem plagued the rural denizens. That problem was the political manifestation of the others. Inasmuch as the new system of power was both economic and political, the beneficiaries of the market's economics also dominated the political arena. The links between government and economy ran deep in the social transformation; indeed, early in the debates over the coming of the railroad and in the disaffection of people from their government in war, those connections had been abundantly self-evident. Moreover, it had been a series of political decisions that had contributed to the debilitation of the farmer—in mortgage laws, in tariffs, in currency and credit, in special benefits for corporations, in taxation, and in virtually every area where authority counted. Thus the problem of the farmers: to solve the problems of life, moral order, and material existence required the mobilization of political resources and the creation of an alternative scheme of social organization. Such a response, no matter what group of people, has never been automatic, predictable, or casual. Indeed, to enter a political arena closely warrened by party and faction was by some reckonings to enter the home territory of the enemy, the territory of those who produced nothing and who presumed to make judgments about the fate of their lessers, judgments which wound up benefiting only those with power.

By popular mythology and with some germ of truth, the calling of the farmer has been traditionally an individualistic, isolated vocation. It is true that the existence was often a solitary one, that the labors in the field knew little of the social discourse and camaraderie of the artisan or merchant in town. It is also true that many a challenge in the course of the labors had to be met alone and that many a decision about the·work had to be made alone, with but one person responsible and but one person and family liable for the consequences of that decision. Yet the individualism of the countryside had its limits. Whether in the carnival of the ante-bellum elections, in the community of the religious observance, or in the shared burdens of charity and mutual responsibility in the wake of calamity or even in the cooperative efforts at harvest time or in barn building, the cooperative and communitarian impulse surged strong. In fact, the system of laws and mores had long served to limit excessive individualism that would disrupt that community. If disappointment were to come, it would less likely be the result of too much solitude and enforced individuality than from too much restraint and enforced mutuality. So too was it that this code, this habit of mutuality was being challenged by an individualistic market that beheld a vision of hard-working tillers of the soil who would be rewarded according to their individual talents and drives and not be protected by the community.

One strain of that gregarious impulse can be located in the agricultural fairs that came to be a routine feature of rural life. From their origins in 1857 with the founding of an agricultural and mechanical association and a fair in the pastures of William Gentry, the fairs offered competition in breeding, crops, and agricultural skills. They also offered entertainment with races, dances, and a general expression of "sociality and the mutual feeling of farmers." John Born reportedly fiddled at each fair for seventy years.[24] Insofar as the fair represented an event of substantial cultural importance for the poor and the isolated, and insofar as the fair, coming as it did immediately after the summer's labors and harvests, punctuated and emphasized the seasonal, cyclical basis of labor, and insofar as the fair provided leisure and entertainment and even indulgence at a relatively abundant time of the year, the fairs retained a connection with the past that served the spirit of mutuality and cultural reinforcement most of all.

Yet the fairs changed in their purpose and attractions. Over the years the fairs underwent a discernable evolution that suggested a tension within the larger agricultural community. The early years of the fairs appear to have been lusty and bawdy occasions of celebration and revelry where drinking and carousing and fighting seemed popular sport.[25] Becoming, however, more sober and restrained and disciplined, the official county history noted in 1881 that "good order and success have crowned the expositions of late years," and the 1885 fair program announced that "no gambling devices will be allowed on the Grounds and peace and order will be preserved at all times."[26] This change ran parallel to another element in which "the methods of conducting fairs have somewhat changed since the *ante-bellum* days."[27] The object and purpose of the fair was spelled out in 1870 in the charter of the Pettis County Agricultural and Mechanical Society; the association existed to promote "improvement in agriculture, manufactures and the raising of stock." In that way fairs could serve as a "standing advertisement of thrift and enterprise."[28] They would be disciplined in the same way other parts of society and behavior were becoming disciplined.

The managers of the fairs were themselves men of prominence, prosperity, and discipline. William Gentry, in whose pastures the first fair opened, president of the fair association in 1866, and always one of the directors of the fair, was not the average dirt farmer. Engaged in stock raising for over forty years, Major Gentry was by the early 1880s "probably the most extensive stock raiser in Pettis County," managed an estate of more than six thousand acres, and had served as a director of the Sedalia Savings Bank and President of the Sedalia, Warsaw & Southern Railroad, as well as briefly serving as a judge on the county court.[29] So too the other directors and officers: merchants, implement dealers, bankers, and the well-born.[30] Their goal was to transform agriculture into a productive science and profitable business. Yet the goal of others, who perhaps found the earlier fairs more to their taste and who occasioned the necessity of rules and prohibitions, was more to hold on to an agrarian past and way of life characterized by sociability and community. The two impulses evident at the fair that pulled against each other, that worked from opposite assumptions, and that suggested far different implications, those impulses would continually divide the community of farmers. The issue was simple, but profound: Exactly what was the object of their labors?

The ambivalent function of the fair lent itself well to the creation of a more overtly political agency that likewise served two contrasting visions. That agency was the Grange—the Order of the Patrons of Husbandry. Of the activities of the Grange in Pettis County little is known. An indefinite number of the local Granges complete with buildings dotted the countryside in the 1870s. Sponsoring various kinds of competitions, active in the fairs, and operating on a basis designed to promote social discourse in the country, the Granges emerged prominently in the lives of the rural population of Pettis County in the early 1870s. And, except for two developments, it could well be that the primary function of the Granges locally was the promotion of social contact and the nurturing of a spirit of mutuality among the isolated farmers of the land. But those salient developments are noteworthy.

The first development is the emergence in 1873 of the Sedalia Cooperative Store Society, an organization with no visible or concrete connection to the Grange but an organization patterned carefully along the exact lines of those sponsored by the Grange in its propagation of cooperatives. Indeed, in its handbook, the Sedalia Co-operative Store Society noted the interest of the Grange in its activities and indicated that "it is probable that some definite action will be taken by the Order, within a short time, for adopting the system."[31] At that cooperative store, members could purchase a variety of provisions with a return of one-half of the net profit on the transaction to the buyer. This was clearly an attempt to lower the cost of purchasing goods. But it was more. It was also a business. The other one-half of the profit was divided equally to be paid as a dividend on stock and to be added to the capital stock. One hundred shares of stock made up the total capital, each share selling for twenty-five dollars, with a limit of four shares per member. The most distinctive component in the structure of this cooperative store, however, was its insistence on cash for payment. Noting sagely that the "evils and loss caused by the credit system, which so generally prevails throughout the country, are incalculable," the store demanded *"immediate cash payment."* On these principles the cooperative store managed to turn a growing profit, pay its bills, and even declare a dividend in its second year of operation. And in its second year it boasted a total of forty-eight members—nearly a score more than had originally founded it.[32] Despite a pattern of growth and increasing sales in this period, however, it was only a short while before the store declined and closed its doors. The experiment had not succeeded.

The meanings of the Sedalia Co-operative Store Society's ephemeral existence are obscure. Partly this is a matter of numbers, inasmuch as the membership of the store never really soared into the ranks of tillers of the soil in the county. But more broadly the significance of the experience is clouded by the ambiguity it represented. It did represent, without qualification, a clear impulse toward cooperation and self-help, a cooperation that explicitly denied the virtues of competition and selfishness at large in the new market society. And it is in that regard that the fraternal practices of the Patrons of Husbandry take on a meaning that is substantially greater than the quaintness sometimes attributed to them. But the material functions of the store and its structure placed limits on how far that cooperation could reach. Especially significant in this regard is its cash requirement. Based on the Rochdale pattern of cooperatives, the cash requirement may have meant a minimum of risk to the store, but it placed an increased burden on its clients, its own members. The ills of the credit system were properly enumerated by the organization for the farmers were in fact suffering and suffering mightily at the hands of the system of legalized usury abetted by deflation. Yet it was not the too easy availability of credit that plagued them so much as the lack of easy credit that made them easy prey to the land and mortgage companies that brought them to conditions of despair. They lacked cash. And without that cash a cooperative store that refused credit was of little use or advantage or, for that matter, of little promise. Indeed, it proved counterproductive, even, as the Sedalia Co-operative Store Society observed proudly that "one good result of the Society is the adoption of the cash system by fifteen grocery firms of this city."[33] It became, as a result of this society, that much more difficult to secure credit for the provisions of daily life—a portentous contribution. This could also explain its limited membership and its short life. In its lack of relevance to the particular circumstances of agrarian life in the 1870s, the cooperative society may well have had its greatest significance. It served as a reminder of the limits of such an enterprise at the same time that it drew upon the active tradition of mutuality. While the cooperative involved a pooling of resources, the available resources to be drawn upon were few. What would be necessary, unless one were to move simply in the direction of the individualistic market, would be either the reformulation of the structure and purposes of the cooperative effort to better conform to the nonmarket, nonprofit orientation evident among some of the rural dwellers or the turn to external sources of help—such as those agencies of government that had aided other groups so generously in their quest for public sanction, funds, and lands.

If the cooperative store holds a precious ambiguity in its meanings the other development associated with the Granger presence in Pettis County yields even more uncertainty. In 1874, at its first convention, the People's Party of Missouri, a product of the political concerns of the Grangers, nominated Major William Gentry of Pettis County for governor. Two conclusions are suggested by this development. One is that Major Gentry was more a man of the people than his wealth, status, and reputation indicate. This conclusion is the common understanding, as, for example, one discussion blandly argues that Gentry was "acceptable to the grangers, since he was a farmer and keenly interested in agricultural problems."[34] Yet Gentry was hardly an average farmer with the problems and worries of the average farmer. The other conclusion, which seems more likely, is that the People's Party was not necessarily comprised of the small farmers. The party did indeed seek restriction of the railroad, a goal often stated by other interests, including merchants and shippers and sometimes even railroads themselves. And it sought economic retrenchment and lower taxes.[35] Aside from a proposal to broaden the availability of free public education, however, the party made barely a gesture in the direction of securing support from the public institutions that could provide the external assistance necessary and that would later provide the agenda for various reform efforts. Supported in 1874 by the Republican Party, the People's Party was anything but a party of the people. In fact, immediately after the nomination of Gentry, membership in the Grange began to decline and in a year and a half had dropped by one-half statewide.[36] The subsequent Greenback Party would easily pick up those disenchanted Grangers.

The Granger experience in Pettis County is riddled with opacity, ambiguity, and not the least—myth. The strains of mutuality and cooperation, evident early in the county's history and nurtured through gatherings and relations of varying degrees of formality and institutionalization, provided the seeds of activism and assistance, and in truth, those strains provided the seeds of the solution to problems that derived not from individual failings but from a collective plight. And whether in the sociability of the early fairs or in the mutual aid of the cooperative store or in the collective pretensions of a third party identifying itself with the farmers, with the people, those seeds were real and held promise of fruit. The seeds were the seeds of community. The seeds were authentic enough and they were natural enough. The problem that led to the impotence of the effort was that those seeds could not be planted in the barren ground of the new order, of the new market society. Those seeds could not be sown in a set of institutions that required, as did the cooperative store, the economic independence of ready cash before one could participate. Nor could those seeds take root in institutions like the Peoples' Party which merged an earlier paternalism with the goals and aspirations of the market. The notions of community protection and assistance, of sacrifice of individual acquisitiveness for community well-being, and of a total set of relations that knew as their basis and goal the relationships of community—those notions proved incompatible with the new fairs, the cash and carry cooperative store that turned a profit, and the political party that purported to speak for the people through the wealthiest farmer in the county. At its bottom, the problem of the community of farmers was that a tension divided them from each other and divided their visions and courses of action as well. The question facing the farming population was whether to hold on to their community or to embrace a new image of the business of farming and a new image of themselves.

By the beginning of the decade of the 1880s the problems facing the farmers were more severe than they had been ten years earlier. But an additional problem now heaped on the existing circumstances of despair. The institutions that seemed appropriate as mechanisms of self-help, political leverage, or mutuality were dominated by people or ideas insensitive to the pressures bearing down upon them, a factor which even enlarged those pressures. The fairs had turned into promotional expositions and disciplining agencies. The cooperative store served to aid those who were already solvent and turned its back on those who needed most the benefits of cooperation. The politics and economics of the Grange faded—happily so in the eyes of those who abandoned the organization, as well as those who stayed—after it pushed Gentry for governor. The activities of the Grange went back to the level of the fraternal order, holding lodge meetings, conferring degrees, sponsoring picnics and lending their buildings for various neighborhood functions.[37] Indeed those buildings, which lasted long, served increasingly as community centers and that was the function that best suited the people who had created them.

iii. Toward the Cooperative Commonwealth

In striking contrast to the ambiguity of the political party mounted by the Grange in 1874, an ambiguity that probably generated an actual division in the ranks of the organization, the Greenback Party held a clear origin and purpose. Based on the social and economic calamity of rural America, the Greenback Party offered an indictment of the system of finance and credit that enriched the banking institutions at the expense of the lives and fortunes of those dependent upon that system. The problem it addressed was twofold. One dimension, the most immediate, was that of deflation. Whereas the convergence of efforts at specie resumption, the demonetization of silver, and the course of economic growth with a simultaneous contraction of the currency, all operated to force debtors to the wall, the Greenback Party proposed the distribution of fiat currency—paper money "greenbacks"—as the basic element of exchange to provide relief from the pressures of deflation. The second dimension of the problem addressed, however, flowed from the deeper analysis of the monetary crisis. The existing currency system, based upon the "intrinsic" value of precious minerals, whether gold or silver, and its obvious consequences and depredations, was still part of a larger system in which money, instead of a medium facilitating the exchange of commodities, had become the *object* of the system. Commodities had become mere instruments of exchange for the accumulation of more money. When the Greenback Party proposed the issuance of fiat paper money, the object was less the immediate one of inflation, although that would have been the effect, but the larger goal of altering the purpose of organized society as it was becoming entrenched and institutionalized in the 1870s and 1880s.

The Greenback Party of Pettis County led a robust life punctuated by meetings, speeches, and picnics, with Sedalia a favorite spot for state conventions and candidates being fielded for countywide and city-offices—and with some success too.[38] They even elected a Congressman, T. M. Rice, whose daughter was the wife of a worker in the railroad shops in Sedalia. As a forum for the discussion of political and economic ideas, as an alternative to the established two political parties, and as a vehicle for the congregation of farmers with like ideas, the local Greenback activity seems to have been popular.

Yet one quality stands out as exceptional. The Greenback movement in the nation has usually been seen as the exclusive domain of the rural population. Perhaps because of its closer relationship to what would later emerge as populism rather than to what would later surface as labor unions, historians have regularly written off the possibility of an intellectual and cultural bridge uniting farmers and workers. Thus even Lawrence Goodwyn, a keenly sympathetic observer of Greenback activity and ideology, notes that, "Either because urban workers accepted the moral criticism of greenbacks, or because the entire matter seemed too difficult to grasp, or because they simply never heard of it, or because they developed other priorities, the soft-money creed proved fairly easy for laboring people to resist." Leon Fink has more sanguinely noted that labor organizations were able to build, in part, by drawing on radical greenback traditions, but in so commenting he departs from the traditional perspective.[39] In Pettis County this much is clear: workers and farmers joined cause. One of the local firebrands for Greenbackism, running for city office in 1880, was Isaac Wright, a bridgebuilder for the railroad.[40] The Greenback Party's city convention in 1880 was held in the East Sedalia Engine House. At that meeting, a depressing gathering because of the number of individuals who declined nominations for city positions because they were either compelled to move on to other places seeking work in the wake of the disastrous strike that spring or they could not afford to serve in public office, the workers termed it, "the party of a living issue."[41] The resonance of worker culture with the ideology of the opposition to the priorities and values of the increasingly market oriented society derived from the similar, but separate, forces and patterns of development among workers. But the bonds of shared experience and tradition made the union natural. When the daughter of Greenback Congressman T. M. Rice married a worker in the Sedalia railroad shops, that wedding was a revealing and symbolic occasion.

By 1886, when the national Greenback Party had run its last candidate for President and had fallen apart never to mount a national campaign again, and when local Greenback activity was a decade old, the state party met for its last time in Sedalia. It met in June when the smoke had not fully cleared from the 1886 strike on the Gould System, a circumstance which makes the selection of Sedalia as the site for the convention especially significant. The meeting was presided over by H. Martin Williams, the Greenback publicist from Springfield, and Congressman T. M. Rice. In its final actions the party endorsed the principles that had been at the core of the national party and the specific planks from the opposition to bank-issued money to the antimonopoly views that had long been salient in this area. The support for the theory and primacy of democracy and popular sovereignty was such that, even though many opposed the doctrine of prohibition, they urged a vote on the prohibition question. And they nominated a St. Louis member of the Knights of Labor, at that time under indictment for strike-related charges, for state railroad commissioner.[42] Indeed, it was difficult in fundamental respects to distinguish between the ideology associated with the Knights of Labor and that of the Greenback Party. But just as that ideology was spreading and maturing, both institutions were declining, soon to be mere shadows of their previous vitality.

It is obvious that there was more to the Greenback movement in this country than the party structure alone. The institution provided a gathering point and a focus for this kind of political and social activity, but it did not limit that activity. Indeed, free thought and discussion was the hallmark of the effort. As a disseminator of specific principles that had already existed and grown locally among farmers and workers, it had served its purpose well. But when the institution died, the ideas and principles did not just vanish. They lived on. Perhaps, as in the strike of 1886, a lesson had been learned.

Exactly how those ideas were sustained and communicated and nurtured in the subsequent years is not clear, although it seems plain enough that those responsible for their growth were both farmers and workers. In 1886 and 1887 a tabloid publication entitled *The Sedalia Labor Union and the Grange* served not so much as a chronicle of local activity as it did as a publicist for ideas associated with Henry George, the Knights of Labor, Greenback currency theory, notions of antimonopoly and as a device for reporting on the activities of kindred efforts elsewhere. Edited by G. B. DeBernardi, of Dresden, a village near Sedalia, the paper prominently displayed, in the one surviving issue of 1887, the political principles of the Knights of Labor and urged support for the Grange.[43] Indeed, despite the outward appearance of an urban worker appeal and orientation, DeBernardi's background and activity (at the time he was an official lecturer for the state Grange) was that of a farmer. This was not a narrowly partisan publication; it took in a wide variety of views and issues. And it included women. Frances Willard's article on "The Labor Question" (which to her meant "more than the temperance and the woman questions combined, for it includes them both") came on page one. The issues of the day were being confronted even if the institutions and organizations of government and politics and economy seemed inappropriate agencies for such discussion.

In fact, given the discouraging history of the ability of such institutions to meet popular needs, workers and farmers demonstrated a remarkable persistence. Despite the sorry outcome of the efforts and energy put into the Knights of Labor, and despite the demise of the Greenback Party, both of which seemed so promising for a while, they continued. In 1888 the local Union Labor Party pressed the same general platform of antimonopoly and antibank sentiments, proposing a government based on popular will and need rather than on vested power. Representing a worker constituency as well as farmers, the delegates to the state convention from Pettis County included Knights of Labor, worker fraternity members, and farmers like DeBernardi too.[44] That activity, in turn, fed yet another organization as the surge toward political involvement expanded. The Agricultural Wheel, soon to combine with the Farmers' Alliance to become the Farmers' and Laborers' Union, appears to have first met in Pettis County in 1888. And it soon expanded, although the precise number of lodges in the county is not known. In May of 1889, however, all of the lodges in the county were present at a secret grand meeting in Lamont.[45] Unabated by institutional inadequacies, determined to shape their own agenda, the farmers and workers surged ahead.

Ahead, however, toward what? The activity was intense. It was widespread. And it had grown substantially from the awkward and faltering steps, whether in Sedalia or out on the farm, of the 1870s. But what was the object of all that turbulence? From the established perspectives of modern historians, the object would have been an increased income. But more money was not the goal. Aside from the theoretical dilemma of how farmers and workers could cooperate in an effort to secure the conflicting goals of higher commodity prices and higher wages, the fact of the case is that the ideology uniting these farmers and workers was fundamentally an antimaterialist ideology. Indeed, it proposed that money be returned to its original status as a means to an end rather than an end in itself. And these themes had long been developed in both the worker and farmer cultures of Pettis County in terms of brotherhood, community responsibility, and the bridling of acquisitive passions. They reached back, even, to the origins of the earliest white settlements in Pettis County. At the end of the 1880s, those themes found explicit, articulate defense.

Among the several who stepped forth to enunciate this ideology, the one who stands out as the most systematic, yet authentic, spokesman was G. B. DeBernardi. Born in the Piedmont Alps in 1831, trained for the priesthood as a child, DeBernardi left his home while still young, migrated through Europe, then to America, and finally settled on a farm near Kansas City before the Civil War. For a while he seems to have lived much as a gentleman farmer; he found ample time to pursue his interests in engineering, mathematics, and political economy. The panic of 1873 ended this. In the wake of financial ruin, he began agitating for the issue of paper money to relieve the economic crisis and soon moved into the ranks of the Greenback Party as an organizer and propagandist. Serving prominently in that party as a lecturer, he also moved into the Grange to continue that function. By the early 1880s he had settled in the small Pettis County village of Dresden, a few miles west of Sedalia on the Missouri Pacific. From here he traveled the state constantly as he lectured to groups of farmers and workers and became an active organizer by the end of the decade for the Wheel and the Alliance. Identified largely with farmers, he reached workers as well because he addressed himself to the broader questions of market society.[46]

By focusing on the importance of cooperation in social relationships, DeBernardi's analysis of society met needs long expressed locally and sharpened the indictment of the existing structure. When the lecturer declared that "cooperation will prove the salvation of labor" he touched upon a moral impulse that had been manifest in a myriad of worker activities from the antimaterialist religious experiences of East Sedalia pietism to the midnight raid to close down the noxious glue factory to the fraternal activity of the AOUW and then most recently the strikes and the cooperative format of the Knights of Labor. And it drew upon the same impulse evident in the rural tradition of neighborly assistance, from the fair to the Grange to the Greenback Party. Cooperation, for DeBernardi,

represented a moral alternative to competition as the basis of human relationships. Competition, he charged, put workers in an unnatural relationship that instead of being mutually helpful was mutually destructive.
The more competitive the workers became, the more they succeeded in
harming their brothers. One injury was obvious: the competition between workers for the same job resulted in one being unemployed and
the other being employed only at a paltry wage. But competition forced
an even more serious problem. In their quest for higher wages, since by
definition they failed to receive the full value of the product of their
labor, they were competing with the purchaser of their labor, ultimately
another worker, for a limited amount of money. The need therefore, he
argued, was for all producers to cooperate, not trade by trade for higher
wages, but together as the producers of value to create an alternative to
the wage system.[47]

DeBernardi expressed the primacy of cooperation in an allegorical
propaganda tract in which workers were preparing to strike for higher
wages only to be cautioned by a person representing DeBernardi's own
position:

> when you demand, in your declaration of principles, higher wages for your-
> selves, be sure and demand, at the same time, that the wages of all other
> trades be kept low; for, if the wages of all other trades, especially of farmers,
> be raised simultaneously, no one will be benefitted by the operation. The
> cost of living would go up, as wages would rise. We therefore, repeat, that if
> the battle of labor is to be fought upon the line of higher money wages, and
> high prices for products, our doom is already sealed. Workingmen must
> learn to respect themselves, and value their own products above any amount
> of money.

This process of learning respect for the dignity of labor and for the products of labor was a process that had been unfolding among Pettis County
producers, especially the workers, for some time, abetted indirectly all
the while by the capitalist proselytism of the gospel of work.[48]

The basis of this cooperation lay in a labor theory of value. With his
comparison of the system of monetary value to this work oriented theory,
he attempted to place the moral impulse for cooperation on a systematic
basis, something also the Sedalia workers and farmers had been attempting for a good while, particularly in their organizational efforts. DeBernardi's focus on money rapidly took the analysis away from the abstract
and into the realm of everyday life. As he solemnly proclaimed that
"money is the root of all evil," he spoke straight from the antimaterial-
ism that operated in the system of pre-Civil War barter, in the Greenback
Party, and in the birth of East Sedalia. But he took it further, as far as
the producers themselves had come. The monetary system was the con-

crete, day to day manifestation of capitalist relationships. Because money was supported by a limited amount of gold and because it mediated all relationships of exchange it had become in itself an important commodity—the most important commodity. Instead of facilitating exchange of true commodities, the products of labor, the medium had become the end for which labor operated. Money was not an instrument of exchange any longer but an instrument of buying low and selling high. Its interest bearing nature "carries the fruits of labor to the wrong parties. It makes millionaires of a few and dooms millions to destitution." Indeed, legal tender was at the source of alienation:

> He who accepts it in exchange for goods or services loses all rights to goods and services . . . . Thus, if a man sells his home for legal tender money he becomes virtually an alien to the world. For him to recover goods, services or another home depends entirely on the will of others.

Money, then, benefited the speculator at the expense of the true producer of wealth, the worker. Within the immediate context of the seemingly endless deflationary tendency of the final third of the nineteenth century DeBernardi's analysis may appear to hinge on a mundane shortage of money. But the shortage of money was not mundane to him. Nor was it mundane to others. The workers had, after all, joined precisely this issue in the strike of 1880 when they attempted to bring the compensation for their labor up from the tight money, crisis level resulting from the panic of 1873. And that is what the Greenback Party had been all about. When DeBernardi argued that labor possessed its own value, that exchange should be exclusively on the basis of direct equivalence of labor without the use of money, he hit a familiar perception in Pettis county.[49]

Perhaps as an example of this alternative system of relationships DeBernardi went so far as to launch an effort to bring it about. His experiment was called simply, The Labor Exchange. It first surfaced locally when Nicholas Romaine, the old cobbler who sponsored labor and free thought meetings in his shop, announced in a letter to the local tabloid *Truth* (which had apparently replaced *The Sedalia Labor Union and Grange*), that he was much impressed by the idea, that he was "in full accord with the objects of the Labor Exchange," and that he believed that the "next change in the order of society will be the Co-operative Commonwealth."[50] Established first in Kansas City and then in Sedalia, the Labor Exchange was simply a device by which individual producers would exchange the products of their labor with each other.[51] Certificates facilitated the exchange, but unlike hard currency, those certificates were the equivalent of an average day's work. The main functions of the officials of the exchange were purely administrative. They kept the accounts of the deposits of the members "expressed in days and fractions of day's labor, or value." When a worker deposited an item or service of his own, he received a deposit certificate in return attesting to the amount of labor on deposit. These were not monetary items in any conventional sense:

> Instead of being final payment for actual wealth parted with, they are evidences that compensation has not yet been made. The farmer who brings a load of produce to market and accepts money, has no further rights on that market. The member of the Labor Exchange who deposits produce in the care of the Association and receives a certificate has not only a right to demand the face value of his certificate in actual wealth, but a further interest in the accumulations of the Association.[52]

The basic point of the operation was of utmost simplicity: to bring producers together instead of driving them apart.

For all its attractiveness as an institutional framework for the culture of Pettis County workers and farmers, the fate of that local culture should not be tied to the fate of the Labor Exchange. The distrust of institutions, whether public or private, corporate or labor, or anything else, had long been an important quality in the lives of those workers and farmers. Indeed, Nicholas Romaine could criticize the Labor Exchange while supporting its principles, ideas he said pointedly that were not new with DeBernardi, because it was ultimately but another institution. He had "very little faith," he said, that the Labor Exchange would be able to bring about the "Co-operative Commonwealth" although it could be a significant step toward it: "The L[abor] E[xchange] is to be an educator in the practical details of cooperation; it is to discipline our forces and give us practical details of experience to a certain limit. Beyond this it will not be allowed to proceed for it has a master."[53] He seemed to suggest that if the institution did not fall of its own weight, its members would pull it down when it started to dominate them or make decisions for them. Certainly that had been the fate of other such organizations. There is an important element in that observation: these people did not regard institutional success as the measure of the strength of their commitment. Much more significant to them were the values, the priorities, the cultural wellsprings that gave birth to such institutions. They seemed to sense that it was the principles by which people lived, rather than the institutions erected to meet specific needs, that mattered most of all. In which case perhaps another conclusion is possible: the cooperative commonwealth had already been made. And it had been made at the most important level, the level of popular thought and attitudes, where people on their own had developed a vision, a vision of a different way of life.

X

The Travail of Sisterhood

It was a man's world. And, in the sense that the values of materialism, aggressiveness, and competitiveness assumed a distinctly masculine association, it was becoming more of a man's world constantly. Yet women entered and coped with that world with greater frequency and visibility. They entered this new set of relationships for a variety of reasons, they encountered experiences understandably viewed as a decline, and they responded to the frustrations and limitations of their experiences in ways that range the full spectrum from lonely, isolated suffering to vigorous activism. And their activism itself ranged from the extension and elaboration of traditional values and roles of domesticity throughout society to efforts to enter the world of men and the market. It is difficult to generalize about so diverse a set of experiences and reactions and to discern the unifying thread of it all. This much, however, can be said: Women in Sedalia had a culture of their own. To some that culture would be a set of obstacles to be overcome. For others, that culture would lead them into battle.

i. The Ordeal of the Doyennes

The boosters of Sedalia often referred to it with pride as "The Queen City of the Prairies," a distinctly feminine association. There was something to this since the city took its name from a woman. Just as his father-in-law, a generation earlier, had the honor of naming Georgetown when that village was platted, so did George R. Smith name the county seat that replaced Georgetown. Where David Thomson looked to the past and recalled fond memories of his home in Kentucky when he chose the name for Georgetown, George Smith looked to his daughter Sarah Elvira, nicknamed Sed. Sarah Elvira Smith, later Cotton, would live until two days past her ninety-ninth birthday in the town that bore her name and with her sister, Martha Elizabeth, the inseparable Smith-Cotton sisters would hold forth in their father's stately house as a source of inspiration, comfort, support, and guidance in a variety of enterprises, social

170

and economic, in the growth of Sedalia. They provided an example to many. By the same token, however, they serve as an example of the perils and frustrations, of the opportunities and fulfillments of womanhood in that society. As daughters and as sisters and as women they sought to fulfill their duties on this earth, and in the midst of an enormous social revolution this proved no easy task.

Perhaps they were fated by the very circumstances in which they began life on this earth. Mileta Ann Thomson married George R. Smith in 1827 and the following year gave birth to a son. This son, named David Thomson Smith, gave his father much hopeful pride but just as quickly brought him grief, sorrow, and despair that would endure decades later. Seven months after his birth, the baby died. Less than a year after that death, however, another child was born to the couple. This child was a daughter, Martha Elizabeth, and then another daughter, Sarah Elvira, came the next year—1831. On these two robust daughters Smith focused much attention, love, and guidance. Still babies when the time came to move from Kentucky to Missouri, they endured the trip and would later recount that experience and the tales they had been told of it as though that really signified the beginnings of life. And so, by their own measure, they started life near where Georgetown would soon be established, in Pettis County, Missouri. Indeed, George R. Smith himself seems to have marked this as the beginning of a new life as well.

While the youth of the Smith daughters in Georgetown seems almost idyllic, to listen to their recollections, the forces at work shaping their development and their own growth and socialization reveal fundamental contours of the creation of women who would later be both distinctive and representative—distinctive in their individual qualities and abilities and representative in their problems and opportunities. Because of the circumstances of the family into which they were born, they held a vantage point few others could claim. Beloved granddaughters of the patriarch of the community and county, accustomed to the presence of slaves for the meeting of their needs, not lacking in the comforts of life that money could buy, blessed with educational opportunities open to few of their sex, the Smith daughters were, to say the least, in a special position. But what really made their situation unique was their father George R. Smith, who, after all, was himself unique.

By all accounts General Smith was in public life a man of stern rectitude, a man of uncompromising principle, a man who commanded loyalty and respect by the sheer force of his will and commitment to cause. Never afraid of isolation on account of his principles, willing to risk all on his own vision of the future, a fighter in countless issues, he was a natural leader, the kind of person many of his contemporaries identified as even a hero. Physically, these traits were reinforced: "a giant in stature, with a look of daring capable of dangerous work, and with the bearing of a man who had won in many hazardous fields of life . . . ." [1] This was the man, whether feared or respected in the community, who fathered Sarah Elvira and Martha Elizabeth.

There is ample reason to believe that General Smith was no less forceful in private life. Sed would write much later that "To my childhood's fancy he seemed a veritable Cid Campeador. Nothing daunted his indomitable spirit."[2] Indeed he nourished bold ambitions in his progeny and pursued a vigorous course to see those dreams realized. They would be educated in their uncle's school and their father crusaded for equal female educational opportunity. In 1840, with still preadolescent daughters, Smith delivered an address on female education which observed that "Abundant homilies have been read upon your amiable weakness and sentimental delicacy, upon your timid gentleness and submissive dependence [and] by these prejudices mothers have been denied the power of instructing their children, wives have not been permitted to share the intellectual pursuits of their husbands and . . . most women had no character at all beyond that of purity and devotion to their families." By virtue of education "man will approach you with profound respect . . . ."[3] In 1846, with teenagers now, Smith wrote his children from Washington that he wanted them to visit the capital "as soon as you finish your education." But, he admonished them,

> when you do I want you to be able to converse fluently upon all subjects and with the most distinguished men and women, for you will meet them. How important, then that you should apply yourselves diligently and energetically to your studies. Now is the time for you to acquire information; and however tempting society may be now, you should resolve and determine, that let others do as they may, for yourselves you will acquire all the knowledge that is possible for you to obtain.

Then he told them exactly how to divide their time so that a third was spent at work, a third with books, and a third for rest.[4] In 1840 George R. Smith had served on the board of directors of a female academy established in Georgetown. In 1848 he hired a teacher to come from Virginia to teach at his permanent academy. The academy was located in George R. Smith's house. Afterwards the daughters went to boarding school in Boonville.[5] His hopes for education, therefore, were not idle hopes. His vision for his daughters was a vision of independence and respect. In fact, it seems reasonable to say that he hoped they would be as assertive as he was. Had his infant son lived, this may well have been a different relationship and vision. Now he had only daughters, though. And George Smith worshipped his daughters.

His daughters worshipped him as well. Domineering he may have been; possessed with a clear vision and high hopes for his daughters he certainly was. General Smith was, nonetheless, a gentle spirit full of so-lace, sympathy, comfort, and love. Sarah Elvira caught the effect neatly: "My timid little mother dreaded the spirited horses which he delighted to drive; but he would say, 'Shut your eyes and I will carry you safely.' This to my young ears was all assuring, and my eyes would close in peaceful serenity."[6] Upon his death Martha Elizabeth, who had early de-veloped a passion for writing poetry, wrote a poem in memory of her father that reflected partly on her childhood:

> For innocent childhood his heart was o'erflowing
> With sweetness and love as pure as their own;
> And tenderly guarding the pure rights of woman,
> The place he assigned her in the world was a throne.[7]

The warmth and the concern for his daughters was evident in every letter he wrote them and seems equally evident when he was at home with them. "His pet names for us children were 'father's child' and 'father's woman;' and whenever his eyes fell on us there was a caress, a sweet word of affection, an overflowing of the full heart. Never were wife and children loved more tenderly than were we."[8]

The influence of their mother paled in comparison to the affection and guidance provided by their father. Her influence, however, supported in all ways but one the father's efforts. One friend noted that Martha Elizabeth's "mother was a constant example to the daughter of what a woman ought to be."[9] The chief qualities in that were the obvious ones. Sarah Elvira observed that "I remember her in my childhood days as one I could not easily get around; a woman keen and vigilant in the manage-ment of her household; a mother tender and loving, kind and sagacious, a wife faithful and true; strict in discipline and holding wisely the reins of power."[10] While these were commonplace enough qualities among eu-logies, the last item mentioned concerning power seems out of place in the household of George R. Smith. The chief quality she brought to bear on her daughters was an attitude toward work, an attitude that lacked universal adherence. Again Sarah Elvira: "Her daughters, she had determined should not be victims to the evils of slavery as she felt that she had been. To this end she bent her efforts daily." She refused to allow opportunity for her children to be idle. "Once when she was mak-ing us work and wait on ourselves, while a slave stood idly looking on, a sister-in-law remonstrated with her, saying: 'Sister Melita, you will ruin that negro!' My mother pleasantly replied: 'Well, I would rather ruin the negro than ruin my children.' " When the daughter tried to argue with her because of the burden of the work her mother simply said that she wished them "to love work."[11] This effort appears to have been con-stant—and successful. In 1843 the thirteen year old Martha Elizabeth—

Bet—wrote her parents who were on a trip East making a particular point to mention: "Mother, I have been at work nearly all the time. I am now sewing for Aunt Melcena [and] day before yesterday I helped grandma make a shirt for grandpa."[12] Even in her absence the will of the mother prevailed with the daughters. This, however, is entirely compatible with the desires of their father.

The one area where there was a clear difference between husband and wife may have been one fraught with ominous implications for the daughters. She kept to herself. Unlike her husband whose activities and movements were constant and significant socially, Melita Ann Smith remained at home. The reasons for this are obscure. At once noting that she was quiet and timid, the daughters based this reticence on avoidance of "the familiarity that breeds contempt." She refused "to borrow under almost any circumstances."[13] And she was respected and esteemed by her neighbors. The ambiguity of this could lead to a dilemma. If she remained at home because this was the proper sphere of a woman she would have been teaching her daughters an important element of their own future roles, an element that contrasted sharply with the qualities articulated by her husband. But it could be equally true that she was teaching them the independence, to be highly valued, that could come only through sacrifice and even loneliness. An ambiguous legacy indeed.

The ambiguity took shape in real life as the two sisters seemed to develop along different lines. Sed stayed home much of the time. Bet yearned to travel and to mix with people. Bet may have been the first to notice Sed's proclivities here. In 1843 when General Thomson struggled with an illness, the entire family had to do its part. Bet and her aunt sat up with Thomson late into the night, and then the next night Sed and another aunt repeated the service. Unlike Bet, who seemed not to relish the chore, she noted that "Sarah was so well pleased with it that if it had been necessary for any one to sit up last night she would have been one of the company."[14] This, significantly, would be the ultimate fate of Sarah Elvira Smith. The development of her sister contrasted with that course. Recalling the days in Georgetown Bet remembered: "I looked with the envy of a child at [her cousins'] rapidly advancing womanhood, and a kind of reverence came over me, as I thought that mine with its privileges would never come." That is the way Sed recalled it too: ". . . my sister grew into a perfect flower of womanhood. Her life in the early years was full of dreams and fancies, characteristic of the girl 'standing with reluctant feet where the brook and river meet.' "[15] Bet would write poetry and entertain others with her singing. Sed would tend to the needs of the family. Bet would socialize. Remembering the courthouse her father built, she was careful to add that "And the ladies could go in, too; for within its walls they had big meetings, great revivals of religion, schools, and sometimes temperance speeches and lyceums."[16]

One can easily see General Smith organizing and speaking at these meetings. One can also easily see Martha Elizabeth Smith steadily making her way the half-mile or so from their home to the courthouse just as regularly. And Bet would travel, taking a grand trip in 1855, apparently in celebration of her twenty-fifth birthday, visiting relatives in Kentucky and going to New York and Canada. While away she urged her sister to join her, "if mother can possibly spare you." If she could not come, Bet pleaded, "sis go *more* into society. Visit Boonville and places where you can have *good* society."[17] But Sed could not go; she was attending to her mother who was in poor health.

The one experience notably lacking in the documents attesting to the development of the Smith sisters is attention to matters of courtship. Both obviously had male friends, and the correspondence on rare occasion mentions disappointment with a flirtation or deeper involvement. But when one friend wrote Sed that she feared that "I am fast becoming an old maid" Sed in fact became even more silent. Her friend protested: "Sed, why do you not tell me your affaires du coeur . . .?" as she had before.[18] The reasons for this absence of discussion or absence of courtship could be explained in many ways. How many truly eligible bachelors could there be in Georgetown in the 1850s? What did these women consider to be an eligible bachelor? Were they, in fact, interested in matrimony? The situation is opaque and renders any explanation tentative. One possibility, however, does find expression in the correspondence of the sisters. The friend quoted above who had been in the habit of sharing secrets ("Sed, you mustn't let anyone but Bet *see* my letters") may have struck on something when she wrote: "I expect to hear soon that either you or Bettie are pluming your wings for a flight from the paternal roof to a snug nest of your own, notwithstanding your father's threats, predictions, or golden offers if you will oblige him by retaining the name of Smith toujours—."[19] George Smith, in fact, *was* sensitive on this point. When writing to hire a teacher for his daughters the central qualification that he probed was his marital status. The poor unmarried teacher could only respond: ". . . if you should consider that an indispensable I can not yet suit you in that respect."[20] At the least Smith was not about to push his daughter into marriage. Perhaps he pushed the other way. The Smith daughters served their father, and by any estimation it would take a rare man to attract them.

There was, however, another that they served and worshipped with the same devotion as their father. Sed, like her father, joined the Christian Church; Bet, with her mother, joined the Disciples of Christ—Campbellites. The religious convictions of these two young women ran deep and they emphasized what Bet called "a firm and unflinching discharge of duty, and perfect confidence and trust in the God of love . . . [and] to endure all things for the glory of Him who suffered on the cross that we might live."[21] Sed was less given to such confessions of faith, and in fact it would only be later that Bet would dwell on her religious sentiments and the duty of following her Holy Father. But the religion was there. And it grew.

The deepening of the spiritual commitment in Bet is easy to see, if also morose in some of its manifestations. Her twenty-fifth birthday seemed to her to mark a sort of threshold or a summit. "Have I nearly gained the zenith of the hill of life?" An awesome question for any age but perhaps especially unnerving at the age of twenty-five, she seemed to have also formulated the answer in the affirmative as she reflected back upon "the beautiful landscape, the sweet memories of the past" as well as "the bright hopes in the future."[22] It was that year that she had special reason to reflect back on the past too. She visited the relatives left behind in Kentucky. But it was not entirely a high-spirited visit. In fact it is at this point that Bet Smith's life became increasingly tinged with melancholy. "Phantom faces haunt me, and voices greet me, both in my sleeping and waking dreams," she wrote her parents from Kentucky. "The spirit longings in this world are unattainable, and only point us to a brighter, purer clime where at the right hand of God, all will be pleasantness and peace. Where happiness will be unalloyed, and tears will be wiped away from every eye."[23] Visiting in Kentucky she had undergone an experience of enormous proportions that moved her deeply to reflect on life—and death. In her journal she wrote down what happened:

> Visited the old home, in Kentucky, where we used to live, and where the ashes of my little brother are buried. I could see the solemn procession follow from the door his little form, move slowly across the yard, and deposit it very near the house, as if human care and love could lessen the chill of death. I tried to imagine the grief of my parents, as the little angel was torn from them before their hearts had learned submission to the will of Him who "chastens whom he loves." I thought of the loneliness in their home deserted by the little prattler, their only child. I thanked God that they and we, their daughters, have not been chastened in vain, that we now look forward to a reunion beyond the grave where the sun is ever shining and separations never come.

She visited the house, then dilapidated, where her family had lived, where she and her sister and brother had been infants. "It was a sacred place to me."[24] The full significance of this experience would be clear only years later when it would form the first element of an eerie, tragic *déja vu*.

However deep this experience ran, it soon was put behind her with more travel and indeed it appeared that her life made a major turn away from the melancholy, away from the brooding. In 1859 Bet married James W. Martin in her father's house. While the occasion was no doubt a happy one, her journal entry belies a nervous tone: "We had a merry little party assembled and all passed off with seeming gaiety, my mother, father, and sister participating. But in our hearts were emotions beyond expression. The beautiful past, the unknown future—gratitude for the one, fear and hope for the other, while above all were unceasing prayer, earnest petition for the blessing of our Father in heaven."[25]

While there is reason to suspect that the gaiety was only seeming, and not genuine, and while the mixture of emotions mentioned—gratitude, fear, and hope—form an ominous combination, many permanent unions have no doubt been formed with less solid bases and more fundamental apprehensions. But Bet continued in her journal: "Three months have passed, three of pleasure, with an occasional earth cloud, but I have reason for much gratitude."[26] The honeymoon was shortlived. The earth clouds began to gather with the force of a storm. Writing shortly afterward to a cousin, Bet's husband had gone to town, leaving her alone. But, she took pains to remark, "I don't get lonely here by myself. I have troops of friends, sweet memories and bright hopes to keep me company—to say nothing of *chickens*, the *sewing* machine, and bustling around *generally*"—the lament of a lonely person, the lament of the daughter of George R. Smith who shared larger aspirations than domesticity could satisfy. Then, commenting on a letter from her sister, she began a different discourse: "There must be a better world than this, where the feelings of the heart are not forced to find expression in cold-meaningless words, when we shall know even as we are known, when in the presence of the Infinite all will be *love* and bliss."[27] The melancholy was back. All was *not* love and bliss.

New hopes came in March, 1860, when Bet delivered a son. The son's name, of course, was George Smith Martin. At four months of age, however, she knew something was wrong: "To his mother he is beautiful, with his golden hair, blue eyes and exquisite complexion. His is not playful, and of course, we think it is because of some extra talent that makes him quiet and sedate." And then she spelled other hopes for young George Smith Martin: "Great sprightliness, or any superficial charm, I am willing to sacrifice to real worth. I should like him to be a man of stern principles, who would rather be right than to occupy high places in this world's honors."[28] She was echoing here what the previous summer she had expressed when she identified for her cousin her father's special qualities: "his stern integrity and uprightness of purpose."[29] The clear hopes that her son would be like her father were dashed. George Smith Martin died in July, 1861—sixteen months old.[30] This would have been a tragedy under any circumstances. But Bet bore the additional weight of having witnessed precisely the same development before with such terror and foreboding. If the future had been uncertain before, the gloom now seemed all around.

The actual course of Bet's life is unclear at this time. Only one certainly exists: there were problems at home, the death of her son aside. At one point she mentions the removal of her father, mother, and sister from Georgetown to the place out on the prairie that would become Sedalia in May, 1859, the time of her own marriage. In the same account, however, she then notes that "In a few months I came back from Saline [County] and became one of the prairie family." That arrangement seems to have existed still in the spring of 1861 when her mother died and then less than three months later when her own son died: ". . . in our home, now doubly darkened, we three, —my father, my sister, and myself, were left alone . . . ."[31] And given the growing circumstances of war, "Life was becoming chaos,"[32] as Bet said. The general and his two daughters fled their home going ultimately to St. Louis, returning to Sedalia at the end of November. Then something even more obscure happened. "Just after our return home in the fall of 1861, a darker cloud than ever before threw its pall about me . . . ."[33] At this point she had been married two and a half years. She had, however, spent precious little time with her new husband. The majority of the time had been with her father and sister. It would be altogether inappropriate and unfair to suggest what was going on. The separation seems to have started early, though. And, protracted as it was, there is nothing to suggest that the husband and wife were able to live together again. Scattered references in court records indicate that James W. Martin was being forced to yield to his wife his courtesy rights to use of land belonging to his wife. And then, on May 4, 1866, after he had sued for divorce and confessed his own adultery, the Pettis County Court granted the divorce proclaiming Martha Elizabeth Martin "the innocent and injured party." James Martin, himself, was given reprieve from the restrictions prohibiting remarriage for a period of five years.[34] The marriage was over.

The questions raised here are large. Why is it that Bet, the innocent party, did not sue for divorce? She seems to have known, to have suffered, at least as early as 1861. The separation was a long one, the difference apparently irreconcilable. What held her back? The chaos and confusion of war could well have contributed to a reluctance to proceed on any permanent domestic course and to a patience, waiting for life to be less strained. Or, Martin could have been in the military; that is not mentioned. Her youth could have had an influence here, although this is not a great likelihood; at the time of her divorce Bet was thirty-six years old. Her father's influence? He was understanding and supportive, but he seems not to have been directing her. She recalled of the period after that dark cloud of late 1861: "my father's deep, divine love, without reproach, without vituperation for any one, went into the shadow with me, and I was safe." His advice to her: "Wherever you want to go, or whatever you want to do, it shall be done."[35] Given his love for his daughter,

given the forcefulness of his personality, and given the unsparing vituperation and recrimination he routinely heaped upon his adversaries, this
counsel reflected uncommon tolerance. Was this the same man who had
shortly before said, "If a man is right, he can not be too radical, and if
he is wrong he can not be too conservative"?[36] Part of the answer to that
could lie in the fact that her own recollection left room for criticism of the
wife as well as of the husband, neither of which Smith chose to pursue.
And that may, in turn, suggest the larger contours of the problem.

It is quite possible that in this moment—which actually lasted more
than half a decade—we can see the limits of Martha Elizabeth Martin,
limits that were not unique to her, limits that derived from no entirely
personal weakness, limits that reflect and reveal a broader pattern of social tensions in relationships between the sexes. The expectations that
formed her own view of the future emphasized on the one hand her
father's pressures and hopes that she become educated, cultivated, and
independent and on the other hand her more traditional role, defined as
she put it, as "a firm and unflinching discharge of duty." These two
impulses would, in marriage, come into conflict. Small wonder, then that
she became apprehensive about the future starting at least at her twenty-
fifth birthday. It was difficult for her to make the decisions between the
two courses and her husband was apparently little help in the matter.
Moreover, she was reluctant to confront the issue directly herself; thus
her veiled references to the frustrations of her role as wife in her letters
and journal. She was caught between the two competing drives in her
own soul, one for independence and respect and the other for the fulfillment of her wifely, womanly duties. In this context it could well be that
the only real choice she had was, in fact, indecision. She could even
prevail through indecision. Since it is obvious that her husband found
another lover, he would not be able to legitimize his new relationship
until he publicly confessed his sin in the old and proclaimed her the
innocent party. In this regard, it appears that Martha Elizabeth Martin
was not just the innocent victim of an unfaithful husband; she was the
victim of a society that drove a wedge between duty to others and independence. And the remarkable thing in the whole episode is not the
depth of her suffering, which was substantial, but that she was able to
defy the narrow choices available to her.

With this new freedom, however, her problems only changed; they
did not cease. In 1861, when General Smith had been serving in St.
Louis as Adjutant General, Bet had been under a doctor's care.[37] This
was the first such treatment she recorded. And, she does not mention the
precise affliction being treated—or even hint at it. In 1868, immediately
after her sister's wedding, General Smith took Bet to the sanitarium and
clinic of Dr. Alexander Hamilton Laidlaw in Hudson City, New Jersey.[38]
She remained there under his treatment for more than a year. She re-

turned again at least in 1873, 1878, and possibly 1882, staying for varying lengths of time. And there appear to have been other physicians consulted as well: she said that her father "took me to many physicians, in the East as well as the West, and tried hard to restore me to health."[39] Whatever the treatment she received elsewhere, under Dr. Laidlaw the treatment involved rest, diet control, and treatment of specific symptoms. Once surgery was contemplated but rejected for fear the tissue would not heal properly. From all appearances Bet had a serious medical problem, or even a series of afflictions.

The precise ailment of this woman and its source elude modern diagnosis given that so few details are ever revealed. In a general reference to this in 1903, at the age of seventy, Bet informed some cousins that "a semi-invalidism has consumed more than half of my life."[40] Perhaps it eluded precise diagnosis at the time. Considering the understanding of medical science in the late nineteenth century, especially concerning what was then generically termed female disorders, this seems not just a possibility but a probability. This is not to suggest, however, that just because the real affliction of Martha Elizabeth Martin was not truly understood that it was not treated clinically. It was. This is to suggest rather that this woman found herself victimized yet again and that this additional subjugation reflects broader problems afflicting females in the nineteenth century. There is, after all, no reason to suspect that Dr. Laidlaw lacked competence. Indeed, he seems to have practiced according to the highest and latest medical wisdom of his day. That is what makes the clinical diagnosis and treatment that much more significant.

Without a doubt the case of Martha Elizabeth Martin was perceived by the medical authorities as a classic case of the hysterical woman.[41] Hysteria was, at the time, both a clinical term describing a variety of symptoms exhibited in the patient and a term of pejorative. The pejorative alluded to the emotional and physical weakness of the patient, the lack of will, the self-indulgence, and the refusal to perform mandated roles. This view prevailed in the medical establishment as an alternative to finding an organic source of the ailment, to finding an actual disease. As a clinical phenomenon, the problem of hysteria seems not to have been something capable of precise definition so much as either a catchall for otherwise inscrutable symptoms (or more likely as a first option for those who chose not to look further) or as a pattern of discrete symptoms. While hysteria was recognized by the late nineteenth century as something that could afflict men, its main body of victims were women from fifteen to forty years of age of the urban middle and upper middle class. In previous years some sort of seizure had been a necessary defining characteristic of the malady, but other symptoms proved by the last third of the century to be as important. The loss of various senses, nausea, headaches, pain, and paralysis of parts of the body provided physical indications of the disorder, but the emotional signs of hysteria were growing larger in its diagnosis. Carroll Smith-Rosenberg has painted a picture of the diagnosis of these emotional symptoms that suggests their relevance to the case at hand. Discussing the importance of depression as a common theme, she notes: "Hysterical symptoms not infrequently followed a death in the family, a miscarriage, some financial setback which forced the patient to become self-supporting; or they were seen by the patient as related to some long-term, unsatisfying life situation—a tired school teacher, a mother unable to cope with the demands of a large family. Most of these women took to their beds because of pain, paralysis or general weakness. Some remained there for years."[42] The chronic melancholia, the death of her mother and then her son, the divorce, the isolation and uncertainty—these were signs anybody could read. A physician could find more.

Dr. Laidlaw found plenty. And he seems to have treated her thoroughly, or at least in a variety of ways, in accordance with accepted medical practice. Rest formed a substantial portion of the treatment and she remained at the health resort for extended periods and she could make occasional trips to New York City, to Saratoga, and other places. But it was more than rest and relaxation (indeed there is an occasional note of boredom in her letters suggesting not relaxation—just a lack of opportunity to do anything. "I must get away from here soon.").[43] It was also an isolation from her own family and home, an isolation that served to remove her from her family and to increase her dependence on the physician himself. This itself is fraught with implications about the purposes of the practitioners. The doctor was an adviser as well. He urged one course of action in particular on Bet Martin: it is necessary, he told her, she wrote her sister, that "we should give no time nor thought to the impossible. Our strength is too limited . . . . "[44] Dr. Laidlaw may have been basing this advice on a meticulous observation of Bet's ambitions and frustrations; or he may have based it on a more general observation about the psychosomatic nature of various ailments; or he may have been talking about the general weakness of women and the general source, therefore, of Bet's problems. It probably was a combination of the three. After solemnly examining her urine he announced: "You have been worrying." While this was an interesting deduction in itself, his logic is no less remarkable: "anxiety of mind always congests the liver, and makes the body sick."[45] Worrying? Possibly. She certainly had ample cause to do so. But the advice was based more than on clinical analysis of her specimen. It was necessary to be less ambitious, he explained, on more general principles. Dr. Laidlaw himself had in his youth "an ambition to do great things." He labored at making dictionaries, taking a coastal survey, engraving, writing for magazines, and other absorbing activities until he was struck by paralysis and consumption and could do nothing for a few years. Then he turned to his medical practice as a gynecologist and "now says his life is play."[46]

Play it may have been, but his practice had more serious dimensions too. The exact contours of the contemplated surgery are never spelled out but the context suggests a hysterectomy. And indeed this would have been a characteristic diagnosis and course for late nineteenth-century physicians.[47] Instead of the hysterectomy, though, "proper treatment" would help her "create healthy organs."[48] By 1878, he had, through whatever treatment, gotten the womb and kidneys about right or "at least ready to get right by time" and then was concentrating his efforts on her piles—itself a problem possibly related to being bedridden and subject to constant rest. The treatment here consisted of painting them with iodine, applying electric shock treatment, and "introducing an instrument for pressure." It should be no surprise that she loathed this: "I have to be *exposed*." After describing all this perhaps there was a note of skepticism in her final comment: "He *thinks* he can cure me."[49] What she was thinking after ten years of this kind of treatment remains unknown. And if there is cause for concern about what was going on in the doctor's examining room, there is perhaps greater cause for concern about what was going on in the doctor's mind. One safe bet could be made: this is not the treatment that brought an end to Dr. Laidlaw's own paralysis.

It is difficult to assess the significance of this ordeal. Given the fact that his medical treatment failed to cure her—she did, after all, continue to suffer from these same symptoms until her death—and given the particular diagnosis and treatment, it would be easy to explain this in terms of the sexual attitudes of a predominantly male medical profession that attempted to restore frustrated women to their "proper" roles of dependence, submission, and domesticity. It is easy because such in fact was the case. But that does not end the matter. Martha Elizabeth Smith (she had her name changed from Martin back to Smith by the New Jersey Legislature in 1873—perhaps the one positive accomplishment of her visits)[50] was nonetheless afflicted. What were the real origins of this affliction? What would have been a reasonable treatment? In approaching these questions one must be careful not to fall into the same habit of Dr. Laidlaw in applying standard prescriptions and formulas reflecting not an understanding of the particular individual at hand but instead a recitation of the established views of the time.

As one considers Martha Elizabeth Smith as an individual woman, there if no escaping the fact that she was beset with difficulties that arose from her own specific upbringing and that arose from being a woman. She was, as early at least as the 1850s, a troubled soul. And, with more frustrations and disappointments and few, if any, satisfactions she became more troubled—deeply troubled. She was literally crippled. With physical ailments that could indeed have possessed biological, organic sources and whose origins escaped diagnosis in the clinics she visited, she was a physical cripple. But she was also crippled socially. Given her position, her education, her travel, her aspirations, her glowing future, her status as the elder daughter of the father of Sedalia, of the senior statesman of the region, of a possessor of wealth and vision, her dreams were bright. But then they crumbled. Her father had glowing dreams of the future for himself that could be realized. Hers could not. Where was the opportunity for a talented, educated woman in this sparsely settled area in the process of industrialization? Where was the opportunity for a woman whose father had already achieved all? What was there for her to do to achieve the kind of fulfillment she sought? If satisfaction could not be found in domesticity, which it clearly could not for her, where then could it be found? Society simply failed to provide such opportunities for satisfaction. She was crippled socially—not by her own limits, but by the limits imposed on her by her environment.

The tragedies run deep in the story of Martha Elizabeth Smith. They start with crushed hopes and dreams and they continue with sexual subjugation veiled as therapy. But the tragedies grew as she became increasingly crippled, increasingly dependent upon others. The dependence was evident enough in the care of Dr. Laidlaw, for it was more than a clinical relationship that he encouraged. His patients, indeed, reciprocated: ". . . for those who are sick and in his care he is all. He is a brother, a father, a comforter, weeps with those who weep, and laughs with those who laugh."[51] The male dependency is obvious, but its specific manifestations here—a father, a brother—are especially significant given the brother she never had and the father she definitely had. She did not mention the other male relationship—the husband.

She did, in fact, become increasingly dependent upon her father. Commenting on her father's assistance in her times of need, she observed that "through it all he watched over me as though I were a little child. Henceforth [from the time that she returned to her home, leaving her husband] I was his charge. In all the beautiful nineteen years that followed, I never seemed for one moment a burden to him . . . He served me with a tenderness, chivalry, and devotion that was sweet and marvelously patient."[52] The dependence was in part financial inasmuch as he provided the considerable sums necessary for her prolonged stays. And it was in many ways simply the earnest love of a daughter. She wrote him in 1869, "Your letters are sacred to me."[53] But there was more than gratitude and love here; she was deeply aware of her dependence, and was even sometimes uncomfortable with it; writing her sister she once said that "how pleasant it would be to be able to watch him tenderly, and minister to his wants as he has so generously done for me. But I cannot."[54] When he died, the emptiness was vast. "I long to be home . . . ," she lamented, "and yet what can we do without our dear father?"[55] Her ultimate tribute came in 1903 and 1904 when the two sisters commissioned a biography of their father. In 1906 Sarah explained it: "My sister is not well, having been for years compelled to be very careful of her health—and strength. Yet she it is who carried the Biography through which altho far short of what we would have it is a consolation to us, feeling as we do that in the absence of sons to perpetuate his name we must not let all his good deeds be lost and forgotten."[56] And this was the only way that his name would be perpetuated. Bet had changed her name from Martin back to Smith, thus fulfilling her father's earlier hope. But in 1907, with the biography done, Martha Elizabeth Smith died.

In the years of her affliction her faith in God deepened. She became crucially dependent upon this spiritual vision of the future. And that spiritual vision focused on two specific aspects: God, the Father; and Death. Her poetry, her letters, her daily thoughts converged on a gloomy, melancholy brooding that could transform any cheerful subject into a dark foreboding. Even her poem "The Child and the Butterfly" which started with a colorful description of beauty and youthful frolicking wound up with death:

> And the little soft hands that our own had kept warm
> And the frolicsome feet we had guarded from harm,
> Grew still and silent; the spirit had fled—
> We were alone with our sanctified dead.
> Like the child for the fly, we call and we wait,
> Looking still toward the sky, standing still at the gate.

She recorded, often in poetry, each birthday as another step closer to the grave. In one poem, entitled "Death" she expressed it bluntly:

> Then let me linger near thy side
>   As friend and friend together go,
> And waiting in thy portal wide,
>   Abide my time 'till all I know.[57]

The equipoise of what would otherwise be an unalloyed streak of morbidity was her faith that death would bring happiness and contentment. "Why should we feel that all else is good but death. That is His appointment as well as life. Why should it not lead to happiness." This was written on her forty-eighth birthday. She continued, developing a Swedenborgian notion of death, that the Father will "finally lead from *this* unhappy existence to higher where we will find our faculties fully adapted to higher and purer spheres."[58] Nearly eleven years later she wrote ambiguously: "Oh how sweet it is to trust in our Father's love and to feel that no time nor circumstance can take us beyond it, and in whatever way Death may come to us it will only take us to Him."[59] An unhappy existence it was for her indeed; no wonder that Death promised happiness and a reunion with God, her Father. She depended on it with her very soul.

Her love and her faith helped her endure. So did her sister. Of Sarah Elvira Smith's personal life less is known. She lived in the shadows of her sister. This was evident early. Sarah was occasionally the poet too, although a far different one, and in 1853 she wrote a poem "To My Sister" which went, in part:

> Yes, sister mine, thy sunny smile
> From memory's twilight dawn
> Has beamed upon the shadowy aisle
> Through which my path hath worn,
> To brighten every joy I knew,
> To gild each passing cloud,
> With heart forever warm and true
> And spirit justly proud.[60]

Her sister recognized this and constantly worked to bring Sarah out, to bring her into society more. On virtually each trip she took she would write back urging Sed to meet her. Sometimes she pleaded. It was important. "So come sis you have been too long confined to the home circle, your own thoughts, and books. You must not think of living so retired any longer and now is such a fine opportunity."[61] But she did not leave, nor is there indication that she escaped the home circle until the home circle had disintegrated. The home circle had kept her occupied.

A model of charity, Sed nursed through poor health and disease every member of the family. When she was a girl Bet had commented on her attraction to this activity when Sed sat up with her grandfather during his illness. In the 1850s it was her mother's health that kept her tied down. That lasted until 1861. Then who was to look after her father and her separated sister who suffered from poor health? Sed was there. Sed was *always* there. Still unmarried at the founding of the town at the age of twenty-six, her father named the town for her. She cared for her father while her sister was gone to the clinics and for her sister when the doctor did not. In February of 1868 she married. Henry S. Cotton, who was four years younger than she, however, was not in good health. She had to attend to him, it seems, almost from the time she got married. By the end of the year Bet, still in New Jersey, would write her father asking twice in the same letter about the health of Brother Henry.[62] Henry S. Cotton died, in January of 1872, less than four years after his marriage. The editor of the religious newspaper that published his obituary wrote

Sed his condolence, saying that "I was not surprised to hear of his death."[63] Bet, in a moment of somber reflection wrote Sed, "I know that your life has been full of care for the last twelve years, since our misfortune of losing our dear mother, and after that the troubles that were mine by reason of a foolish marriage, and your having to give up society and devote yourself to me, and having to take up the burden of the family." A month later she wrote her sister again urging her to go east for a visit: "you should leave home for rest, after the melancholy time you have had in nursing thru so long a sickness and losing your dear husband."[64] After this it was her father who weakened, dying in 1879. And then her sister's paralysis. This chore, though a labor of love, lasted more than a quarter century—perhaps substantially longer. And it was more than just occasional help. In 1903 Bet wrote relatives that she had been weak for years, that she required a *"home atmosphere"* when traveling and that her sister was unable to travel as well: "because my inability controls my sister's movements . . . . 'Smith and Cotton' seem almost incapable of voluntary separation."[65]

These two women lived together, grew old together, and suffered together. This was not the life their father had in mind for them. It should not be surprising that they, like other women, turned their suffering, their sacrifices, and their fulfillment of obligations into signs of divine favor and tests to be rewarded. The lessons of the trials of Job helped make sense of calamity and misfortune. Their mother had done this. In 1846 while the future was still far from certain in their new home in Missouri she worried that the catastrophes of the past—the loss of their son and the loss of her husband's inheritance in a bank failure—still troubled her husband: "your fondest hopes were blasted, your brightest prospects faded, the joyous visions of youth too early vanished, leaving in their stead the sad realities of life. But should we not look upon our reverses as blessings in disguise? In what better way could we be brought to a sense of our dependence upon a Supreme Being? 'He chasteneth whom he loveth.' "[66] The children had learned their lessons well. A quarter century later Bet would write Sed in reference to the difficulties of their marriages, "But sister it may be we needed the discipline. It may be one of the flames to purify our gold so that the face of the Redeemer may shine resplendently in our lives. It may be one of the 'Rods' we have to 'pass under,' it may be one of the chastenings that seemeth now grievous but afterward shall yield peaceable fruits . . . ." As for Sed's ministering to the needs of her family so constantly, Bet was emphatically confident: "God *will bless you*."[67]

But the sacrifice and suffering moved beyond a trial by God to be rewarded and actually became a virtue in itself. In 1868 during her stay at the sanitarium, Bet became withdrawn and did not write her sister and brother-in-law for an extended time. When they reproved her she responded that by refraining from writing she "was giving myself the greater privation, and really deriving some pleasure from the *sacrifice* because I thought [I] was not intruding so often my letters upon the home folks." And at the same time that she declined to write she also felt that she was still too outspoken about her suffering: ". . . I should be more resigned and bear more quietly my afflictions and keep them more to myself."[68] Her occasional doubts ultimately confirmed and deepened her convictions. The doubt came out in one of Bet's poems: "Invalid Reveries."

> My morning was bright with a glorious sky,
> And I joined the toilers hurrying by;
> But my hands were soon idle, my feet became still,
> Impatient, I cried, "is it really God's will?"[69]

She concluded that indeed it was God's will. There is in this suffering, even, a crucifixion allegory complete with doubts and the only line of Scripture she ever quoted in her letters: "Father *forgive* them they *know not* what they do." The result of this introspection, this doubt, this deepening of devotion, and commitment to suffering as a virtue was a transformation from a Job-like suffering to what N. M. Ragland, her minister and old friend of the family termed at her death: a "Christlike endurance of affliction."[70]

Moreover, a sense of mission accompanied the suffering. The mission: to alleviate the suffering of others. Philanthropy and charity proved to be forms of sacrifice that both sisters could share and that could allow both, confined at home as they were, to improve the world. They had the money and land left them by their father and mother. They decided to use this for reform and assistance. Sometimes this aid went simply to needy individuals, especially widows, and they helped young women to pursue their education and to travel.[71] And they did help women in organized efforts as well. Temperance advocates from birth under the influence of their father, they continued their efforts in this cause. How many organizations they kept alive by their financial support there is no telling. In soliciting additional support for the Missouri Women's Christian Temperance Union, which the Smith-Cotton sisters had helped previously, Clara C. Hoffman, the president of the organization, commented "Now I know how many demands are made on you two women all the time." The appeal she made, however, was one bound to strike a responsive chord in George Smith's house: "More than all other agencies combined the W.C.T.U. is making women *think* for themselves. More than all other agencies the W.C.T.U. is *breaking* the priestly chains that have so long held women in bondage."[72] Clara C. Hoffman had just visited them in their home. Frances Willard visited at their home as well and "we recognized in her a friend and sister."[73] Women's rights and women's needs provided a focal point for their efforts, but their concerns encompassed others too. They sponsored the creation of a new institution built in Sedalia: The George R. Smith College, a college for blacks.[74] They corresponded with Jane Addams about donating a large house locally "for the purpose of starting a philanthropic work similar to that at 'Hull House.' "[75] The large house is not identified, but their willingness to sacrifice could have made it their own. They donated land and money to allow the construction of a Carnegie library.[76] The sacrifice and the duty were abundant. Their mission, their duty in this world was large.

In 1907 Martha Elizabeth Smith died. Her last sentiments were appropriate. To a close friend, she said, "I am glad you are doing your duty in the world." And then: "What will we do with sister?"[77] Her sister lived another twenty-three years. Before she died she gave the land where her house was located for the construction of a new high school for Sedalia. Then the house of George R. Smith, the house of the Smith-Cotton sisters, the house that knew wealth and power, that knew affliction and humility, the house that knew tragedy and victory, that house was razed. It was no more. The family of George R. Smith was no more. The ordeal was over.

In reflecting on the meaning of the lives of the daughters of George R. Smith, it is worth stating the obvious: Had Martha Elizabeth Smith and Sarah Elvira Smith been males or had David Thomson Smith lived, the story above would have been enormously different. For this is the experience not just of two children of George Smith, but of two women. Such is the power of gender. The experiences of these women were of necessity far removed from the experiences of men. So too were the values and awareness of themselves that they generated different from those of their male contemporaries.

The consciousness they developed focused on a purification of the soul, the sanctification of suffering, and the urgency of a mission of redemption. To the extent that their own visions of the self and soul provided satisfaction, to the extent that their concept of purity and sanctification provided a sense of community with others of their sex, to that extent their efforts could be judged successful. And indeed given the strength and breadth of the forces working against community, purity, and charity and given the maze of frustrations and obstacles confronting them, this is a substantial achievement. At a very minimum they had defied the choices narrowly available to them—to fit the role of domestic submission or to fit the role of their father as an ambitious and assertive conqueror (the comparison with El Cid was perhaps the most telling).

In another perspective, however, as those choices were defied in great personal triumph, so were other, broader, obligations evaded—the obligation of confronting not just the problems of women in a world of sin but the problems of women in industrial market society. Just as the experiences of these sisters were different from those of men by virtue of their gender, so were their experiences different from other women, women who were even more vulnerable because of their position in the market, because of their lack of the material independence which the Smith-Cotton sisters could assume even with their charitable dispensation of their means. For other women the purity of the heart and the life of the white flower would not be enough.

ii. The World of Women and the World of the Market

In the nineteenth century the curse of Adam and Eve had been paraphrased to the rhythm of "For men must work, and women must weep, And there's little to earn and many to keep." While this formula may have put it too miserably, with the expansion of market society it became increasingly possible and likely that women could do both: work and weep. Women moved increasingly into the world of the market, the world of men. Why they did that and what they found there are questions that need to be asked as well of other ventures like marriage, but the problem takes on a special relevance in the consideration of the larger pattern of social change that had revolutionized other relationships. Women were caught between the two worlds of domesticity and the market. So long as they remained before the hearth the frustrations were real and the difficulties of realizing the demands made of them were more difficult than in an earlier form of organization that emphasized a moral economy or universal productivity within the family. But to leave the home and encounter the world of employment, competition, and wage labor generated additional complications. And more and more women did this.

As one seeks the origins of this shift in role performance it appears that a variety of forces operated to create the circumstances conducive to such a change. A flat law explaining this process does not surface. But it does seem definite that the move into the market came seldom as the result of a decision of women opting for a role of independence and opportunity without regard to what was being left behind. The forces of push, in the balance, outweighed the forces of pull. Consider the opportunities available to women. They were few and not terribly attractive. The census returns tabulating the products of industry and their places of manufacture for 1880 indicated four females over fifteen years employed. Before that none had been indicated. But by 1890 around one hundred ninety women over fifteen years were employed in manufacturing, either as clerks, operatives, or pieceworkers. This would compare with around fifteen hundred male employees in the same industries.[78] While the census material may well be correct in the proportions assigned to male and female employment, it does not, of course, touch upon many areas of employment that are distant from manufacturing. And indeed, the service areas of the local economy may well have accounted for most female employment and at any rate was a female dominated sector. Washing, sewing, cooking, teaching, housework, and other female oriented pursuits fail to show up in those statistics; they also, each and everyone, serve as simple extensions of domestic skills and duties—not as innovations.[79] Woman's work, the same at home or in the market, with lower wages than the male counterparts, hardly represented a glittering path of opportunity. Woman's work was, still, woman's work.

The quest for new employment becomes more comprehensible when considered against the backdrop of other circumstances. Those circumstances ranged from the process of socialization to the raw compulsions of poverty or ostracism. Those factors are visible at many points. Emma Klein's background before she went to work in the home of N. L. Norton, north of Sedalia, was specifically identified when she suddenly disappeared. She had been "taught to believe that an indispensable step to womanhood is to learn to work, and that to do so properly, is to go away from home to work out . . . ."[80] The altogether common phenomenon of widowhood prompted others to seek a means of support, usually with a sense of desperation and urgency. Equally common, though, were the women who had been deserted, either for a short term or for good. Reports of washerwomen who encountered enormous difficulties supporting their children because husbands left during strikes, during business downturns, during the winter slowdown of local business were frequent and they came at personal times of tribulation as well (as with one woman whose husband in East Sedalia deserted her because he had cancer). Or sheer internal discord in the family—quite aside from the need for supplemental income—appears to have motivated some. There is, for example, the case of a machinist in East Sedalia who refused to provide for his wife and two children and apparently otherwise abused them. When his wife attempted to take in sewing he forbade that. She sold all her flowers and their son ran a lemonade stand on the corner to provide support. In another instance a woman took in washing for a living while her crippled son gathered rags to sell while the husband, for whatever reason, did nothing.[81] In these various situations, clearly the compulsions loomed larger than the attractions of the market, or at a minimum they made the market look attractive only when compared to its alternative.

There is, however, one other circumstance that brings light to bear on the entry of more females into the market. Frequent reports of women seeking employment in Sedalia noted, as a lesson to local young women, that they had come from other communities and had been forced from their homes because they had been shamed, their reputations sullied, and their downfall begun. These instances were most visible when the woman was pregnant. And in those circumstances the employment found would ordinarily terminate upon the discovery of the pregnancy. The story of one woman is poignant: she was promised marriage on a moonlight picnic near Boonville and gave up her virtue and "she left that area shamed" and came to Sedalia and found a position working in a local home—until she was discovered pregnant. Her fate after that—the news report commented on her plans to go to St. Louis—is unknown but it seems to have been no more promising than her other experiences.[82] Indeed, the one sanctuary preserved to women—if coercively—was now denied. When Julia Fisher became pregnant, her mother cared for her but upon discovering the source of her physical troubles she "positively refused to have anything to do with her, and would not let her enter her house."[83] In those instances the redemption of the prodigal seemed out of the question and employment outside the home was but the only alternative. Aside from the stark double standard displayed in this behavior, and apart from the assumed coercions, the denial of choices for either the pure or the sinners, reflected in this set of circumstances, another quality is also evident. To enter the world of the market seems to have been viewed almost universally as a punishment—not an opportunity—a punishment for transgressions that seemed a parallel to the original sin. These women had to suffer not only the curse of Eve but the curse of Adam as well. To that extent this pattern of shaming and ostracism reflects a masculine society's self-indictment: the punishment for sin is to enter masculine relationships of work.

"Legitimate" work itself could be hard to find and, once found, short-lived, given the origins of the necessity for such work. Other work opportunities, however, filled the void. The chief among these was prostitution and prostitution thrived in Sedalia. The documentation of the brothels in Sedalia remains understandably sketchy but the houses surfaced enough in the news accounts for the incidents transpiring there to confirm their presence. In 1870, Lizzie Cook and Maggie Howard each ran bagnios but by 1875 Cook had apparently merged with a Madam Ballard in the Junction House. This house still operated at least as late as 1878 but other houses eclipsed it including one operated by Madam Hicks in the early 1880s, Mollie West's after that, and Clara Parks' and an array of others at varying times like the Union House and Lillie Calahan's Happy Hollow.[84] Others appear more subdued under the guise of boarding houses, hotels, or even private residences. One millinery shop apparently did double duty as an assignation house as did several hotels and businesses.[85] And then there were the street walkers, some of them operating obviously as independents in the trade. Despite regular campaigns to rid the town of the presence of this sexual trafficking, the whorehouses stayed. Ordinarily it appears that the houses would pay a monthly fine to the authorities for both the madam and the boarders.

The penalty for nonpayment of the fine was a raid.[86] And the raid would arrest the male clients as well as the female employees, a circumstance that could do much to damage business. In the main, prostitution seems to have been present in Sedalia, and at times to have flourished. And so too did opportunities for employment in this trade abound.

In the formation of the pool of women this trade was able to draw upon for the provision of its services two distinct sets of circumstances are involved and both derive from powerful compulsions. For some, those who had been disgraced, whoredom seemed to be the only alternative. Indeed, a continual reading of the accounts of the *Bazoo* suggests that prostitution was the automatic and certain fate of the woman who became sexually active or indiscrete or casually or deliberately violated the narrow code of Victorian morality. Such was the penalty of seduction for the seduced.[87] The other circumstance was that normally referred to as white slavery. The details of this practice do not appear until the second half of the 1880s which may indicate either a greater sensitivity to the business or an increase or beginning of the practice. Ordinarily employment would be offered women that promised good pay and light work. In 1885 a group from Joplin appeared in Sedalia recruiting for such vague an enterprise only to be betrayed by a woman with them. One young woman who had come to town from the outlying areas to get a job signed on to do housework only to discover too late the kind of institution that had employed her and what her employers actually had in mind for her to do. Ultimately, of course, she was able to depart but only vigorous publicity and legal intervention secured her the possession of her belongings left there.[88] Less fortunate was another young woman who had been kept in a brothel against her will after being enticed into the house. It took a police raid to liberate her.[89] The business of prostitution may be used to signify many things, but it seems fair to say that it did not represent a real opportunity for most women. And to the extent that it did actually represent an opportunity it did so only for those who had already been made pariahs or who suffered the most egregious forms of degradation and humiliation. A man's world indeed.

What is so striking about the actual contours of women's entry into the market, the quest for employment, and the securing of some kind of position is that the women involved seemed so little inclined to articulate or to identify their problems in the internal terms of labor and position and wages and working conditions but to view the large process of entry into the market as itself the problem. The objective basis for work discontent was real: wages at a lower rate than for males, the minimal opportunities for employment or advancement, the onerous piecework system that prevailed among the trades associated with female labor, the sewing and washing, and the unequal treatment they found in work. On the one hand this could easily be explained—as it has often been before—simply as the yearning for domesticity, the craving for home life and its "natural" duties. This however, is inadequate inasmuch as the domestic situation itself had changed and proved unsatisfactory to many and in fact even drove some to the market. On the other hand, there may be a germ of that same analysis that deserves examination. The decline was not so much from the domestic system that existed in the 1870s and 1880s; it was from a domestic system that had prevailed at an earlier time that included men and women as functional and satisfiable participants and that was based on a sense of mutual responsibilities—if within a context of patriarchy—rather than individual rights and opportunities and ambitions. The problem of women as they perceived their entry into the market in terms of downfall and decline was not therefore a personal problem alone; it was that society itself had fallen. The moral world that women were supposed to represent served, as the men well perceived, as a testimony to the distance the material world had moved from where it could be. The world of women and the world of the market remained alien to each other, even when they intersected. The distinctive culture of women, whether identified as a culture of domesticity or a culture of morality and purity thus served to intensify the problems experienced by women, objectively and subjectively. It could also serve as a way to deal with those problems.

iii. The Redeemers and the Seeds of Feminism

The sheer existence of a separate women's culture that focused on morality and purity and that also included the notion of large mission in this world made that culture substantially more than a passive indictment of masculine, material, secular society and culture; it also provided an ideological lever to transform the world. The redemption of the individual's— and society's—sins has ever been one of the driving forces bringing people together and driving them apart. And to a degree this question would plague the women's causes of Sedalia in the Gilded Age; the irony, however, is that the tensions that would surface over the commitment to the cause would be both tensions between male and female and tensions between women themselves. That issue would be fraught with a long lasting significance.

There was never any question about the precise problem women's culture would scrutinize most carefully and respond to most vigorously. It was the same problem in Sedalia that it was throughout the nation: Demon Rum. Nor was there anything new about this evil. It had been around since the earliest days of the country. This had been one of the offensive connotations of the electoral process that appalled General Smith's daughters in the 1840s and 1850s. General Smith himself had agitated the issue speaking on the cause of temperance in the 1840s, a

cause that struck him as unique. It was not just a case of righteous mor-
alizing, he argued, to preach against alcohol. It was, rather, an awareness
of the growing interconnectedness of human relations, something he developed with almost a Melville-like prescience, that he said would make
it "criminal, may I not say suicidal . . . to remain an idle spectator much
less to take sides against the temperance cause."[90] And the issue had
lingered and grown much as the adherents of the temperance cause figured they had seen the evil itself grow. Aside from the frequent use of
the subject as the basis of a sermon or editorial, temperance cropped up
periodically at the renewal of saloon or dram shop licenses and at times of
public outrage as in the incident in which Joseph Wood murdered a man
while he was drunk in 1867. It also occasionally took institutional form,
as in the formation of the I.O.G.T. And it could hold an electric potential as a public cause that could transcend others and blur other loyalties
and identities as it had during the 1877 Murphy temperance movement
riot and railroad strike. But in one place it held a special significance and
that significance grew. Just as women's culture, whether defined in terms
of domesticity or morality, became increasingly associated with the spiritual and nonmaterial world so too did the issue of alcohol provide a
mechanism defining the separateness of women as they declined to par-
take of the beverages and thereby also a mechanism of intensifying and
symbolizing the purity of the moral code entrusted to women. No other
issue could do this—thus the attractiveness of the cause and the image of
the cause as preeminently a female cause.

On the heels of the Murphy movement, agitation moved in several
circles for the continuation and institutionalization of the cause that had
stimulated such energy, commitment, and public involvement when it
was a temporary revival. In January of 1878 those efforts bore fruit. The
Sedalia Women's Christian Temperance Union was launched and membership was open to those who would pay twenty-five cents and subscribe
to the pledge: "With malice toward none, and charity for all, I, the un-
dersigned, do PLEDGE my word and honor, GOD HELPING ME, to abstain
from ALL Intoxicating Liquors as a beverage, and that I will, by all honorable means, encourage others to abstain."[91] Such a pledge held an
enormous significance. It would be especially a moment of personal introspection and commitment to those who were the most identifiable victims of the problem of alcohol. The unequivocal statement of the pledge
could, after all, provide a moment of personal redemption for those people and actually turn lives around, and by extension could also redeem
society. But it held a different significance for those who made the least
personal change in such personal redemption and commitment. It
bonded them together in an explicit, articulate mission that the mythology of sex alone could not provide. And, in fact, the Sedalia Women's
Christian Temperance Union was the first organization in the area, aside

from churches, to claim as its members a substantial number of women. Women had found a place perfectly compatible with their sexual role yet that place was outside the home. And the object of their activity was nothing less than the redemption of society.

In the following years the WCTU and the CTU kept active on a number of fronts ranging from appearing in court protesting the renewal of saloon licenses, circulating petitions remonstrating against such renewals, to circulating the cards pledging individuals to abstinence. Education and conversion, however, remained the basic mechanism of securing reform, even when the ultimate object was to educate people for the purpose of securing prohibition legally. "The influence of woman," as it was commonly put, would surely prevail in this precious area through her unique leverage. As one speaker (a male) at the state meeting of the WCTU held in Sedalia expressed it: "The mother can instill into the mind of the boy at her knee such sentiments as she most desires. The young woman can direct and control her lover in his actions and sentiments. The wife can plead with her husband and her prayerful supplications will not be fruitless. In short woman in any and all positions of life is all powerful when she earnestly desires the accomplishment of any particular point."[92] Without the right to vote, perhaps this nonpolitical pressure—or hope—was all that could be expected and the emphasis on moral persuasion as the path to victory could simply be an effort to make the best of a bad situation. But there seems more to it than that. It was, first, consistent with the larger traditional role of woman as teacher, carrier of moral tradition, and nourisher of culture. If traditional female economic functions were simply extended into society beyond the home so too were traditional female moral duties now carried beyond the home into society. It also, and, at the same time, reflected an assumption that women were indeed somehow different from males, both in terms of values and power. The seeds of a separate identity with a strikingly modern potential were thereby revealed. But perhaps of equal significance, such an emphasis on moral suasion as the key to a better world reflected a broad conception of political relationships that transcended the narrow confines of the institutions of government and organized party. In this view, these women demonstrated a fundamental faith in democracy, both in the efficacy of the popular will and in the faith that their cause would meet an enthusiastic reception among the people. What at first appears to be mere acceptance of a means only because it was the only possible route may in fact have been a careful selection and combination of views both traditional and modern. The mixture could be revolutionary.

The means and the ends of the movement were always close and never completely separate. And if the means of the effort were distinctly female in conception, the object of it all was female with a vengeance. The object of the temperance movement, after all, was not really temperance and moderation in the consumption of alcohol. It was complete and total abstinence. This was new. A generation earlier General Smith campaigned for temperance and he spoke of his own association with alcohol: "I do not crave it [and] indeed I do not even think of it unless some friend invites and then I only quaff the nectared poison to pledge my friendship to a friend."[93] As it became regularly female in its constituency and base, it also became increasingly absolute in its demands. When General Smith's daughters went to Europe in 1888 Martha Elizabeth wrote a friend of her surprise and disgust at the drinking common in France. Although the wine served at every meal played an important part "we sit with ours untouched and enjoy it more I think than they do. . . . I should like to make them a *temperance speech*, but think I shall forego the pleasure and let them go on to destruction."[94] They were not alone in this sentiment since the temperance pledge itself explicitly required its adherents to abstain from *all* intoxicants. The movement had been intensified; the goal had become absolute and uncompromising, as uncompromising indeed as a woman's virtue. The goal was purity. The greatest tribute one could receive in this framework was probably that given Martha Elizabeth Smith on her death: "She was a woman who wore the white flower of a blameless life."[95] And these are the goals put into a series of symbols: "the white flower;" "the unsullied heart;" "the white life;" "the blameless life." In the WCTU Frances Willard headed the Department of Social Purity. When Frances Willard spoke in Sedalia "she spoke of her theme, a pure life, a life of holiness, a rational service to humanity and to God." And, according to the Smith-Cotton sisters, "her style was chaste" and "she had kindled a fire whose purifying flames will burn 'till the goal she has set before this people will be won."[96] The goal was not temperance. Nor was it even abstinence. The goal was a pure life. Nothing less, even, than a pure society.

Appropriately enough, the women's movement went beyond the issue of alcohol to the purification of society in other ways. In 1882 a group of prominent women established what they called a Working Women's Home. They contributed their money to it and they hired a matron to operate the institution and they launched an effort to make the home self-sustaining.[97] For at least several years the Working Women's Home operated and found considerable support among the women of Sedalia. Its functions were several. When women needed temporary assistance the institution provided them a temporary home and then it helped them find employment. Its income was derived from the sales of women's and children's clothing which seems to have been taken in as donations and then recirculated to the poorer women of the city at bargain prices. The number of inmates of the home varied, with about three appearing the norm. And it seems to have functioned well. On one occasion three young women had been promised employment as domestics but when they arrived in town and reported for work they were refused employment. The women running the Working Women's Home gave them assistance to help them through the difficult times and then helped them locate jobs.[98] The Working Women's Home was exactly what the three words in its name suggested. And other organizations followed. A Women's Benevolent Association organized at the YMCA in 1885 to work on poverty cases with apparently a special focus on women's needs.[99] And it had a counterpart in East Sedalia—the railroad department of the WCTU.[100] And the WCTU's mission in East Sedalia had yet a further adjunct, a children's organization, a Band of Hope. A woman's culture, a distinctly female culture, and an aggressive women's culture flourished in Sedalia by the late 1880s.

A proper understanding of this activity could focus on a number of specific qualities, each with a separate set of implications. Charity? In fact, charity looms as one of the most explicit of the qualities of assistance underlying these various actions. It is also a quality promptly identified as feminine. Sacrifice? Certainly the sacrifice was evident here in terms of money, time, effort, and goods donated to the cause. Yet the sacrifice in the larger sense of an effort that heals the soul, that demonstrates commitment, the humbling of pride and the rejection of hubris— this kind of sacrifice seems to have been the more substantial. That too was something that, in the suffering and the affliction, could generate a spiritual satisfaction that ran counter to the forms of satisfaction being touted in masculine circles. A sense of mission? Without a doubt the spread of womanly qualities throughout society here was the same as it was in the effort to rid society of the thralldom of alcohol. Sisterhood? These efforts provide one of the best examples of the efforts of women to unite *as women* across class lines on a strictly women's set of issues and concerns. Their loyalties were to each other and to their common culture and values. Each of these qualities seems to work individually as explanations. Yet to isolate any of these components bends that culture into another shape and distorts its meaning. The fundamental object of all of these things was plainly their totality: the effort of women, uniting together, on the basis of qualities long associated with domesticity, to use their influence and power to purify society, to rid it of evil. Their conception was not that of patronizing charity to ameliorate social tensions or that of overbearing sympathy for their lessers to reinforce their own status. Their conception was literally to rid society of evil. Consider the charity, consider the sympathy, consider the sense of mission, the sacrifice, and the whole array of sentimental qualities that could be produced to explain these actions. Then consider the statement of the editorial of the *Weekly Bazoo*: "If there were more Working Woman's Homes, there would be fewer houses of prostitution."[101] It was obvious then, if not now, what was going on. These women viewed women as victims of a society organized around masculine and material values and they set about to change this by uniting as women along the lines of traditional women's culture, helping out members of their own sex, and then moving to alter the entire society, to bring social relationships into line with moral relationships, to purify society. The white life would be for all.

Such a goal, associated as it is with absolutism, with altruism, with sentimentalism, and with femininity, has often stimulated responses of derision, contempt, and amusement. And indeed from the jaundiced perspective of the 1980s, it does sometimes seem difficult to take such ambitious schemes and visions seriously. But these women were earnestly serious and they deserve better treatment than they have often received. Granted, some of the origins of this vision and crusade can be found in the intense frustrations of many women whose experiences paralleled those of the Smith-Cotton sisters in emotional and spiritual intensity, but that only serves to suggest the breadth and the reality of those experiences, not to discredit them as products of a weaker sex moving beyond the pale. And, while it may be true, as Barbara Epstein has suggested insofar as the white life also encouraged a minimal sexual intimacy within as well as outside marriage, that this vision can be traced partly to a Victorian fear of sex, there is far more to this vision of purification than chastity could ever be capable of symbolizing.[102] There was, after all, the other side of the Victorian double standard that was the specific subject of attack in that effort. Nor does the "domesticity" of this vision, encompassing as it does qualities and virtues that had traditionally been assigned to women and that had been increasingly used as tools of subjugation, necessarily demonstrate that women's equality and the conventional morality were inimical. They were, perhaps, but only in the context of a market society where equality would be associated with materialistic aspirations and ambitions. And that is precisely the significance of the crusade to purify society. Market society was inimical not just to conventional morality but to any standard of morality that was not derived from material estimations of the worth of the individual. In this sense the crusade for the redemption of society represents a pointed and fundamental resistance to the secularization of society, to the growing materialistic emphasis of society, to the laissez-faire morality of society in which purpose, and mission, and essence of life on earth were relegated to a status inferior to secular, material pursuits. The crusade for the redemption of society affirmed the primacy of other values and of other relationships, and such redemption would come about through sisterhood.

The rigors of living each day, privately and publicly, an intense commitment to a philosophical, emotional, and spiritual cause could be draining and even exhausting for those who shared the faith. For others with doubts it could be alienating. The demands of self-sacrifice might

be fulfilling for some; to others those demands just denied the self satisfaction they sought. Yet herein lay a perplexing situation: if women
were justified in speaking out in behalf of this cause only because of the
sanctions of domesticity and righteousness it was able to summon, how
could other women dissent? To dissent would be to fall into a double trap
of moving outside woman's traditional sphere for it would involve first the
development of a public forum—a trap the crusaders had avoided only by
the substance of their politics—and secondly the articulation of goals decidedly undomestic and unrighteous by definition. But some women did
this.

The women who moved in another direction had a leader, an articulate spokesperson. Sometimes she went by the name May Myrtle. Other
times she was called Rosa Pearle. And still other times she called herself
Aunt Fuller. And there were probably other names as well. But her real
name was Elizabeth Dugan. Elizabeth Dugan's husband, George Dugan,
was a painter but he never surfaced in her activities and she seems to
have maintained a careful and deliberate independence at all times. In
the late 1870s she started writing "society" news for the *Bazoo* and published frequent poems there as well. Her poetry was usually quaint and
touching rather than moving or polemical and sometimes consisted of little more than ditties and doggerel.[103] But it usually possessed a definite
female perspective in some sense or another and it often seems that
Dugan actively cultivated that perspective. Socially and politically, she
took her duties seriously and was the most outspoken of several com-
plainants in 1882 about corporal punishment in school. Fiercely independent, she kept her daughter away from school over the issue. It was never
clearly developed publicly if her daughter had been personally mistreated
in school, although it appears that her mother felt she had, but the school
board's position was crystal clear; the board maintained that parents were
not making their children obey sufficiently at home so the schools were
having to do the job for them.[104] Dugan's temperament could not abide
this. It could be that her daughter in fact was mistreated (the principal of
one school was accused of hitting a pupil in the head with the school
bell) or it could be that she was distressed by the principle of the
matter—that organized society was not only usurping functions of the
home, especially the educational function of the mother, but was performing that function shabbily. She may have even been the parent who
took the issue of corporal punishment in the schools to court since she
was not one to value submissiveness or domesticity as the automatic role
of a woman.[105] She also seems to have had reservations about the WCTU
when it was being launched in town although at one point she appears to
have taken side with it.[106]

By 1885 she had become firmly established in the city's journalistic
efforts and continued her poetry and managed the society news for the

Democrat.[107] Then, however, she started writing for a new newspaper called *The Earth*, "the original family, literary and society paper." She wrote her poetry and she wrote lengthy columns that seemed to be the core of the paper. During the 1886 strike she used virtually every opportunity to lecture the Knights of Labor on the error of their ways. While this was conventional enough it also allowed her to develop her own social views and values. She found divine sanction for the gospel of work and the work ethic, the notion of reward for merit, and she noted that "mental toil is far more wearing to the physical system than manual labor" and had no use for fanaticism or "the crack-brained Don Quixote."[108] And when, as in this case, "it is aristocracy on one side and mobocracy on the other—the despotism of money or the despotism of the commune," she said it is the "conservative element of the country, the middle classes, who must keep the peace and settle the controversy."[109] Her loyalties were clear. So too were her prejudices and her reasons for looking askance at the efforts of her sisters in the crusade to purify society—perhaps a Quixote-like effort, perhaps even tinged with fanaticism.

May Myrtle, Rosa Pearle, Aunt Fuller, and especially Elizabeth Dugan came into their own with the advent of *Rosa Pearle's Paper* in 1894.[110] Perhaps the new woman was coming into her own as well. The beginnings were inauspicious as the tabloid appeared to be a sterile high society journal. Its reception by women around Sedalia caught its spirit accurately: "Your paper is nice, neat and attractive." "Your paper is very nice and very pretty in every particular." "We all like the paper; it is very nice." "Your paper is neat, well edited and very nice." "I like your paper; it is so nice and neat and pretty."[111] It seemed to be unanimous that *Rosa Pearle's Paper* was very nice—and little else. The only controversy in its pages focused on who was left out of the "list of pretty girls." Yet the paper was different. It was edited by a woman and in fact some lore has it that the people who worked at the newspaper were all women or that a majority were. Dugan's niece, Alice M. Dugan, was associate editor—printer, and foreman too. The paper had a potential and given Rosa Pearle's independent spirit it would not be long before that potential would surface.

Rosa Pearle had a sharp wit and a sharp tongue. She could speak gently and she could speak acidly on the one subject that occupied her increasingly: the role of woman in society, especially the relationship between men and women. At one time she could announce that it was a time for thanksgiving since "never within the memory of the oldest inhabitant has there be so many styles to choose from."[112] At another moment she would list the qualities of of the "woman of to-day." "the woman of to-day reads Ibsen, but she knows how to cook a dinner and nurse the sick." "The woman of to-day wears a corset, but she wears shoes with sensible soles." "The woman of to-day is not afraid to refuse a disreputable man's acquaintance because he has money and position." "The woman of to-day likes her preacher, but she don't fall down and worship him instead of Omnipotence." "The woman of to-day is not bound to worship a mean husband, or live with him either."[113] In column after column Rosa Pearle and Aunt Fuller delicately lacerated the double standard, reported on wife-cheaters, agitated for more equitable domestic arrangements, and encouraged women to enter the business world. When war erupted between Japan and China in 1894 she announced that "Sedalia could spare more than a 'major' in the war . . . —she could spare several able-bodied loafers whose wives are at present supporting them."[114] When she discussed the situation where husbands would not allow their wives any money, even though the husbands paid the bills and provided for them, she referred to these women as paupers and suggested obliquely that they sell their old clothes for the money, buy plenty of dry goods to be billed to the husband and sell those dry goods too: ". . . why any wife will permit herself to be made into a spiritless creature, for the sake of any man living is a mystery to me and beyond finding out by even the most astute." And further: "I declare any man that would reduce his wife to such a condition of things ought to be imprisoned for life."[115] The new woman was being increasingly defined by Rosa Pearle. Once she listed a series of questions reflecting the old and the new attitudes. Instead of the old question "Does your wife approve of your smoking?" the new one "Do you approve of your wife smoking?" Instead of "Does you wife take an interest in your politics?" the new was "Do you take an interest in your wife's politics."[116] Indeed the consistent theme in the definition of the new woman by Rosa Pearle was the ability of women to decide for themselves, to take the initiative, and to move into society on an even footing with their male counterparts.

The seeds of feminism had been sown and they even seemed to be flourishing and starting to bud. And certainly this was a different tack than that espoused by the crusaders of the WCTU. Indeed, they looked upon each other with grave apprehensions and they found fundamental problems, at least implicitly, in the perspective offered by the other. The problem with the approach of the redeemers may have been that it accepted far too much of the roles and rituals of domesticity in their crusade. Certainly there was little of this in Rosa Pearle's approach. But the problem with the latter was that it involved exactly what Rosa Pearle boasted as a goal: moving into society. That society was precisely the market society of masculine qualities that the moralists rejected and hoped to revolutionize. Where the redeemers had hoped to restructure relationships throughout society to bring them into conformity to a clear moral code, the incipient feminists like Rosa Pearle wanted to change the position of women in the existing set of relations. What each sought, the other condemned. Where the redeemers yearned for a society of rigid moralism and righteousness the women's rights advocates wanted fewer obligations and more freedoms, an open, laissez-faire society based on the market of talents and the wishes of individuals ranging from economic independence to areas of lifestyle that border on narcissism—just like males. While sacrifice was a virtue for the redeemers, self-denial was a sin for their more "modern" sisters.

The dilemma facing both approaches was fundamental. They could view each other as the malefactors of society or, possibly, together view men as the devil force in society. Alternatively they could, however, seek in the system the source of their frustrations, a system that now presented to them the limited choice of the denial of self or the denial of others as the road to fulfillment. Ironically, given their opposing stances, they were both close to doing just this. They both clamored for a soul to be at rest. Such would be the fate of women—and men—in the new society.

PART FOUR

Conclusion

XI

A Way of Life Forsaken?

It seems a world long ago, when one reflects on the world of the Pettis Countians in the nineteenth century—not just the world that had long passed for them in the making of industrial society, but the one which had been made by these people as they moved into the last decade of the century. Whether perceived as a simpler, more comprehensible world or as a time when people were closer to each other in their sense of community, it can easily appear as a forsaken world, one whose central and defining qualities seem so remote from our own organization of the patterns of life.

The signs of that forsaken world abound in Pettis County and Sedalia. The dam on Muddy Creek that formed the basis for the mill and the community at St. Helena is gone. Only a timber that had been part of that dam remains visible and serves as a reminder of what once was there. David Thomson's house remains as imposing as when it was first built in the 1840s. In it and around it are the marks of a way of life that often went undocumented but that bear a more telling, though mute, testimony. The skill of Absalom McVey is evident in the joining and fitting of the wood. And the craft of the masons is obvious in the brickwork. Elsewhere in the county a few weathered and worn mill wheels, each with its distinctive cutting pattern still plainly discernible, still survive, themselves victims of and witnesses to an enormous transformation. Remains of old roads, old fences, ancient fords and trails all bear witness to the lives and dreams of an earlier time, at least for those who look and see. In town, where the pressures of change from renovation, growth, and modernization have borne down in a concentrated way, the marks of the past are equally subtle—and haunting. Some old buildings, including Smith's Opera House, are but shells and symbols of an earlier day. The names of the businesses often summon memories of the past and echo the dramas of a century ago. But the railroad shops are gone and so are the roundhouses. The stockyards, the college, and the home of the Smith-Cotton sisters have all disappeared as have many of the other less conspicuous landmarks of Sedalia and Pettis County.

The graves are there, as though keeping watch on the present and counseling remembrance of the past. Out in the country, in the city cemetery, in places where one would not expect, in small family plots and in grand settings, the graves bear the names of prominent families and the names of the next to anonymous. Some markers bear the icons of the Ancient Order of United Workmen and other fraternal orders. Some are ostentatious; many are so plain that the names are barely readable. All reveal something about life in this world and sometimes hopes for the next. There lies the entire Smith family, including David Thomson Smith and George Smith Martin. There lies the past. Just above the Pettis County line by the Heath's Creek Baptist Church the headstone over the grave of H. M. Ramsey, almost eighteen years old at his death in 1865, still carries the meaning of his death: "Murdered by the Missouri State Militia." There too lies the past. Great and small, famous and humble, predators and prey, they rest as equals. But the meanings of their lives, the legacies of the communities these mortals made, are not buried.

What these people left is primarily a legacy of plain, unpretentious people, in ways both bold and subtle, in private and public life alike, and often against the forces of institutions and powers completely alien to their purposes and values, seeking a life of respect and dignity and pride with mutual respect and harmony between individual and community, and where social relationships coincided with popular values. What makes this legacy so notable, as modest as it seems, is that it became increasingly difficult to live that kind of life and it became increasingly difficult even to behold a vision of that kind of life.

Two vastly different perspectives on this period, and on the process of transformation central to it, suggest irreconcilable images—one of progress, the other of decline. In the consideration of how the material needs of people were met, there can be little denial that there was some advance. The long term costs of those advances aside, certainly the quantities of production increased and the speed of production quickened. The production process itself became more sophisticated and complicated, although the complexity and sophistication of organic, natural and preindustrial technologies should never be underestimated. In the terms of an earlier generation, the basic measure of progress was that nature had been conquered, that human society was no longer subject to the domination of nature. This does, then, represent a kind of progress.

There is another focus, however, that provides a completely different assessment of the changes evident in the nineteenth century. That focus is on the needs of the people, though not just the material needs, those necessary for physical survival. The nonmaterial needs are less easily categorized or quantified, a quality which by some lights makes them less legitimate. They are nonetheless real and nonetheless important. Whether conceived as the pride generated by an individual or community in the quality of work and life, or the sense of satisfaction emanating from certain kinds of relationships and activities, or that comes from adherence to traditional standards and mores, the nonmaterial qualities do not fit with the conceptions of progress at large in the reshaping of this nineteenth century world. The core elements of those nonmaterial needs, concepts like satisfaction, responsibility, and the harmony of individuals with each other and with their environment, do not fit because they are not subject to the same kinds of long term measurement and collective determination by economic, demographic, or what often passes for political, standards.

The intriguing point about those separate perspectives, however, is that they are not necessarily separate. Individuals do not, after all, live their lives in ways that draw lines dividing the nonmaterial and the material spheres of activity from each other as they go different, and indeed opposite, ways in their daily passages. The fundamental object of life in early Pettis County was precisely the fusion of material and nonmaterial relationships in such a way that a harmony was achieved through reciprocal obligations and the elevation of the community above the prerogatives of the individual. Those material and nonmaterial qualities merged in subtle ways as the system of production was oriented toward the use of the product, by the people who produced it or by someone they knew, instead of for a market and for a profit, as the system of currency (or lack of currency) generated relationships of trust and good faith and nearly universal indebtedness as the technology—whether that of the "majestically slow" oxen or the watermill ever subject to the whim of nature—proved sufficient to meet the material needs of these people but not so bountiful as to require the creation of new needs to be satisfied to justify that production nor so powerful as to require that the people using these tools become extensions of the machine process rather than the machines the extensions of the people. And perhaps at its most fundamental, there was probably never any doubt about the purpose of life—disagreement over what it should be, sometimes; doubt over what it was, never. The purpose was the promotion of the welfare of the community and the adherence to traditional standards of right and wrong and decency. And that required the subordination of the economy and those powerful individuals who sought their own gain at the expense of others. For the community was based on nonmaterial assumptions of propriety and purpose.

This is not to say, obviously, that this generated a utopia or that those relationships produced universal satisfaction. Patently they did not. A whole race of people and an entire gender could testify to the inequities of such a system. Yet to say that such a structure and such a purpose is the source of those inequities is to ignore completely the inequities and injustices endured by women and blacks, among others, since the demise of that community-oriented structure. The frustrations they experienced in this early society, indeed, bear a striking resemblance to the frustrations that their white male counterparts also expressed. In that society, truly, as Milton Thomson wrote home, "man is born to disappointment." And only an enormous, universal, overarching sense of purpose and sense of commitment could make that disappointment tolerable.

What happened, ultimately, is that the fulfillment of those material and nonmaterial needs became contradictory and required a choice as to which would be satisfied. It was not so much that the material *needs* had been subordinated to the nonmaterial values of the community in the early days; actually the two existed in mutually supporting, harmonious ways. It was rather that individual material *ambitions* were suppressed. The material aspect of life had not been incompatible with its moral goals. The pursuit of wealth and power at the expense of others in the community, however, had been. And when the social structure became identified with exactly that pursuit as its central purpose, the social structure became incompatible with the values, purposes, and assumptions of the traditional world these people had known. At that point it became virtually impossible for the individual to meet material and nonmaterial needs at the same time or even to satisfy either with the preservation of any integrity. While society was being altered to provide a minimum of protections for the weak and a maximum of opportunities for the powerful—both in the name of greater individual responsibility—it became that much more difficult for that same individual to exercise responsibility over the various dimensions of life. It became that much more difficult for a person to conceive the system of production as an integral element of the life of the individual and the community as the purpose of those lives had long been defined and accepted. It became that much more difficult for the sense of pride and satisfaction, whether in work or life, to derive from the accumulation of property and power. It became that much more likely that those two needs would not just be incompatible. They would be diametrically opposed to each other in mortal conflict.

That conflict produced no neat demographic divisions—as if the category in which one "objectively" falls could generate either conformity or dissonance. The community was divided, at odds with itself, over what kind of fate that society would shape. Businessmen held opposing visions of the future from each other. The tension in the workers' community, among farmers, and among women, likewise, was not a tension that normally reached articulate manifestations, although on occasion they too emerged. Rather, the tension was over the vision of the future that guided them in their daily activities and that made them feel apart from the people they previously had been close to. It was this kind of tension, in fact, that divided the individual, that seared the soul of those grappling with the question of which direction the future.

There are several tragedies in this tension. One is that the community that once had been was gone forever. The harmony had been replaced by a systematic acrimony, the cooperation replaced by competition. Or, as Nicholas Romaine sagely observed in 1889 about the past of his community writ large: "In a new country where the people are on an equality they co-operate in building their houses, cutting their wood, killing their hogs, etc., but as capitalism creeps in, co-operation creeps out."[1] The neighbors would now charge each other, for a gain, for their services. Second, the tension, being opaque and noninstitutional in its ordinary form, has caused historians—and leaders and officials more generally— to identify the public's needs and desires with those of the people at the top who understandably viewed the new system with approval and cheer, and to view the dissenters as cranks, minorities, and outcasts, a view which may even have become a self-fulfilling prophecy given the shortsighted view of the past and the unquestioning view of the present perpetuated by the media and the schools. Third, this tension created countless individual tragedies as people in their efforts to fuse the quest for dignity and their yearnings for respect and their strivings for good character with the material circumstances of their society have even been called upon to equate those marks of character with the accumulation of property, wealth, and power only to find out belatedly that the satisfaction of material possessions is not the same as the satisfaction of harmonious relationships, that indeed they are elusive, ever growing, and ultimately insatiable in the appetites they whet. But finally, the largest tragedy of all is that the tension is not necessary, is the result of an artificial choice. The choice became sufficiently narrowed in the new system to a loyalty to oneself or to one's obligations to others that the possibility that those obligations were entirely compatible became increasingly remote a perception. Yet with a poet's sense of irony, precisely that circumstance meant that when the perception of that relationship between the material and the nonmaterial, between the individual and the community, surfaced it did so in a conscious way. That meant that such relationships were not—as they once had been—bonds and purposes to be assumed, but actually goals and lives to strive for. It was at that point that it was no longer just defending a way of life but actually trying to define a new one in which the material and spiritual needs of the individual and the community merged.

Yet those divisions, those tensions proceeded with the force of the economy that drove them. The result was a series of wedges between the individual and the community, between different parts of the community, between work and play, between the secular and the spiritual, be-

tween people and the institutions that are supposed to serve them, and
between the past and the present. The issues that separated the world of
the industrial society of 1890 from the world of the early settlers were
thus not just policy differences, but identity differences.

Those people who resisted the changes toward a greater material emphasis in the structure and purpose of life, those people who retained an
identity grounded in traditions in which they had a sense of purpose
beyond aggrandizement and domination—those people were hardly radicals or revolutionaries. They were modest people with limited goals. But
they did value honesty and authenticity in their relationships. Perhaps
that is sufficient to make them some kind of radicals; it certainly was
sufficient to make them incompatible with the new society of industrial
capitalism.

The heritage of the past spoke plainly enough to those people grappling with the question of the fate of their society in 1890; so too does
it speak to us today, nearly a century later. The main effort of those
people who resisted the onslaught on the past, who attempted to retain
qualities of that older community in their own lives was to preserve or
recapture not the isolated parts of that earlier life but the bonds and relations of the unified whole that gave meaning to the total scheme of
things. Indeed, it was precisely that unity that had been sacrificed in
a fundamental reversal of the priorities of organized society. Where previously individual ambition had been sacrificed for a larger community
harmony, it came to be that exactly that harmony was sacrificed to un-
leash individual ambition. Because the costs of such a reversal were
so large, so devastating, and so evident, many people resisted. Yet in
the intervening years those costs have become both more subtle and
more deeply felt, though not always in an articulate sense, as the sacrifices demanded by such an organized society have taken on new dimensions.

This is not to suggest a crude dichotomy between the individual and
the community. Such a polarity would neglect the delicacy of the relationship of the two, since it was not the individual that was sacrificed, but
individual material ambitions that threatened the welfare of the community which were suppressed. Indeed in the years since that individual
was supposedly liberated, individualism has been sacrificed, suppressed,
and restricted in ways more subtle, more powerful, and more destructive
than possible or imagined in ante-bellum Pettis County. Where material
security and advancement are by definition commodities to be rewarded
sparingly, as analysts from William H. Whyte to C. Wright Mills have
pointed out, people are called upon to suppress any individuality, their
own personalities, their own distinctiveness, as they conform to the roles
prescribed for them by the market and by the institutions which have
power over them. In so doing a redefinition of individual needs becomes

apparent, a redefinition in fact that leads to different kinds of relationships and perceptions which themselves lack authenticity in origins and consequences.

And those consequences are enormous. They can be seen in the ways in which those who have learned the habits of the market sufficiently look upon the opportunities of life in terms of investment potential and resale value, or those others who yearn for acceptance and who thus define their needs within the framework of the expectations of those who have made it, and who then anticipate the broad range of possible reactions to attitudes and actions so as not to offend, so as to satisfy others and thereby receive approval and acceptance. Often it is possible to detect an aura of confidence, despite the self-denial, a confidence however fragile, that the rewards, the satisfactions and compensations for the abnegation, though not quite in reach now, will be there in the future—always in the future. The frailty of that confidence is betrayed by the simultaneous fear that usually goes unspoken, the fear like that expressed in Arthur Miller's poignant drama that the game will be over at any moment, that the acceptance of and the need and desire for an individual will evaporate quite as easily as it was created. Bolstered by myths, by deceptions, and by the accumulation of material commodities in ritual style, life can be not only tolerable but have moments of triumph as well. But stripped of the charades and the lies and the self-deceit—whether compulsive, coerced, or deliberate in origin—what is left is a vast hollowness and an enormous loneliness. It is not the loneliness that comes from being physically apart from people, but the more debilitating loneliness that comes from being with people, or among people, and remaining unsatisfied and unfulfilled with a distance placed between people by the fear and distrust and acrimony guiding social relationships. It is the kind of loneliness that emerges from an isolated struggle for individual success, as John Womack, Jr., has said, with "each one against the others, to fulfill one's dream of pride in oneself." Given the already sufficiently bruised egos, the rituals of success through enhanced status and incomes and the limited rewards those qualities can generate—greater power over others and more things to consume—those rituals are comprehensible enough, if they do but barely lighten the burdens of loneliness, fear, and artificiality. That these personal problems are in fact social problems is in fact as readily apparent in the 1980s as in the 1880s; they are problems that are inextricably connected with the larger structure of social relationships. For the society that encourages people to view their neighbors with fear as competitors, with derision as undeserving, with insincerity as so much material in one's own ambitions, that society leaves little room for broad relations of intimacy, honesty, and authenticity. That, by now, established society built upon such disingenuous concepts as saving by spending, peace through war and armed might, contentment through acquisition, freedom through curtailed responsibility, and salvation through institutionalization operates at both the individual and collective level with a force undreamed a century ago.

As entrenched as that society has become, however, the challenge remains very much the same after all these years. The fundamental challenge is simply to see an alternative to that set of relationships. And that, not surprisingly, comes easily enough. Even those who have developed an identity that converges with the established system have often failed to yield completely to its demands. Those people who have a stake, any stake, in relations of friendship, brotherhood, and sisterhood, who have a stake in any set of mutual obligations and respect, who, in fact, have a sense of self-respect based upon their own refusal to be intimidated and cowed by the external structure, or perhaps most of all, in the unselfconscious ways of understanding the limits and opportunities of life, those people represent the limits of the established order. They also present a challenge to it. The persistence of traditional values, of relations characterized by intimate trust and respect and love, of individual responsibility instead of dependence on institutions, actually undermine the expansive demands of obedience and sacrifice. Indeed, to seek the community unfragmented by the divisions and sacrifices demanded by a society defined by its materialistic purposes is literally to live in that community. And it is precisely at that point that the experiences of those people in Pettis County and Sedalia speak most directly to us now. When one seeks that community where the material and the nonmaterial realms are not in conflict, where the individual and the community form a unified whole that is greater than the sum of its parts, that person finds it; that person makes it. And then a satisfying way of life is not forsaken. Nor is it just defended. It is created.

A Note on Historiography

In the preparation of this work I have been ever conscious of the implications the study of a single community might have in the broader effort to comprehend the past. Clearly this study of Sedalia and Pettis County is designed less as a chronicle of the development of that area in Missouri than as a case study whereby larger questions are focused, questions that require for their determination exactly such a local history effort. In the framing of those larger questions and in the contemplation of how to proceed in the inquiry I have been fortunate in being able to draw upon a body of literature that has proved to be sophisticated, exciting, and innovative in the approximate quarter century since it emerged with clarity and distinction.

The fundamental perception in this body of work is that the process of industrialization, as we have been familiar with its contours, requires a broader consideration for it to become more than a self-satisfying tautology; it requires consideration within a broader context to become comprehensible in human terms. Two elements of that context are especially important: one is the set of relationships of exchange which drive the decisions made in that industrialization process, particularly those relationships of the market; the other is that the strictly economic manifestations of change associated with the rise of industrial capitalism hold powerful implications for other relationships that appear quite remote from the province of economic forces and that themselves hold implications for those economic relations.

The work of E. P. Thompson has been especially insightful and powerful here. His *The Making of the English Working Class* (New York, 1963) presented the course of development by which workers in England resisted "the annunciation of economic man." By transforming the process of industrialization from a set of alterations in economic forms to a broader social transformation, the process takes on different dimensions. Indeed, the object of the process is in one sense greater production for the economy, but as the economy moves from being only an aspect of social relations and activities to the core around which the rest of society

213

is organized, the process also becomes one with the object of narrowing and reducing people to economic units to be regulated by markets and relationships of property and power in those markets instead of governed by custom, morality, tradition, or other noneconomically derived standards.

The Making of the English Working Class has rightfully been termed a classic and a landmark study. It has been responsible for the recharting of the course of labor history in the world and indeed for a reconsideration of social history as well. In this effort, however, Thompson has received intellectual support from a number of areas. C. B. Macpherson's *The Political Theory of Possessive Individualism: Hobbes to Locke* (New York, 1962) analyzes the ideology, and its relationship to the social structure, of market society in a tight and systematic manner that places it in a real historical context by demonstrating the revolutionary assumptions for traditional society of the cluster of ideas associated with possessive individualism. Particularly helpful in Macpherson's discussion is his schematic of the relationships characterizing different forms of social organization, to wit: the traditional or customary society, the simple market society and the possessive market society. In the last form mentioned, it is not just the ability to enter into relationships of exchange and negotiation in the determination of individual fates that separates it from other patterns, but the requirement and necessity of doing so by virtue of the definition of labor as a commodity, the *only* commodity of a significant portion of the population, which can be used as a resource for survival. And the inequitable distribution of power this represents as others have different resources—such as land and money—upon which they can draw for a very different kind of existence in this world further separates it from those patterns. This can be augmented with reference to Karl Polanyi's *The Great Transformation* (Boston, 1957), an anthropological study that I have found especially useful for its description of the subtlety and power of the wrenching effects the transformation of money, land, and labor into commodities held. These three studies, in fact, quite independent and with ample room for dissent among them, are each prepared with such power and intellectual force that they hold the potential for reorienting the approach to the rise of industrial capitalism. What happens when that new approach is generated is that it becomes a people's history rather than a chronicle of inexorable progress.

Locating the people's history poses a significant challenge to the historian attempting to understand this course of change. At one time it was often performed at a real cost of substance and perspective. The documents of organizations, of leaders in the government and economy, and indeed of the literati all provided a comprehensive view of society, but a skewed picture emerged that was heavily weighted to the side of those who emerged on top, those who dominated the particular organization of society that resulted, albeit one which they quite characteristically saw as benevolent and fair and open and natural. In this process not only were the aspirations and values of other parts of society either neglected or assumed, but the whole culture as it came together suffered distortion.

In the past several decades as historians have attempted to move, as Eric Hobsbawm urged, "From Social History to the History of Society," *Daedalus*, 100 (1971), a number of revisions of the history of portions of American society have altered dramatically our understanding of both the separate parts and the whole. Not the least of these parts is the business community itself. Embracing ideals of individual success and self-determination, these people have too often been subjected to the priorities of others that valued the gains of consolidation over the satisfactions of autonomy and broadly dispersed power in the economy. I would note two examples of work that penetrates the social values some attached to the competitive market: James Willard Hurst's notion of "The Release of Energy," presented in *Law and the Conditions of Freedom in the Nineteenth-Century United States* (Madison, 1956), remains an invigorating appreciation of a set of values that caused people to break loose from the restraints imposed by society (that I have discussed above more sympathetically) and that would impel them to resist similar restraints when imposed by the course of business consolidation itself. William Appleman Williams, in *The Contours of American History* (New York, 1961), perceives that world of individualism of the midnineteenth century, not just with passion and insight, but in a context of change where the culture of the individual entrepreneur is increasingly eroded and challenged by corporate capitalism. Hurst and Williams, obviously, wind up at very much different points in their discussions, but along the way they have given the lie to the classical economists' persistent drawing of the individualistic nature of the modern economy, a fact with implications profound in the consideration of tensions a century ago.

While this is an insight of great importance, there is nothing particularly revolutionary about the observation that American business, in its early forms and expressions, believed that markets, competition, and the work-ethic provided the path to success, satisfaction, and freedom. Certainly evidence abounds on this point. The problem is that this view of a particular part of society has too often been taken as an expression of the whole of society. Indeed Hurst argues this, both in *Law and the Conditions of Freedom* and in *Law and Social Process in United States History* (Ann Arbor, 1960), and Williams finds a striking congruity in the individualistic cultures of business and agriculture. This is understandable enough, given the power and presence of the idea that American history has lacked the conflict over fundamental values and priorities that has plagued less fortunate nations in Europe and Asia. The consensus interpretation of the past has been challenged sufficiently in the years since the 1950s when it held full swing, but the residues of this perspective linger in assumptions about the other parts of society for which expressions of alternate views are not so readily visible because of the simple omission of conventional documents testifying to such. Actually, of course, those documents *are* available; autobiographies, letters, journals, newspapers, speeches, and other forms of evidence that indicate a vibrant alternative culture abound. But when they surface they are often dismissed as exceptional; more commonly they are simply ignored as signs of cranks, subversives, or quaint but misguided altruists.

By this point it has become a commonplace that various groups of people in American history have been understood (or misunderstood) more through the assertion of a series of assumptions than through careful investigation. Those who were once held, with some pomp and sense of rediscovery, to be the "inarticulate" have turned out to be not nearly so inarticulate; the problem has been more the disinclination of historians to listen than for the sources to be silent.

This has been most evident among workers. Again E. P. Thompson provided a significant starting point. But in the endeavor, the contributions of others have been critical. Eric Hobsbawm had indeed previously launched forays into the world of people he termed *Primitive Rebels* (New York, 1959) and George Rudé explored *The Crowd in History: A Study of Popular Disturbances in France and England* (New York, 1964). With a very much different timbre Charles Tilly examined the process of counterrevolution in *The Vendee* (New York, 1964). And the work of Eric Hobsbawm in his recent volume of essays, *Workers: Worlds of Labor* (New York, 1984), and especially the essay in that volume, "The Making of the Working Class 1870–1914," and Gareth Stedman Jones, *Languages of Class: Studies in English Working Class History 1832–1982* (New York, 1983), has brought much of this earlier effort into a new dimension by exploring the *remaking* of the working class by examining the relationship between social consciousness and social being. In each instance the effort has been to mine the culture of people, especially of workers, by examining conventional historical source material and also the patterns of collective behavior which reveal assumptions and beliefs and priorities about the proper and improper forms of social organization by considering those patterns in the precise social context in which they appear. Raymond Williams, accordingly, urged the search in culture for a "structure of feeling," the consistency of purpose connecting the institutions that a group of people builds, the values it develops, the discipline it respects, and the activities it sanctions and encourages. Several of Williams' works are especially useful on this point: *The Long Revolution* (New York, 1961); Williams, *Culture and Society 1780–1950* (New York, 1958); and Williams, *Keywords: A Vocabulary of Culture and Society* (New York, 1976). Eric Hobsbawm referred to much the same pattern as "fitting together." Thus it is that Hobsbawm's extended studies of social bandits bring political and social significance to forms of behavior which previously had been taken seriously only by those historians with a penchant for the personal qualities or drama reflected in the episodes of outlawry that occasionally punctuate the history of society. Hobsbawm, in *Primitive Rebels* and *Bandits* (New York, 1969) and *Revolutionaries: Contemporary Essays* (New York, 1973), and others, like John Womack, *Zapata and the Mexican Revolution* (New York 1968), have managed to do so by examining the myths that surround the outlaws, by considering the circumstances in which they operate (what kinds of changes and problems beset the people in that environment), by noting the selection of targets of the outlaws, and who benefits and who suffers from the act. Indeed, Hobsbawm asks the same questions of the outlaws as many would ask of the lawmakers themselves.

Yet more conceptually, the study of workers is undertaken with a precise sense of context that links otherwise innocuous and insignificant data to patterns that reveal much about the workers and the society of which they are a part. This involves a sensitivity to not just the breadth with which workers felt the changes proceeding in the course of industrialization, and not just the breadth of the challenges these alterations in habits and customs and priorities presented to communities, but a sensitivity as well to the varieties and breadth of the responses workers offered to those changes. And what has been noticeable in the work of these historians is first their departure from the angle of vision of the labor economists who found in the formation of trade unions and the quest for collective bargaining the distinctive and welcome solution of the American labor movement, and secondly, their location of a course of development in the response. The central feature of that development has been the move to an increasingly disciplined, self-conscious political movement. Thompson, as usual, expressed it poignantly: "It is . . . this collective self-consciousness, with its corresponding theory, institutions, discipline, and community values which distinguishes the 19th-century *working class* from the 18th-century *mob*." This developmental focus has not been nearly so vital a concern of American historians as it has been among their English counterparts. For example, the pioneering work of Herbert Gutman literally endeavored to "balkanize" the examination and fragmented time as well as events in his *Work, Culture, and Society in Industrializing America: Essays in American Working-Class and Social History* (New York, 1976). Other historians have focused on specific aspects of worker culture as they examine workers in the directness of their own lives both at work and in the larger society. A brief run through the pages of *Labor History* and an examination of some of the recent books indicates the richness of recent developments in this area: Paul Johnson, *A Shopkeeper's Millennium: Society and Revivals in Rochester, New York 1815–1837* (New York, 1978); Leon Fink, *Workingmen's Democracy: The Knights of Labor and American Politics* (Urbana, 1983); John Bodnar, *Immigration and Industrialization: Ethnicity in an American Mill Town, 1870–1940* (Pittsburgh, 1977); Daniel Walkowitz, *Worker City, Company Town: Iron and Cotton Worker Protest in Troy and Cohoes, New York, 1855–84* (Urbana, 1978); Paul Faler, *Mechanics and Manufacturers in the early Industrial Revolution: Lynn, Massachusetts 1780–1860* (Albany, 1981); Alan Dawley, *Class and Community: The Industrial Revolution in Lynn* (Cambridge, Mass., 1976); John T. Cumbler, *Working-Class Community in Industrial America: Work, Leisure, and Struggle in two Industrial Cities, 1800–1930* (Westport, 1979); Sean Wilentz, *Chants Democratic: New York City & the Rise of the American Working Class, 1788–1850* (New York, 1984); Charles G. Steffen, *The Mechanics of Baltimore: Workers and Politics in the Age of Revolution 1763–1812* (Urbana, 1984); Bruce Laurie, *Working People of Philadelphia, 1800–1850* (Philadelphia, 1980). In this growing and substantial body of work the isolated themes and insights are often significant and revealing, but the result tends toward a kaleidoscopic vision rather than a focused view of worker history that brings the different economic, cultural, and structural elements into perspective. Whether this integrated picture of the history of American workers is pursued within specific communities or within the nation, the challenge remains a foreboding one.

Too often we neglect the simple observation that the history of American society in the middle years of the nineteenth century is also largely the history of agriculture. And too often we neglect to move beyond the history of markets and production in the countryside to the history of life. Most commonly that life has been penetrated mainly on its peripheries when historians have sought to explore specific elements of the economy, or such issues as race and slavery, environmental issues, or to explore local nostalgia and origins. The tendency remains largely fixed to the pattern set by Richard Hofstadter in *The Age of Reform* (New York, 1955) whereby farmers are viewed by the light shed on them from distant and not always representative sources. Thus, the state history journals continue to provide the best sources for agricultural life.

That life, however, was undermined by a set of forces tied to the economy that increasingly pointed to the political explosion we know as populism. Fred Shannon's persistently unreconstructed populist views in his analysis of the economic forces besetting *The Farmer's Last Frontier: Agriculture: 1860–1897* (New York, 1945) remain an important starting point for an understanding of the problems those people dealt with in a daily life that knew few mercies but that also produced nonmaterial satisfactions, and not the least, a vision of a new society. Despite all the attention to the economics of agriculture, to the political movement of the farmers, and to the culture of farmers, it is inexplicable how these forces were related to other parts of society such as workers. Lawrence Goodwyn's *Democratic Promise: The Populist Moment in American History*

(New York, 1976) comes closest to approaching this but even he contends that the cultural bridges between workers and farmers were absent. Perhaps a study of the cultural progression of Greenbackism to the Union Labor Party and the splinters on and off associated with this rural/urban movement can provide the key to that bridge. Goodwyn's bibliographical essay presents a solid discussion of historiographical issues relevant to this study of one county.

In this study I have touched upon, but only touched upon, the particular problems, opportunities, and responses of women to the changes transforming their society. Simply put, I have found the appropriate framework for this discussion, as it regards women, to be that employed in the discussion of other groups, like farmers, workers, and business advocates. Society was changing—all of it—and while the particular forms of change varied from individual to individual and group to group, the core set of demands, the domination and definition of life by material priorities, provided the context in which other questions had to be posed. And in that context questions of domesticity, of morality, indeed, of freedom, while facing both sexes, confronted women with a greater immediacy and with powerful and different political implications.

In the recent studies of women in nineteenth century America, the collection of brief biographies written by Margaret Forster in her book *Significant Sisters: The Grassroots of Active Feminism, 1830–1939* (London, 1984) is especially helpful. She probes large questions that know so many individual answers, and indeed explores, with vivid grace and imagination, the nebulous social entrapment of women. In the study of the plight of women, it bears repeating yet again, the personal *is* the political. The literature available on medical diagnosis and treatment of women in the late nineteenth century, which I have cited in the notes above, I have found valuable, not just because of the particulars and the details of that aspect of life, but because of its allegorical nature. As one reads between the lines of the medical practices of a century ago and of current discussions of those practices, we find that the index of freedom and self-respect may be best revealed in society's penalties and maledictions for those seeking greater strength. In another vein, the work of Barbara Leslie Epstein, *The Politics of Domesticity: Women, Evangelism, and Temperance in Nineteenth-Century America* (Middletown, Conn., 1981), reveals a powerful crucible in the crusading zeal of women by bringing together a cluster of elements that contributed to the reform impulse within feminine circles. In all this, again, the transformation to industrial capitalism provides not just a backdrop unrelated to the dynamics of the forces encircling females on the farms, in the towns, and in the villages of the nation, but a critical vector shaping the choices available to them and, as I argued above, often denying them the opportunities it simultaneously held forth.

The question of race has been but slightly addressed in this study. I have developed those issues in my *Legacy of Fear: American Race Relations to 1900* (Westport, Conn., 1984) and *Chains of Fear: American Race Relations since Reconstruction* (Westport, Conn., 1985), both collections of documents with an interpretation. Indeed a critical element in this interpretation derives from a document originating in this community—a letter from a slave in Texas to his parents in Pettis County—and upon which I commented at length as it bears upon the scholarship relevant to the slave family and the larger context of cultural and economic history of which it is a part, in an essay, "Slaves, Families, and 'Living Space': A Note on Evidence and Historical Context," *Southern Studies: An Interdisciplinary Journal of the South*, XVII (Summer 1978).

The leading studies on this subject that directly bear on this work are those that concern slavery and its aftermath. Eugene Genovese's effort in *The World the Slaveholders Made: Two Essays in Interpretation* (New York, 1969) to relate George Fitzhugh's coda of slavery to the models of society sketched by C. B. Macpherson is both inspired and rigid. Genovese's *Roll, Jordan, Roll: The World the Slaves Made* (New York, 1974) is properly considered a tour de force, marred only by the author's reliance on the concept of hegemony at too many points; so too Herbert Gutman's *The Black Family in Slavery and Freedom* (New York, 1976) shed important light on an area of slavery where a personal "living space" knew substantial autonomy. The bitter dispute between Genovese and Gutman was occasionally illuminating, but too often involved extraneous and unspoken agendas. Lawrence Levine's study of *Black Culture and Black Consciousness* (New York, 1977), the result of close observation of nuance and hidden meanings within black culture, is filled with insight; it is also devoid of any discussion of class as a factor shaping that racial consciousness.

It would be of little use to make short comments on the historiography of these groups in American history were it not for one additional comment. One of the objectives of the present study has been not to provide a complete analysis of each group but to suggest a context in which they might individually be understood differently from conventional treatments and in which the relationships between the several at least start to assume a coherent pattern. For this is one of the central problems of current American social history: Bernard Bailyn recently observed (*The Chronicle of Higher Education*, September 4, 1985) that since the dramatic developments in American social history about fifteen years ago, "social history has been going off in many different directions. It has generated a lot of new information, but it has also contributed significantly to the incoherence of the whole historical picture. Instead of a general picture of how the present situation has emerged out of the past, we have a lot of highly technical histories." The fracturing of the past, which has produced so much new information about particular groupings of people, has also sacrificed the general context linking them together.

While the effort to confront the problem of synthesis posed here has been only recently addressed, it has been approached with vigor and care especially in the work of Thomas Bender. Aside from his book *Community and Social Change in America* (New Brunswick, N.J., 1978) in which the issue is raised, his essay, "Wholes and Parts: The Need for Synthesis in American History," *Journal of American History*, 73 (June 1986) sparked a discussion in the *Journal of American History*, 74 (June 1987) that permitted Bender to expand on the concept of a public culture as a path to an historical synthesis. I would also suggest, for a productive insight with considerable potential in this quest for a general context, David Montgomery's study of *Workers' Control in America: Studies in the History of Work, Technology, and Labor Struggles* (New York, 1979). "Workers' control," Montgomery says, "was not a condition or state of affairs which existed at any point in time, but a struggle, a chronic battle in industrial life which assumed a variety of forms." Montgomery writes "of powers which working people have lost in this century, of popular values antagonistic to acquisitive individualism which have been snuffed out, of workers' regulation of hiring, work arrangements, and dismissal which have been vanquished in the name of progress, and of continuing traditions of working-class struggle, which have been far broader in scope than the union bargaining sanctioned by government and 'public opinion.'" He writes of a system of control that is economic, political, educational, psychological, and social. He writes of the same challenge that E. P. Thompson described that was presented to the weavers at the end of the nineteenth century in England, the challenge by factory owners "to stand at their command," a challenge which Thompson maintains "was the most deeply resented indignity." Clearly this question of control is one that is not restricted to the wage laborer, the machine tender, and the factory hand. It is a question vital to democracy itself in relations with authority, however defined—economic, gender, race, political, or social. It is even a metaphor of alienation, one that derives not from hard economic relationships that can be calculated in terms of surplus value, but that derives from the control that individuals and communities have over their own lives. If we transform Montgomery's concept slightly from workers' control to peoples' control we will have approached ever more closely a common context in which the struggles of individuals and particular groups become more comprehensible and fit together.

The key to the study then becomes the notion of agency—the ability of people to *act*, to control their lives. It is agency that is challenged in the process of industrialization. It is agency that is at issue in the rise of a fragmented society that centralizes power. It is agency that is the goal of popular movements until they become institutionalized. And it is agency that is manifest when people engage in that search for control itself. (For a discussion of this process, see Cassity, "Modernization and Social Crisis: The Knights of Labor and a Midwest Community, 1885–1886," *Journal of American History*, 66 [June 1979].) In 1958 E. P. Thompson raised this issue in his essay, "Agency and Choice," *The New Reasoner*, No. 5 (1958), 89–106 and in 1976 Thompson (in Henry Abelove, Betsy Blackmar, Peter Dimock, and Johnathan Schneer [MARHO: The Radical Historians Organization], eds., *Visions of History* [New York, 1983]) assessed his own contribution to worker history as one involving "a vocabulary of agency and moral choice" which had been pushed out of "mainstream orthodox Marxism" and which in Western capitalist ideology "got completely lost." To see that the historical concept of agency is not lost again remains a significant challenge.

Finally, the work of David Thelen on Missouri deserves a special comment because it examines the social and economic developments I have been concerned with and does so on a statewide level, and that state is Missouri. It is a brilliant example of the forms that political history can take. It also suggests how Sedalia fit into a statewide pattern. In *Paths of Resistance: Tradition and Dignity in Industrializing Missouri* (New York, 1986), Thelen builds upon the framework of political upheaval at the turn of the century that he had initially developed in *The New Citizenship: Origins of Progressivism in Wisconsin, 1885–1900* (Columbia, Mo., 1970) and in his biography of *Robert M. La Follette and the Insurgent Spirit* (Boston, 1976), a framework which turned on consumer consciousness as the origin of a new political awareness whereby citizens sought to decentralize the concentrations of economic and political power that controlled their lives. The signal development in *Paths of Resistance* that makes it expressly significant for the present work is Thelen's continuing quest for the historical origins of that political movement with a strikingly democratic potential and he has located it in the violence with which the principles and practices of the new economic order of industrial capitalism wrenched traditional social patterns and structural arrangements and then the resistance of people, from a wide assortment of callings and stations and traditions, to those changes.

In the completed works that we have each produced Thelen and I have crossed paths at many points. In the research that we both conducted along the way we did so as well. Indeed, we have shared ideas and sources too often to assay each other as competitors in the pursuit of how *really* we got to where we are today. So it is that our understanding of the process of transformation to the new, modern organization of life derives from a similar conceptual and historiographical base. So it is that our calculation of the costs of change, while never identical, bears a kinship.

Yet the differences in interpretation remain. Those differences have given me cause for reflection and contemplation. Ultimately I suspect that they have more to do with his emphasis on public life and the institutions important in its composition and my own focus on social relationships at a more immediate, even personal, level. Political institutions perform a secondary role in this work; they are important insofar as they reinforce or undermine a vision of society. It is that vision, which is obviously a political critique in its broad forms, with which I am primarily concerned. It is a search for identity, if that be a form of class consciousness (again in its broad Thompson-like configuration) or if that be the identity of the Ishmaelite, or if that takes some other pattern, that strikes me as the most enduring legacy in the make-up of modern society. For it is the defense of a way of life opposed to that of the market, opposed to the loss of power to distant agencies, even when in the name of responding to popular needs, opposed to the material definition of the goals and rewards of life—it is that way of life that represents the ultimate challenge and that provides at the same time the path of fulfillment.

Notes

Chapter I: Origins and Traditions

1. *The History of Pettis County, Missouri* (n.p., 1882), 806. Cf. also the overlapping treatments offered in a series of sketches of early Pettis County developed anonymously by the Federal Writers Project under the Works Progress Administration in the 1930s including: "Pettis County Soil," file #8977; "Topography of Pettis County," file #8976; "Historical Sketch," file #8971; and "Indian Archaeology—Pettis County," file #8969. This collection is contained in the Western Historical Manuscripts Collection in Columbia, Missouri. Future references will simply note WPA file.

2. "Historical Sketch," WPA file #8971; "Pettis County: Earliest History," WPA file #8969; untitled draft, WPA file #8962; *History of Pettis County*, 211–213, 801–803; William E. Foley, *A History of Missouri*, Volume I, *1673–1820* (Columbia, Missouri, 1971).

3. "Historical Sketch," WPA file #8971; untitled drafts, WPA files #8962 and #8967.

4. Untitled draft, WPA file #8969, suggests the presence even of British activity in the area because of the remains of a British officer preserved in an Indian burial mound. The story and speculation surrounding this tomb have been repeated and modified many times.

5. *History of Pettis County*, 860–861.

6. *Ibid.*, 861, 873–874.

7. "Early Settlement—Pettis County," WPA file #8962; "Towns and Villages in Pettis County," WPA file #8973; untitled draft, WPA file #8962; Ramsey file of place names, State Historical Society of Missouri, Columbia. It would be easy to overstate the importance of this commercial activity; it was at times prudent to close the Sappington store for two or three months. D. D. Garrett to E. D. Sappington, December 19, 1832. Sappington Papers, Missouri Historical Society, St. Louis. Also, cf. Lewis Atherton, *The Frontier Merchant in Mid-America* (Columbia, Mo., 1971).

8. Laura J. Yeater, *General David Thomson* (n.p., n.d.), 12, 15–17; James Wooldridge Powell, *Edgewood: The Story of a Family and their House* (n.p., 1978), 35–48.

Chapter II: The Pattern of Community

1. Untitled manuscript (p. 1) examining early years of Pettis County in Henry Lamm Papers, Western Historical Manuscripts Collection, University of Missouri, Columbia, Missouri; Samuel Bannister Harding, *Life of George R. Smith, Founder of Sedalia, Mo.* (Sedalia, Missouri, 1904), 21–22.

2. Letter, Absalom McVey to wife, March 12, 1837. Letter in possession of W. A. McVey, Sedalia, Missouri.

3. Harding, *Life of George R. Smith*, 21–22.

4. *Ibid.*, 47-48, 38.

5. Letter, Absalom McVey to Mr. Edmondson, his father-in-law, November 21, 1847. Letter in possession of W. A. McVey, Sedalia, Missouri.

6. *Ibid.*

7. Absalom McVey to wife, March 12, 1837.

8. Harding, *Life of George R. Smith*, 36, 26.

9. Pettis County Industrial Census for 1850. The entire industrial census for 1850 fit on one page.

10. Pettis County Agricultural Census, 1850, ms. pp. 615–616, 635–636.

11. *History of Pettis County*, 219.

12. Samuel M. Jordan, "Farming as it Used To Be, and as it Is in Missouri," *Missouri Historical Review*, 22 (October 1927), 14–15.

13. Untitled manuscript, Lamm Papers, 5–6; Jordan, "Farming as it Used To Be," 14–15; *History of Pettis County*, 219–220, 1010.

14. Jordan, "Farming as it Used To Be", 15.

15. *Ibid.*, 17.

16. *Records of the County Court*, Pettis County, Volume A–1; 455, November 7, 1842; 495, May 2, 1843; 503–504, August 7, 1843.

17. County Court records, by noting the terms of credit available on the settlement of estates through sales of property, continually confirm Martha Elizabeth Smith's observation that "The old system of credit prevailed in those times to such an extent that merchants' and grocers' bills and all expenses of the family were settled up only once a year, and sometimes not so often." Moreover, in that recollection Smith was referring to credit as it was at the end of the 1850s, a sign of its durability. Harding, *Life of George R. Smith*, 287.

18. *Ibid.*, 41.

19. *History of Pettis County*, 217.

20. Harding, *Life of George R. Smith*, 26.

21. Jordan, "Farming as it Used to Be," 20; Harding, *Life of George R. Smith*, 23.

22. Absalom McVey to wife, March 12, 1837.

23. Jordan, "Farming as it Used to Be," 14.

24. Harding, *Life of George R. Smith*, 28–29.

25. This, of course, is but one example of such craftmanship. See the Pettis County Historic Sites file at the State Historical Society of Missouri for other instances.

26. *Records of the County Court*, Pettis County, Volume A–1: 68, May 6, 1839; 424, May 13, 1842; 574–575, May 7, 1844; 547, February 5, 1844; Volume B–2: 119, May 4, 1846.

27. Untitled manuscript, Lamm Papers, 1; Jordan, "Farming as it Used to Be," 16–18.

28. C. M. Cravins to M. M. Marmaduke, June 12, 1837, Sappington Papers, Missouri Historical Society, St. Louis, Mo.

29. *History of Pettis County*, 1010.

30. *Records of the County Court*, Pettis County, Volume A–1: 180–185, August 11, 1840.

31. *History of Pettis County*, 1013–1014. This lack of money is further suggested by the vast majority of purchases made on credit at the dry-goods store operated by Marmaduke and Sappington at St. Helena at the beginning of the 1830s. See St. Helena firm Account Book, 1832–1833, Missouri Historical Society, St. Louis, Mo.

32. "Pettis (County Court and Clerk)," WPA file #8957. The last of these functions is not one to be taken lightly. Before the organization of Pettis County such a bounty had been voluntarily offered by the neighbors in the St. Helena area. See the records of those bounties dated May 10, and May 15, 1832 in the Sappington Papers, Missouri Historical Society.

33. See, for example, the disposition of the case of Polly Rutledge, "a blind and helpless female," *Records of the County Court*, Pettis County, Volume B–2: 7 August 6, 1844; 52–53, February 6, 1845.

34. W. A. McVey, *Yester Years: A Study of Missouri's First Roads and Transportation Systems in Central Missouri* (n.p., 1973). See also the official description of one of the early roads which ran "to General Hogan's then leaving that turning

through the right hand land there on past the widow Wallace's place on the right
thence on to Higgins & McCormick's mill, from that on past Abraham McCormick's leaving Michael Goodnight's farm on the right thence to the head of walnut creek thence on to spring fork at Henry Parrish's house thence on to the
Benton County line." *Records of the County Court*, Pettis County, Volume A–1:
26–27, May 8, 1838.

35. Harding, *Life of George R. Smith*, 39, 50–54.

36. *History of Pettis County*, 257.

37. Bingham's close association with Pettis County can be seen not only in
his travel in the same political circles as George Smith and in his own physical
proximity to Pettis County but in more direct ways as well. The estate of Lewis
Redd Major paid George Bingham $15.00 due the artist when Major died in
1845. *Records of the County Court*, Pettis County, Volume B–2: 95–6, November 4,
1845. For information concerning Bingham and the background for his paintings
County Election, Stump Speaking, and *Canvassing for a Vote* see John Francis Mc-
Dermott, *George Caleb Bingham: River Portraitist* (Norman, Oklahoma, 1959), 62–
67, 87–114; E. Maurice Bloch, *George Caleb Bingham: The Evolution of an Artist*
(Berkeley, 1967), 128–168; and Albert Christ-Janer, *George Caleb Bingham: Frontier
Painter of Missouri* (New York, 1975).

38. McDermott, *George Caleb Bingham*, 99–100.

39. *Ibid.*, 107–108.

40. *History of Pettis County*, 260–262.

41. *History of Pettis County*, 260–263; U. S. Census, manuscript returns of
enumeration of slave inhabitants of Pettis County, 1850 and 1860, State Historical
Society of Missouri.

42. *History of Pettis County*, 248; Slave census manuscripts for Pettis County,
1850 and 1860, State Historical Society of Missouri.

43. Laura J. Yeater, *General David Thomson* (n.p., n.d.), *11*.

44. *Ibid.*, 11, 16–18; Harding, *Life of George R. Smith*, 34; James Wooldridge
Powell, *Edgewood: The Story of a Family and Their House* (n.p., 1978), 53.

45. Harding, *Life of George R. Smith*, 24–26, 32.

46. Letter written by Mildred Thomson to Milton Thomson, February 10,
1851, Berry—Thomson—Walker Family Papers, Western Historical Manuscripts
Collection, University of Missouri, Columbia, Missouri.

47. Yeater, *General David Thomson*, 24–26.

48. Harding, *Life of George R. Smith*, 52. Mildred Thomson to Milton
Thomson, February 10, 1851; Milton Thomson to Mildred Thomson, May 17,
1851, Berry-Thomson-Walker Family Papers.

49. *History of Pettis County*, 220.

50. Powell, *Edgewood*, 43–45; Yeater, *General David Thomson*, 19.

51. David Thomson to Milton Thomson, January 31, 1847, Berry-Thomson-Walder Family Papers.

52. Yeater, *General David Thomson*, 27–28.

53. Harding, *Life of George R. Smith*, 44.

54. *Ibid.*, 20.

55. Harding, *Life of George R. Smith*, 51–52.

56. See, for example, the reply to Milton Thomson's request that a slave buyer from Boonville be sent to purchase one of his slaves, Wilson Brown (?) to Milton Thomson, July 11, 1844. Berry-Thomson-Walker Family Papers.

57. Martha Elizabeth Smith to family, June 12, 1855, Smith-Cotton Papers, Western Historical Manuscripts Collection.

58. T. T. Bradley to A. Higgans, July 11, 1859, T. T. Bradley Letters, State Historical Society of Missouri, Columbia, Missouri. Portions of this letter have been reprinted in Michael J. Cassity, "Slaves, Families, and 'Living Space': A Note on Evidence and Historical Context," *Southern Studies*, XVII (Summer 1978), 209; Additionally one should note that the first recorded death in Green Ridge Township was that of Solomon Cofer, a black man "in the family of Robert Means, Sr." The fact that Cofer maintained his own distinctive surname instead of doing without or assuming the name of his owner suggests further the coherence of black family life in the area. *History of Pettis County*, 1043.

59. Harding, *Life of George R. Smith*, 52,20.

60. See for example the interview with Anderson Powell (again the distinctive surname) who described slave life in Pettis County after he was brought into the county as a slave of Thomas Joplin in 1836. Included in this is his account of slaves attending the same church services as the masters. Sedalia *Weekly Bazoo*, May 24, 1887.

61. Harding, *Life of George R. Smith*, 20–21.

62. *Ibid.*, 49.

63. Bacon Montgomery manuscript, genealogical file in George R. Smith Papers, Missouri Historical Society, St. Louis.

64. *Ibid.*, 31, 32, 43; *History of Pettis County*, 927–8.

65. *History of Pettis County*, 213–214.

66. Harding, *Life of George R. Smith*, 31.

Chapter III: The Crisis of Change and War

1. Samuel Bannister Harding, *Life of George R. Smith, Founder of Sedalia, Mo.* (Sedalia, Missouri, 1904), 50.

2. *The History of Pettis County, Missouri* (n.p., 1882), 1044.

3. The nearest competitor to Smith for this singularity was John S. Jones, a speculator, trader, and planter. Unlike Smith, who in fact had even gone into partnership with Jones, Jones did not follow his beliefs into politics, wound up broke instead of wealthy and left the area as the war erupted jeopardizing himself and his family for their slave-owning principles (Jones was even related by marriage to Jefferson Davis and managed a plantation for Davis in Mississippi whose name he appropriated for his own in Pettis County: "Deer Park"). William B. Claycomb, "John S. Jones: Farmer, Freighter, Frontier Promoter," *Missouri Historical Review*, LXXIII (July 1979), 434–450.

4. Harding, *Life of George R. Smith*, 57.

5. *Ibid.*, 57–58.

6. *Ibid.*, 68–69.

7. *Ibid.*, 90–95.

8. *Ibid.*, 103.

9. *Ibid.*, 60.

10. *Ibid.*, 156–158; *History of Pettis County*, 421–422.

11. Harding, *Life of George R. Smith*, 163–167.

12. The penetrating conception of the market as a set of relationships at once economic, political, and social, presented by James Willard Hurst, *Law and the Conditions of Freedom in the Nineteenth-Century United States* (Madison, 1956), Chapter I, "The Release of Energy," suggests the limitations of the relevant studies of economic change in early Missouri that focus mainly on organizations and financial growth (e.g., James Neal Primm, *Economic Policy in the Development of a Western State: Missouri 1820–1860* [Cambridge, Mass., 1954]). At the same time, however, it should be noted that in the particular relationship between law and popular attitudes assumed by Hurst he takes the victor's view of history and glosses over real opposition to that view. Harry N. Scheiber, "At the Borderland of Law and Economic History: The Contributions of Willard Hurst," *American Historical Review*, LXXXV (February 1970), 755. For a full development of the logic of market society and the changes it pressed in a theoretical context see C. B. Macpherson, *The Political Theory of Possessive Individualism: Hobbes to Locke* (Oxford, 1962) and especially his models of different forms of social organization, 46–70.

13. *Jefferson Inquirer* (Jefferson City, Missouri), September 23, 1854; Harding, *Life of George R. Smith*, 176–7.

230 NOTES

14. Harding, *Life of George R. Smith*, 177–9.

15. Reminiscences of Martha Elizabeth Smith in *ibid.*, 50–52.

16. Perry McCandless, *A History of Missouri* : Volume II, *1820–1860* (Columbia, Mo., 1972), 270–271; Harrison A. Trexler, *Slavery in Missouri 1804–1865* (Baltimore, 1914), 204–5.

17. Besides the original works of Fitzhugh, see the discussion of his critique by Eugene Genovese in *The World the Slaveholders Made: Two Essays in Interpretation* (New York, 1969), Part II, "The Logical Outcome of the Slaveholders' Philosophy."

18. James S. Rollins to George R. Smith, May 24, 1855, printed in Harding, *Life of George R. Smith*, 224–226; McCandless, History of Missouri, 270.

19. T. K. Smith, "The Organization of the Blue Lodges and Border Ruffians," ms. in Jonas Viles Papers, Western Historical Manuscripts Collection, University of Missouri, Columbia, Mo.; Harding, *Life of George R. Smith*, 211–12.

20. Mark McGruder, *History of Pettis County, Missouri* (Topeka, 1919), 204; McCandless, *History of Missouri*, 272–274; Harding, *Life of George R. Smith*, 210–233; *The History of Pettis County, Missouri*, 424.

21. George G. Vest to unidentified "My Dear Sir," February 2, 1885, printed in Harding, *Life of George R. Smith*, 225 (the original of the letter is in the George R. Smith Papers, Missouri Historical Society, St. Louis, Mo.); Sedalia *Sunday Morning Bazoo*, March 1, 1885; *Jefferson Inquirer*, May 30, 1856; *The History of Pettis County, Missouri*, 840, 931–2. Conflicts abound in the above accounts and an added dimension is provided in the epitaph given the slain white woman, Elizabeth A. Raines: "Her death was caused from blows inflicted by H. France's negro Boy. The public opinion is that his master abetted the murder." Nowhere else is this factor mentioned and I am grateful to Van Jones for providing me a photograph of the tombstone as well as other information concerning the incident.

22. Harding, *Life of George R. Smith*, 193–209; *Jefferson Inquirer*, May 30, 1856.

23. Harding, Life of George R. Smith, 251–5, 271–7, 281–2; *Jefferson Inquirer*, May 17, 1856. For an index of deepening tension see the letter from Lizzie to Sis, July 20, 1859, in neighboring Saline County noting that two blacks were hanged, one burned and five ran away, or, as the local people preferred to believe, were abducted. Joseph Marshall Family Papers, Western Historical Manuscripts Collection, University of Missouri, Columbia, Missouri.

24. Reminiscences of Martha Elizabeth Smith in Harding, *Life of George R. Smith*, 283, 285–6; *History of Pettis County*, 402–3.

25. Harding, *Life of George R. Smith*, 287–294, 298–303.

26. *Ibid.*, 304–318.

27. *Ibid.*, 295; James Wooldridge Powell, *Edgewood: The Story of a Family and their House* (n.p., 1978), 74–5.

28. Harding, *Life of George R. Smith*, 322–335; reminiscence of G. S. Grover in *ibid.*, 318; *History of Pettis County*, 425.

29. Letter from Orville to Mary [McEwen], January 30, 1862, McEwen Papers, Missouri Historical Society, St. Louis, Missouri.

30. James E. Love to Molly, October 10, 1861, James E. Love Papers, Missouri Historical Society, St. Louis, Missouri.

31. Kate or Lily Faulhaber, "Sedalia," ms. in Nellie Ingram Scrapbook, Volume I, State Historical Society of Missouri, Columbia, Missouri.

32. Harding, *Life of George R. Smith*, 332; W. Wayne Smith, "An Experiment in Counterinsurgency: The Assessment of Confederate Sympathizers in Missouri," *Journal of Southern History*, XXXV (August 1969), 376; *History of Pettis County*, 379–380.

33. Catharine Luckett Family Scrapbook, Western Historical Manuscripts Collection, University of Missouri, Columbia, Mo.

34. *History of Pettis County*, 450–453.

35. Richard Field, *Richard Field: A brief Story of his Life, Written by Himself* (Lexington, Mo., 1930), 16–19. I am grateful to William B. Claycomb who mentioned this incident to me and then provided a copy of the autobiography of Field's son who was at the home when his father was taken away and killed.

36. W. A. McVey, "Capture of Sedalia, October 1864," unpublished manuscript (1978) in possession of author; *History of Pettis County*, 434–450.

37. Harding, *Life of George R. Smith*, 339–352; *History of Pettis County*, 425–426, 458.

Chapter IV: The Engines of Economic Growth

1. See the Pettis County letters to Governor Fletcher from G. R. Smith (January 1, 1866), Jos. L. Gage (December 31, 1865), and others in uncatalogued file, Missouri State Archives, Jefferson City.

2. *Missouri State Times* (Jefferson City), January 11, 1867; William E. Parrish, *Missouri Under Radical Rule: 1865–1870* (Columbia, Mo., 1965), 1–75; Fred DeArmond, "Reconstruction in Missouri," *Missouri Historical Review*, LXI (April 1967), 364–377; Thomas S. Barclay, "The Test Oath for the Clergy in Missouri," *ibid.*, XVIII (April 1924), 345–381; Thomas S. Barclay, *The Liberal Republican Movement in Missouri 1865–1871* (Columbia, Mo., 1926), 143. See the copy of the oath signed by George R. Smith in the Missouri State Archives, Jefferson City, f. 12405.

3. *The History of Pettis County, Missouri*, (n.p., 1882), 417.

232   NOTES

4. Letter from Sedalia from "UxS" in *The People's Tribune* (Jefferson City), December 6, 1865 (emphasis in original); Sedalia *Weekly Times*, December 27, 1868. Herbert G. Gutman admirably developed the historical importance of the effort of the institutions of the new industrial order to establish legitimacy in protracted conflicts involved in this transformation, in his study of "Class, Status, and Community Power in Nineteenth-Century American Industrial Cities— Paterson, New Jersey: A Case Study," in Frederic Cople Jaher (ed.), *The Age of Industrialism in America: Essays in Social Structure and Cultural Values* (New York, 1968).

5. Sedalia *Weekly Times*, November 21, 1867; Sedalia *Independent Press*, November 15, 1866; Clifford D. Carpenter, "The Early Cattle Industry in Missouri," *Missouri Historical Review*, XLVII (April 1953), 202–13.

6. Sedalia *Weekly Times*, April 6, 13, 1866, February 2, 7, May 11, July 4, 1867.

7. Missouri *State Times*, November 15, 1867; Sedalia *Weekly Times*, June 27, August 8, October 3, 10, 1867, February 2, March 26, 1868; Sedalia *Weekly Bazoo*, May 30, 1876.

8. *History of Pettis County, Missouri*, 525–526, 532–535.

9. Missouri *State Times*, June 14, 1867; Sedalia *Weekly Times*, April 27, 1866; December 5, 1867, January 9, April 16, May 7, 1868; Sedalia *Daily Bazoo* , November 11, 1869, March 1, 1870, August 15, October 24, 1871.

10. See the summary of railroad projects involving Sedalia and Pettis County in the tables provided by Edwin L. Lopata, *Local Aid to Railroads in Missouri* (New York, 1937), 135–135; Sedalia *Weekly Times*, February 21, 1867, April 9, 16, 1868.

11. *The People's Tribune*, March 14, June 27, July 4, 1866.

12. Sedalia *Weekly Times*, September 19, 26, 1867, January 23, February 13, May 21, 1868; *History of Pettis County*, 516.

13. Lopata, *Local Aid to Railroads*, 36–37; Sedalia *Daily Bazoo*, October 5, 6, 14, 1869. Bacon Montgomery had also been appointed to the county office of registration by the governor following the purge. Sedalia *Weekly Times*, February 9, 1866.

14. Sedalia *Daily Democrat*, November 4, 1869.

15. Sedalia *Daily Democrat*, November 4, 1869; Sedalia *Daily Bazoo*, November 2, 1869; Sedalia *Weekly Times*, November 4, 11, 1869; Lopata, *Local Aid to Railroads*, 105–107.

16. Sedalia *Daily Bazoo*, January 18, 1870; Sedalia *Weekly Bazoo*, January 30, 1872; Lopata, *Local Aid to Railroads*, 132.

17. Sedalia *Weekly Bazoo*, January 2, 1872.

18. Sedalia *Weekly Times*, April 9, 1868; Sedalia *Daily Bazoo*, December 1, 1869, February 23, December 19, 1870; Sedalia *Weekly Bazoo*, December 24, 1872, January 21, 1873.

19. Sedalia *Daily Bazoo*, September 24, October 13, 1869, January 28, October 18, November 23, 1870; Sedalia *Weekly Bazoo*, November 14, 21, 1871.

20. Sedalia *Weekly Bazoo*, October 15, 1870, August 15, 22, September 19, October 24, 1871, February 27, June 18, 25, July 2, 1872, May 13, 1873; Sedalia Board of Trade Proceedings, 1872–1888, State Historical Society of Missouri, Columbia, Missouri.

21. Sedalia *Daily Bazoo*, December 8, 20, 1869; *History of Pettis County*, 469.

22. Sedalia *Weekly Times*, February 21, October 24, 1867, February 28, December 19, 30, 1870, September 19, 1871, May 20, 1873; Parrish, *Missouri Under Radical Rule*, 161–165.

23. Sedalia Board of Trade Proceedings, meeting of June 19, 1873, State Historical Society of Missouri, Columbia.

24. U. S. Census, Products of Industry manuscript for Pettis County, 1850, State Historical Society of Missouri.

25. This discussion relies, aside from the examination of the mill sites and stones still in the county, on the cogent discussion in John Reynolds, *Windmills & Watermills* (New York, 1970), especially 44–49.

26. U. S. Census *Manufactures of the United States in 1860* (Washington, 1865), 307; U. S. Census, *Ninth Census—Volume III: Statistics of the Wealth and Industry of the United States* (Washington, 1872), 539; see also the manuscript census materials, indicating the individual establishments, in the State Historical Society of Missouri.

27. Newspaper clipping in F. A. Sampson Scrapbooks, Vol. III, p. 4, State Historical Society of Missouri.

28. Sedalia *Weekly Bazoo*, July 22, 1872; newspaper clipping in F. A. Sampson Scrapbooks, Vol. I. p. 97, State Historical Society of Missouri.

29. Sedalia *Weekly Bazoo*, July 22, 1872.

30. Newspaper clipping, F. A. Sampson Scrapbooks, Vol. III, p. 7.

31. Newspaper clipping, F. A. Sampson Scrapbooks, Vol. I, p. 73.

32. U. S. Census, *Manufactures . . . in 1860*, 307; U. S. Census, *Ninth Census—Volume III*, 539; U. S. Census, *Report on the Manufactures of the United States at the Tenth Census*, Vol. II (Washington, 1883), 142 (this census was omitted from the figures cited since the category changed definition and the manuscript census does little to provide consistency); U. S. Census, *Report on Manufacturing Industries in the United States at the Eleventh Census: 1890*, Part I (Washington, 1895), 496–497.

33. F. A. North, *The Hand-Book of Sedalia, Missouri, including a Carefully Compiled History and Business Directory* (Sedalia, 1882), 126–127.

34. *Ibid.*, 127–128.

Chapter V: God and Mammon: The Birth of East Sedalia

1. "The Washerwoman's Song," Sedalia *Weekly Bazoo*, February 1, 1876; this poem was reprinted from the Ft. Scott *Monitor* without author attribution. The author, one Ironquill (Eugene F. Ware), was a Ft. Scott attorney and sometime writer of verse. See James C. Malin, "Ironquill's 'The Washerwoman's Song'," *Kansas Historical Quarterly*, XXV (Autumn 1959), 257–282.

2. Although this transformation has been one of the major themes of Western civilization, its American manifestations, long neglected, are receiving increased attention. The work on law and the changing social order has moved beyond the pathbreaking work of James Willard Hurst to a much more critical perspective by Morton J. Horwitz, *The Transformation of American Law* (Cambridge, Mass., 1977). Studies by a new generation of historians on the resistance to this change presented in society, especially by workers, exhibit an impressive and challenging beginning (though not to say a unanimous one) in this direction.

3. Sedalia *Independent Press*, March 28, 1867; *The History of Pettis County, Missouri* (n.p., 1882), 474–476.

4. Letters from "Temperance" and "A Good Templar" in Sedalia *Weekly Times*, February 9, 1866; the resolution following the lynching calling for temperance was published in *ibid.*, April 18, 1867.

5. Sedalia *Weekly Times*, February 23, December 14, 1866, February 20, 1868; Sedalia *Daily Bazoo*, February 16, 1870.

6. Sedalia *Weekly Bazoo*, September 18, 1871; *The History of Pettis County, Missouri*, 546–547, 565–566. The one thrust of this moral code, that of the support it lends industrial capitalism has become, since Max Weber's heralded findings, virtually a cliche. Its other functions have been approached in a creative manner in Richard Jensen, *The Winning of the Midwest: Social and Political Conflict, 1888–1896* (Chicago, 1971) and Ronald P. Formisano, *The Birth of Mass Political Parties: Michigan, 1827–1861* (Princeton, 1971). These two studies contrast two religious impulses generalized to world views: for Jensen, the pietists vs. the liturgicals; for Formisano, evangelicals vs. ritualistic, laissez-faire ethics. As penetrating as these studies are, they have not, at least at the relevant points, surpassed Herbert Gutman's "Protestantism and the American Labor Movement: The Christian Spirit in the Gilded Age," *American Historical Review*, LXXII (October 1966), 74–101. Mainly this results from Formisano's and Jensen's approach which provides religious attitudes a determinative function without probing the larger social context from which those attitudes are derived. In particular, they have failed to consider what needs may have been fulfilled by various religious experiences.

7. J. M. Van Wagner, like his son who succeeded him, A. J. Van Wagner, held a strong advantage over most of the other city ministers. The local press afforded him much attention. Any number of his sermons, and, after he left Sedalia, his letters, appeared in full in the newspapers, making his theology by far the easiest to reconstruct. The most pointed, concisely argued and systematically developed discussion relevant here, yet completely consistent with his earlier sermons, came in a speech on the work ethic to a public assembly when he returned to Sedalia in 1886, Sedalia *Daily Bazoo*, April 20, 1886; *History of Pettis County*, 547–548.

8. Sedalia *Weekly Bazoo*, July 2, 1872; *History of Pettis County*, 577, 566.

9. *History of Pettis County*, 503–504, 543–544, 620–622.

10. *Ibid.*, 560–562, 620–622. The barriers separating East Sedalia from Sedalia proper were such that the secular and religious activity of the workers' community received only oblique attention in the press. The crucial point of the conversion into a holy world separate from a secular world which was breaking down in its traditional structural and cultural certainties was one that had an important historical antecedent in the Puritan Revolution: cf. Michael Walzer, *The Revolution of the Saints: A Study in the Origins of Radical Politics* (New York, 1968).

11. Sedalia *Weekly Bazoo*, February 6, 1872; Sedalia *Weekly Democrat*, February 15, 1872; M. M. "Brick" Pomeroy, *Our Saturday Nights* (New York, 1870), 153, 126–127; Irwin Unger, *The Greenback Era: A Social and Political History of American Finance, 1865–1879* (Princeton, 1964), 74–75.

Chapter VI: A Vale of Tears: The Experiences of Change

1. For an example of a different approach see Stephan Thernstrom's study of social mobility, which, he says, "requires the use of objective criteria of social status." The assumptions concerning the "objective" analysis of the lives of other people in another historical period are, at the least, questionable. More troublesome, however, is the use of the conception of mobility in a discussion of a social context in which mobility may not have had positive relevance. Stephan Thernstrom, *Poverty and Progress: Social Mobility in a Nineteenth Century City* (New York, 1970), 84.

2. Samuel Bannister Harding, *Life of George R. Smith* (Sedalia, 1904), 287; Sedalia *Weekly Bazoo*, February 13, 1883; E. P. Thompson, "Time, Work-Discipline, and Industrial Capitalism," *Past and Present*, No. 38 (December 1967), 56–97.

3. *Ibid.*; Sedalia *Daily Democrat*, September 18, 1885; Sedalia *Weekly Bazoo*, October 3, 1871; Robert E. Riegel, "Standard Time in the United States," *American Historical Review*, XXXIII (October 1927), 84–89; Lewis Mumford, *The Myth of the Machine: Technics and Human Development* (New York, 1966), 286.

4. *The History of Pettis County, Missouri*, (n.p., 1882), 482. No effort has been made to compile the grim statistics of rail fatalities and injuries. It would,

however, be safe to say that by the 1880s when the city press began to record them, scarcely a week passed without such incidents.

5. Sedalia *Weekly Bazoo*, February 13, 1883.

6. Sedalia *Weekly Bazoo*, April 4, 1871, May 5, 1876, March 13, April 3, 1877, January 22, 1878, January 6, 1880, March 29, 1881.

7. Sedalia *Weekly Bazoo*, January 21, 1873, April 3, 1877, January 22, 1878, January 6, 1880, March 29, 1881.

8. Sedalia *Weekly Bazoo*, May 4, 1880, October 18, 1881, May 8, May 15, 1883, October 10, 1884, June 25, July 30, 1889; Sedalia *Daily Democrat*, November 25, December 29, 30, 1885.

9. Sedalia *Weekly Bazoo*, October 24, December 12, 1871, February 18, 1873, December 12, 1876, July 8, 1884, January 8, December 8, 1885, April 30, 1889.

10. Sedalia *Weekly Bazoo*, May 6, 1879, January 24, 1882; Barbara Welter, "The Cult of True Womanhood: 1820–1860," *American Quarterly*, XVIII (Summer 1966), 151–174; William E. Bridges, "Family Patterns and Social Values in America, 1825–1875," *American Quarterly*, XVII (Spring 1965), 3–11.

11. Sedalia, *Weekly Bazoo*, May 6, August 12, 1879, December 13, 1881, January 31, June 13, December 19, 1882, July 26, 1887; Welter, "The Cult of True Womanhood," 161–164, 171–174.

12. Sedalia *Weekly Bazoo*, April 24, May 9, 1873, March 25, July 1, 1884, July 9, 1889; Sedalia *Daily Democrat*, April 21, May 11, 1888.

13. Sedalia *Weekly Bazoo*, April 10, 1877, June 25, 1878, January 21, 1879, February 2, November 9, 1880, August 23, 1881, April 25, May 9, June 13, August 22, 1882, August 14, 1883, January 8, 1884, April 9, 1889.

14. Sedalia *Weekly Bazoo*, February 17, 1885.

15. Sedalia *Weekly Bazoo*, February 24, 1885.

16. *Ibid.*

17. Keith Thomas, *Religion and the Decline of Magic* (New York, 1971), 89.

18. Sedalia *Weekly Bazoo*, February 1, 1887.

19. Sedalia *Weekly Bazoo*, May 21, 1876.

20. Sedalia *Weekly Bazoo*, November 29, 1881.

21. Sedalia *Weekly Bazoo*, December 27, 1881.

22. Robert Blauner, "Death and Social Structure," *Psychiatry*, 29 (November 1966), 381.

23. *The Truth*, February 21, 1889.

24. Blauner, "Death and Social Structure," 381.

25. Max Gluckman, *Politics, Law and Ritual in Tribal Society* (Chicago, 1965), 7–8.

26. Sedalia *Weekly Bazoo*, November 2, 1880.

27. Sedalia *Weekly Bazoo*, May 31, 1887, June 7, 1887.

28. Sedalia *Weekly Bazoo*, August 7, 1883. That this was not restricted to a single, short period of time and that it may have possessed a distinctly working class quality is indicated by the frequent references of E. T. Behrens' wife to her consultations with a fortune teller in the 1920s and 1930s. Behrens was a local labor leader in Sedalia at the turn of the century. E. T. Behrens Papers, Western Historical Manuscripts Collection, University of Missouri, Columbia.

29. Thomas, *Religion and the Decline of Magic*, 191.

30. Sedalia *Weekly Bazoo*, August 19, 1884.

Chapter VII: The Businessmen and the Market

1. Sedalia *Weekly Bazoo*, February 29, 1876.

2. *Ibid.*, August 15, 29, 1876; Sedalia *Weekly Democrat*, August 24, 1876.

3. Sedalia *Weekly Bazoo*, August 15, 1876.

4. *Ibid.*, May 2, 9, 16, 1876.

5. *Ibid.*, January 7, 1879.

6. *Ibid.*, November 30, 1880, November 29, 1881, April 8, May 27, 1884.

7. *The History of Pettis County, Missouri* (n.p., 1882), 572–587; Sedalia *Weekly Bazoo*, September 14, 1872, September 28, 1875, April 11, 1876, June 3, 1879, September 21, 1880.

8. Sedalia *Daily Bazoo*, August 1, 11, 1879; Sedalia *Weekly Bazoo*, August 12, 1879.

9. Sedalia *Weekly Bazoo*, January 13, 1880.

10. *Ibid.*, March 15, 22, 1881.

11. *The History of Pettis County, Missouri*, 515–518, provides valuable information concerning the changing management of the railroads serving Sedalia.

12. Sedalia *Daily Bazoo*, August 17, 1875; Sedalia *Weekly Bazoo*, August 18, 1875.

13. Julius Grodinsky, *Jay Gould: His Business Career 1867–1892* (Philadelphia, 1957), 198–200, 234–237; Sedalia *Weekly Bazoo*, November 23, December 7, 14, 1880; Sedalia *Daily Bazoo*, August 5, 1879.

14. *The History of Pettis County, Missouri*, 522; Sedalia *Weekly Bazoo*, January 28, May 6, August 12, September 23, 1879; Sedalia *Daily Bazoo* August 13, 1879. The effort to connect Sedalia and Warsaw with a railroad began in 1877 but only the campaign to move the state capital launched early in 1879 could provide the railroad project sufficient impetus. See the Sedalia *Weekly Democrat*, September 20, November 22, 1877.

15. Sedalia *Daily Democrat*, November 10, 1877; Sedalia *Weekly Democrat*, November 15, 1877; Sedalia *Weekly Bazoo*, February 14, 1882.

16. Sedalia *Weekly Bazoo*, November 18, 1884.

17. *Ibid.*, January 20, February 17, 1885; Sedalia *Daily Bazoo*, February 28, March 3, 6, 7, 10, 17, 1885; Sedalia *Sunday Morning Bazoo*, March 8, 1885; Sedalia *Daily Democrat*, March 6, 7, 10, 1885.

18. Sedalia *Daily Bazoo*, March 10, 11, 12, 1885; Sedalia *Sunday Morning Bazoo*, March 15, 1885; Sedalia *Daily Democrat*, March 10, 11, 12, 14, 1885.

19. Sedalia *Daily Bazoo*, March 10, 11, 1885; Sedalia *Daily Democrat*, March 10, 11, 12, 1885.

20. Sedalia *Daily Democrat*, March 13, 14, 17, 1885; Sedalia *Daily Bazoo*, March 11, 12, 13, 14, 1885; Sedalia *Sunday Morning Bazoo*, March 15, 1885; Sedalia *Bazoo* Extra Edition, March 16, 1885; U. S. Congress, House of Representatives, 49th Cong., 2d Session, Report No. 4174, *Investigation of Labor Troubles in Missouri, Arkansas, Texas and Illinois*, 1887, pp. iii–iv.

21. Sedalia *Daily Bazoo*, March 15, 1885; Sedalia *Daily Democrat*, March 10, 11, 17, 1885.

22. Testimony of Martin Irons, in U.S. Congress, *Investigation of Labor Troubles*, Part II, 436–437; Terence V. Powderly, *The Path I Trod: The Autobiography of Terence V. Powderly*, ed. by Harry J. Carman, Henry David and Paul N. Guthrie (New York, 1940), 118–124; Ruth A. Allen, *The Great Southwest Strike* (Austin, 1942), 57; Sedalia *Daily Bazoo*, March 9, 10, 11, 12, 17, 19, 1886.

23. Sedalia *Daily Bazoo*, March 9, 11, 1886.

24. *Ibid.*, March 23, 24, 1886; Testimony of W. B. Lyons (pp.265–266), J. J. Frey (pp. 267–269), R. Rockwell (pp.273–274), and W. H. Mason (p. 275), in Congress, *Investigation of Labor Troubles*, Part I; May Myrtle, "An Open Letter to the People of Sedalia," *The Earth*, March 27, 1886 (*The Earth* was a society paper that began publication about the same time as the strike.); Sedalia *Weekly Bazoo*, April 19, 1887, contains testimony in the trial of four strikers charged with train wrecking.

25. Sedalia *Daily Bazoo*, March 10, 11, 12, 25, 27, 1886; Sedalia *Weekly Bazoo*, April 20, 1886.

26. Sedalia *Daily Democrat*, October 2, 6, 7, 9, 1885; Sedalia *Daily Bazoo*, February 26, March 9, 11, 31, April 1, 2, 6, 7, 1886; Sedalia *Journal*, April 4, 1886.

27. Sedalia *Daily Bazoo*, March 31, April 1, 2, 6, 9, 10, 1886.

28. Sedalia *Weekly Bazoo*, May 4, 1886.

Chapter VIII: The Community of Workers

1. This particular hymn was one sung at one of the Reverend Van Wagner's revivals. Sedalia *Weekly Bazoo*, August 24, 1875.

2. Sedalia *Weekly Bazoo*, December 12, 1871, February 1, May 16, 1876, February 6, 1877.

3. The Junction house was only the most obvious and the most permanent of a number of brothels known to exist in Sedalia. Fights and raids frequently brought them into public view. Sedalia *Weekly Bazoo*, November 8, 1870, July 18, 1871, May 9, 1873, June 22, August 10, 1875.

4. Two brilliant examples of this process of "projection" can be found in Winthrop Jordan, *White Over Black: American Attitudes Toward the Negro, 1550–1812* (Chapel Hill, 1968) pp. 150–154, concerning the projection of sexual passions by whites onto blacks, and E. P. Thompson, *The Making of the English Working Class* (New York, 1964), especially pp. 365–374, focusing on the displacement of social energies into religious channels. On the fight see Sedalia *Weekly Democrat*, June 7, 1877.

5. Sedalia *Weekly Bazoo*, May 16, 1876.

6. See, for a discussion on the James legend, William A. Settle, Jr., *Jesse James Was Him Name* (Columbia, Mo., 1966) and especially pp. 120–121, concerning Edwards' response to the murder of Jesse James. Besides the considerable attention Edwards' Sedalia *Democrat* gave the local response to the murder, even the hostile *Bazoo* acknowledged the public support for the collection of James' widow. Sedalia *Weekly Bazoo*, May 16, 1882. Placing these activities of Frank and Jesse James and their followers in a broader context of political and economic transformation of Missouri is David Thelen, *Paths of Resistance: Tradition and Dignity in Industrializing Missouri* (New York, 1986), 70–77. The larger theme of social banditry, with the James brothers as but one instance, is one that has been treated effectively in the context of the transformation to capitalist forms of social relationship by Eric J. Hobsbawm, *Primitive Rebels: Studies in Archaic Forms of Social Movement in the 19th and 20th Centuries* (New York, 1959) and Hobsbawm, *Bandits* (New York, 1969).

7. Settle, *Jesse James Was His Name*, 88–91; Sedalia *Weekly Bazoo*, July 11, 1876.

8. Sedalia *Weekly Bazoo*, August 26, 1876; Sedalia *Daily Democrat*, August 27, 1876.

9. Sedalia *Weekly Bazoo*, October 28, 1878.

10. Sedalia *Daily Democrat*, July 6, 12, 14, 15, 1877.

11. *Ibid.*, July 12, 13, 17, 18, 1877.

12. *Ibid.*

13. *Ibid.*, July 22, 23, 27, 29, 1877; Sedalia *Daily Bazoo*, July 23, 27, 29, 1877.

14. Sedalia *Daily Democrat*, July 24, 1877.

15. *Ibid.*, July 25, 26, 1877.

16. *Ibid.*, July 26, 27, 1877; Sedalia *Daily Bazoo*, July 26, 27, 1877.

17. Sedalia *Daily Democrat*, July 28, 29, 1877; Sedalia *Daily Bazoo*, July 28, 29, 1877.

18. Sedalia *Weekly Bazoo*, March 5, 1878.

19. Sedalia *Daily Democrat*, December 29, 1877. J. J. Upchurch, *The Life, Labors and Travels of Father J. J. Upchurch, Founder of the Ancient Order of United Workmen* (San Francisco, 1887) provides important knowledge of the functions of the AOUW.

20. Sedalia *Daily Democrat*, March 19, 1880.

21. *Ibid.*, March 20, 1880.

22. *Ibid.*, March 21, 23, 25, 26, 28, 1880; Sedalia *Weekly Bazoo*, March 23, 1880.

23. Sedalia *Daily Democrat*, March 21, 23, 1880.

24. Sedalia *Weekly Bazoo*, May 24, 1881, May 8, 1883.

25. *Ibid.*, March 30, 1880.

26. Sedalia *Daily Democrat*, March 17, 20, 1885; manuscript dated December 30, 1944, pp. 4–6, E. T. Behrens Collection, State Historical Society of Missouri, Columbia, Mo. E. T. Behrens at the time was eighteen years old and active in several worker organizations. He later edited a worker newspaper in Sedalia, served as president of the state A. F. of L. and ran for governor as a Socialist. This particular document appears to be the draft of a letter recounting his experiences in the Sedalia labor movement.

27. Sedalia *Daily Bazoo*, March 10, 14, 1885; Sedalia *Daily Democrat*, March 10, 1885.

28. Sedalia *Daily Democrat*, March 11, 14, 17, 1885; Sedalia *Daily Bazoo*, March 14, 17, 1885; Sedalia *Sunday Morning Bazoo*, March 15, 1885.

29. Sedalia *Daily Democrat*, March 13, 1885; Sedalia *Daily Bazoo*, March 11, 12, 13, 1885.

30. Sedalia *Daily Democrat*, March 10, 11, 17, 19, 21, 1885; Sedalia *Daily Bazoo*, March 17, 1885; Sedalia *Sunday Morning Bazoo*, March 15, 22, 1885.

31. Sedalia *Daily Bazoo*, March 17, 1885; Sedalia *Daily Democrat*, March 17, 20, 1885.

32. *Journal of United Labor*, November 10, 1884, April 10, May 10, August 10, 1885; *Record of the Proceedings of the Ninth Regular Session of the General Assembly, held at Hamilton, Ont., Oct. 5–13, 1885*, 206–25; Sedalia *Sunday Morning Bazoo*, March 8, 1885.

33. Sedalia *Daily Democrat*, March 17, 1885; Joseph R. Buchanan, *The Story of a Labor Agitator* (New York, 1903), 142–148. While Buchanan claims considerable responsibility for his organizational efforts as an influence in the final settlement of the strike, local coverage places his visit and effort at the very end of the strike, on the day of the St. Louis meeting which concluded the strike.

34. Sedalia *Daily Democrat*, July 23, 29, 31, August 1, 11, 14, 29, 1885; "Program of Memorial Services in Honor of General Grant," in "Sedalia, Fraternal Associations," State Historical Society of Missouri, Columbia, Missouri.

35. Sedalia *Daily Democrat*, April 10, 17, June 19, July 29, September 5, 1885; Sedalia *Daily Bazoo*, April 7, 1885.

36. Norman J. Ware, *The Labor Movement in the United States 1860–1895* (New York, 1929), 140–145; Testimony of E. K. Sibley in U. S. Congress, *Investigation of Labor Troubles*, Part I, 250–252.

37. Sedalia *Daily Democrat*, September 5, 1885; Testimony of Martin Irons, U. S. Congress, *Investigation of Labor Troubles*, Part II, 437, 448.

38. Ruth A. Allen, *The Great Southwest Strike* (Austin, 1942), 35–43; Martin Irons, "My Experiences in the Labor Movement," *Lippincott's Magazine*, XXXVIII (June, 1886), 618–627; Testimony of Martin Irons, U. S. Congress, *Investigation of Labor Troubles*, Part II, 436–437.

39. Sedalia *Daily Bazoo*, March 11, 1885; Sedalia *Daily Democrat*, March 17, 20, September 5, 15, October 20, November 22, December 22, 30, 1885.

40. Sedalia *Daily Democrat*, September 23, October 3, 17, November 26, 1885; newspaper clippings and programs in Nellie Ingram Scrapbook, Western Historical Manuscripts Collection, University of Missouri, Columbia, Missouri.

41. Sedalia *Daily Democrat*, September 17, 29, 1885.

42. Sedalia *Daily Democrat*, October 7, 23, 30, November 3, 25, December 8, 23, 1885.

43. Testimony of Martin Irons, U. S. Congress, *Investigation of Labor Troubles*, Part II, 438–442; "The Way the Southwestern Strike Was Ordered," *The Nation*, XLII (May 20, 1886), 418–419; Terence V. Powderly much later claimed that Irons told him of mysterious circumstances surrounding the strike order including a gunpoint command to order the walkout, presumably by agents of the corporation in an effort to break the power of the Knights. Powderly, *The Path I Trod*, 118–124. Irons also told the same tale to E. T. Behrens, a Sedalia Knight who knew Irons, and who then provided the same interpretation to Ruth A. Allen. Allen, *The Great Southwest Strike*, 57. Whether that interpretation is an accurate description of the origins of the strike or merely an excuse that Irons, after the strike an outcast, fabricated to diminish his own responsibility in the dismal outcome of the strike cannot be resolved. In either event, it is clear from Irons' testimony and published remarks that the action was entirely consistent with his own philosophy.

44. Sedalia *Daily Bazoo*, March 9, 10, 11, 12, 1886; Testimony of Oscar von Kotchtitzky, U. S. Congress, *Investigation of Labor Troubles*, Part I, 300–304. In that testimony (p.301), Kotchtitzky even declared that some of the strikers in Sedalia and other points assured him that they were not in sympathy with the strike and "would freely return to work if they could."

45. Sedalia *Daily Bazoo*, March 9, 11, 1886.

46. Sedalia *Daily Bazoo*, March 9, 10, 11, 17, 19, 1886; testimony of Martin Irons, U. S. Congress, *Investigation of Labor Troubles*, Part II, 441. While Irons reportedly was willing to accept arbitration, he preferred that the governors use their influence to "bring about a meeting of the railroad officials and the executive board of District No. 101."

47. Sedalia *Daily Bazoo*, March 9, 11, 12, 13, 16, 17, 19, 1886.

48. Sedalia *Daily Bazoo*, March 20, 1886.

49. Sedalia *Daily Bazoo*, March 23, 24, 1886; Testimony of W. B. Lyons (pp. 265–266), J. J. Frey (pp. 267–269), R. Rockwell (pp. 273–274), and W. H. Mason (p. 275) in U. S. Congress, *Investigation of Labor Troubles*, Part I; May Myrtle, "An Open Letter to the People of Sedalia," *The* [Sedalia] *Earth*, March 27, 1886. The Sedalia *Weekly Bazoo*, April 19, 1887, contains a partial transcript of the trial of four strikers charged with train wrecking. The trial ended in a hung jury and the case was not retried.

50. Sedalia *Daily Bazoo*, March 12, 1886.

51. Sedalia *Daily Bazoo*, March 9, 17, 20, 23, 30, April 6, 1886; Powderly, *The Path I Trod*, 129–131; Bureau of Labor Statistics and Inspection of Missouri, *Great Strike of 1886*, 71.

52. Henry C. Fike Diaries, March 31, 1886, Western Historical Manuscripts Collection, University of Missouri, Columbia, Missouri; Sedalia *Daily Bazoo*, March 24, 27, 30, April 3, 6, 1886.

53. Sedalia *Daily Bazoo*, March 31, April 1, 2, 9, 10, 17, 21, 28, 1886; Sedalia *Weekly Bazoo*, April 20, 1886. The same internalization of the despair, frustration, and apparent purposelessness of their effort that in this case led to violence, has been brilliantly analyzed in the more recent context of the bureaucratization of the civil rights movement: Robert Coles, "Social Struggle and Weariness," *Psychiatry*, 27 (November 1964), 305–315.

54. Sedalia *Weekly Bazoo*, April 20, 1886. These remarks were in sharp contrast with Debs' later eulogy of Irons: "Martin Irons, Martyr," (December 9, 1900) in *Debs: His Life and Speeches* (Chicago, 1908), 273–75.

55. Sedalia *Daily Bazoo*, May 4, 1886.

56. Sedalia *Weekly Bazoo*, April 13, 1886; Sedalia *Daily Bazoo*, April 22, 1886.

57. Sedalia *Weekly Bazoo*, September 14, 1886; Sedalia *Daily Democrat*, June 27, 1888.

58. Sedalia *Daily Democrat*, February 24, 1885; E. T. Behrens, "I Been Workin' On A Railroad," *The Railway Clerk*, February 1940, 64–65, 83; pencilled manuscript in E. T. Behrens Collection.

59. Sedalia *Daily Democrat*, May 1, 5, 1888.

60. Sedalia *Daily Democrat*, May 4, 1888.

Chapter IX: The Agrarian Commonweal

1. Fred A. Shannon, *The Farmer's Last Frontier: Agriculture: 1860–1897* (New York, 1945).

2. *The History of Pettis County, Missouri* (n.p., 1882), 880.

3. *Ibid.*, 963.

4. *Ibid.*, 1044.

5. R. M. R. Kemp to brother and sister, November 2, 1854 in *Pioneers of Pettis, III* (mimeographed volume in State Historical Society of Missouri, Columbia, Missouri), 53–54.

6. Productions of Agriculture in Pettis County in 1850, and Productions of Agriculture in Pettis County in 1860, census manuscripts located in State Historical Society of Missouri.

7. U. S. Census, *The Statistics of The Wealth and Industry of the United States* (Washington, 1872), 192–195; U. S. Census, *Report on the Productions of Agriculture* (Washington, 1883), 124, 196.

8. U. S. Census, *Agriculture of the United States in 1860* (Washington, 1864), 92; *Statistics of Wealth and Industry of the United States* [1870], 192; *Report on the Productions of Agriculture* [1880], 124.

9. *Agriculture of the United States in 1860*, 92; *Report on the Productions of Agriculture* [1880], 161.

10. George F. Lemmer, "Farm Machinery in Ante-Bellum Missouri," *Missouri Historical Quarterly*, (July 1946), 470.

11. *Statistics of Wealth and Industry of the United States* [1870], 192–193, 356; *Report on the Productions of Agriculture* [1880], 68–69, 124.

12. Missouri Bureau of Labor Statistics, *Fifth Annual Report* (Jefferson City, 1883), 60.

13. *Agriculture of the United States in 1860*, 192, 207; *Statistics of Wealth and Industry of the United States* [1870], 192, 356.

14. Sedalia *Weekly Times*, January 9, 1868; Thomas J. Pressly and William H. Scofield (eds.) *Farm Real Estate Values in the United States by Counties 1850–1959* (Seattle, 1965), 36.

15. Sedalia *Weekly Bazoo*, November 1, 1869, March 1, 1870, August 15, 1871.

16. *History of Pettis County*, 272.

17. J. Q. Newbill to nephew, February 16, 1875, and J. W. Newbill to sister, March 28, 1876, both in *Pioneers of Pettis*, III, 58–60.

18. Missouri Bureau of Labor Statistics, *First Annual Report* (Jefferson City, 1880), 31, 51.

19. U. S. Census, *Reports on the Statistics of Agriculture* (Jefferson City, 1880) 31, 51.

20. U. S. Census, *Report on Farms and Homes: Proprietorship and Indebtedness* (Washington, 1896), 346 and map following that section. See also, however, the varieties and technicalities involved in the system generally referred to as sharecropping evident in the land transactions, tax papers, and sharecrop contracts in the Pettis County Papers of the Missouri Historical Society in St. Louis. Examples would be the agreements between W. P. Haley and G. S. Franklin (August 27, 1889), W. P. Haley and Lewis and Charlie Stevens (August 4, 1886), and Mariah F. Haley and J. B. Robinson (1888).

21. According to the calculations of the Missouri Bureau of Labor Statistics, by the end of the 1880s 88% of the taxed land in the county had been mortgaged. Missouri Bureau of Labor Statistics, *Fourteenth Annual Report* (Jefferson City, 1892), 316.

22. Missouri Trust Company, *Farm Loans* (Sedalia [1885]), pamphlet in State Historical Society of Missouri, Columbia, Missouri.

23. Shannon, *The Farmer's Last Frontier*, 303.

24. *History of Pettis County*, 349, 350, 928.

25. See, for example the summary of the offical and unoffical happenings at the 1867 fair in the Sedalia *Daily Evening Press*, October 4, 1867.

26. *Ibid.*, 349; Sedalia Industrial & Art Exposition Association, *Premium List*, 1885, (Sedalia, 1885) in State Historical Society of Missouri, Columbia, Mo.

27. *History of Pettis County*, 349.

28. *Charter, Constitution & By-Laws of the Pettis County Agricultural and Mechanical Society* (Sedalia, Mo., 1870) in State Historical Society of Missouri, Columbia, Mo.; *History of Pettis County*, 348–349.

29. *History of Pettis County*, 279, 352, 359–60, 373, 472, 482, 522, 526, 928–930. The Sedalia *Daily Bazoo* listed Gentry as the wealthiest farmer in the county, March 2, 1886. See also the eulogy of William Gentry, Sedalia *Weekly Bazoo*, May 7, 1889. The distance between Gentry and other farmers in the area can be noted in one small detail. Gentry was known for the fox hounds he kept for the hunt; the "poorer classes" of the same neighborhood were known for the dogs they kept that preyed upon Gentry's sheep. *History of Pettis County*, 929–30, 957.

30. See the lists of association directors in the fair guides cited above and also the endorsements of farm machinery by prominent farmers in local advertisements, as for example, the endorsement of Hill's Hay Ricking Apparatus by William Gentry, J. R. Barnett, and M. H. Siberts.

31. *Handbook of the Sedalia Co-Operative Store Society* (Sedalia, Mo., 1874), 16, State Historical Society of Missouri, Columbia, Mo.

32. *Ibid.*, 4, 13.

33. *Ibid.*, 15. It is not clear, however, how many of those institutions continued that practice. Others like the East Sedalia Co-operative Store, which catered mainly to workers, and the store operated by Norton & Norton on Ohio Street seem to have been more successful and longer-lived, a fact which would have resulted from different business practices. The 1876 city directory for Sedalia discusses (208) the East Sedalia Co-operative Store; in 1877 that store enlarged its building and stock. Sedalia *Daily Democrat*, July 6, 1877. Norton & Norton, whose origins are not known, was still operating in 1883. Sedalia *Weekly Bazoo*, January 2, 1883.

34. Edwin C. McReynolds, *Missouri: A History of the Crossroads State* (Norman, Oklahoma, 1962), 287. See also Solon J. Buck's, discussion of the Missouri Independent political activity of 1874 in Buck, *The Granger Movement: A Study of Agricultural Organization and Its Political, Economic, and Social Manifestations, 1870–1880* (Lincoln, Nebraska, 1963), 194–6. Also, Walter B. Stevens, "The Political Turmoil of 1874 in Missouri," *Missouri Historical Review*, XXXI (October 1936), 3–9.

35. Duane G. Meyer, *The Heritage of Missouri* (St. Louis, 1983), 427.

36. Buck, *The Granger Movement*, 58–59.

NOTES

37. See especially the reports of Grange activities in the Sedalia *Weekly Bazoo*, May 30, 1876; Sedalia *Daily Democrat*, July 31, 1877; *History of Pettis County*, 1043.

38. The local Greenback Party was able, significantly, to draw upon people who left both the Republican and the Democratic Parties. O. A. Crandall, a prominent Democrat in the late 1860s and 1870s, became a common spokesman and nominee for the Greenback Party in Sedalia after 1880. L. L. Bridges, a Republican Presidential Elector in 1876 was nominated for Congress at the Greenback convention but declined and nominated T. M. Rice who won. In 1881 Bridges was elected city attorney as a Greenback and later served in the state legislature as well. *History of Pettis County*, 619, 633–4. See also coverage of particular Greenback activities: Sedalia *Daily Bazoo*, September 11, 1879, April 5, 1881; Sedalia *Weekly Bazoo*, May 16, 1876, June 25, 1878, March 30, 1880, May 4, 1880, August 17, 1880, April 5, 1881, October 24, 1882, May 20, 1884; Sedalia *Daily Democrat*, March 26, 1880, May 2, 1881.

39. Lawrence Goodwyn, *Democratic Promise: The Populist Moment in America* (New York, 1976), 17; Leon Fink, *Workingmen's Democracy: The Knights of Labor and American Politics* (Urbana, 1983), 39.

40. Wright's occupation was never clearly indicated in the news reports covering his political activities, a factor which suggests further the blurred distinctions locally between farmers and workers. His position was stated in an announcement upon his death in 1889; he had been run over and killed by the train. Sedalia *Weekly Bazoo*, March 30, 1880; April 2, 1889.

41. Sedalia *Daily Democrat*, April 4, 1880; Sedalia *Weekly Bazoo*, April 6, 1880.

42. Sedalia *Weekly Bazoo*, June 8, 1886.

43. The sole remaining issue of the *Sedalia Labor Union and Grange*, January 8, 1887 (vol. 2, No. 50), is in the State Historical Society of Missouri, Columbia, Mo.

44. Sedalia *Daily Democrat*, May 4, May 18, June 8, 1888.

45. R. V. Denny, the secretary of the Pettis County Farmers' and Laborers' Alliance, joined the Wheel in the county in March, 1888. *History of the Farmers' Alliance, the Agricultural Wheel, the Farmers' and Laborers' Union, the Farmers' Mutual Benefit Association, the Patrons of Husbandry, and other Farmers' Organizations* (St. Louis, 1890), 198. Sedalia *Weekly Bazoo*, May 14, 1889. See also the tariff reform activities, political protests, and Wheel and Alliance meetings reported in Sedalia *Weekly Bazoo*, January 29, 1889, June 18, 1889, August 20, 1889, September 3, 1889, September 24, 1889.

46. "G. B. DeBernardi: A Sketch and an Appreciation of his Life" (n.p., n.d.), pamphlet in reference library, State Historical Society of Missouri, Columbia, Mo.

47. G. B. DeBernardi, *Trials and Triumphs of Labor* (Marshall, Mo., 1890).

48. *Ibid.*, 150–1.

49. G. B. DeBernardi, "Synopsis of the Labor Exchange" (Independence, Mo., n.d.), 11. This pamphlet is also found in the reference library, State Historical Society of Missouri, Columbia, Mo.

50. *Truth*, March 7, 1889. This free thought paper, published by E. T. Behrens and edited by U. F. Sargent in Sedalia, is in the Western Historical Manuscripts Collection of the University of Missouri, Columbia, Mo.

51. Jefferson City *Daily Tribune*, March 2, 1890. For the institutional history of the Labor Exchange see Missouri Bureau of Labor Statistics, *Twentieth Annual Report* (Jefferson City, 1898), 198, 212, and H. Roger Grant, "Blueprints for Co-operative Communities: The Labor Exchange and the Colorado Cooperative Company," *Journal of the West*, XIII (July 1974), 75–78.

52. DeBernardi, *Trials and Triumph of Labor*, 211–24.

53. *Truth*, March 7, 1889.

Chapter X: The Travail of Sisterhood

1. Alexander Hamilton Laidlaw quoted in Samuel Bannister Harding, *Life of George R. Smith, Founder of Sedalia, Mo.* (Sedalia, Missouri, 1904) 389–390.

2. S. E. Cotton in *ibid.*, 386.

3. This speech was partially published in *ibid.*, 43–47, but I have drawn upon the original handwritten copy in the George R. Smith Papers in the Missouri Historical Society in St. Louis.

4. G. R. Smith to Sarah E. Smith, April 26, 1846, Smith Papers in the Missouri Historical Society, St. Louis.

5. M. E. Smith in Harding, *Life of George R. Smith*, 46.

6. S. E. Cotton in *ibid.*, 386.

7. N. M. Ragland, *"Dear old Georgetown,"* or *Memoirs of Mrs. Martha Elizabeth Smith* (St. Louis, n.d.), 23.

8. S. E. Cotton in Harding, *Life of George R. Smith*, 387.

9. Ragland, *"Dear old Georgetown"*, 27.

10. This recollection has been printed several places; see *ibid.*, 30 ff.

11. *Ibid.*

12. M. E. Smith to parents, October 18, 1843, G. R. Smith Papers, Missouri Historical Society, St. Louis.

13. Ragland, *"Dear old Georgetown"*, 30.

14. M. E. Smith to parents, October 18, 1843, G. R. Smith Papers, Missouri Historical Society, St. Louis.

15. Ragland, *"Dear old Georgetown"*, 47–48, 60.

16. M. E. Smith in *ibid.*, 66–67.

17. M. E. Smith to family, June 12, 1855, Smith-Cotton Papers, Western Historical Manuscripts Collection, University of Missouri, Columbia.

18. Anna I. M[onroe] to S. E. Smith, April 10, 1851, Smith-Cotton Papers, Western Historical Manuscripts Collection, Columbia.

19. Anna I. M[onroe] to S. E. Smith, December 7, 1850 and April 10, 1851, Smith-Cotton Papers, Western Historical Manuscripts Collection, Columbia.

20. James N. Carpenter to G. R. Smith, November 20, 1848, G. R. Smith Papers, Missouri Historical Society. Apparently Smith did not hire Carpenter; he hired a female teacher instead.

21. Ragland, *"Dear old Georgetown"*, 67, 76.

22. *Ibid.*, 76.

23. M. E. Smith to family, June 12, 1855, Smith-Cotton Papers, Western Historical Manuscripts Collection.

24. Ragland, *"Dear old Georgetown"*, 79.

25. *Ibid.*, 81.

26. *Ibid.*

27. M. E. Martin to Willie, September 3, 1859, Smith-Cotton Papers, Western Historical Manuscripts Collection.

28. Ragland, *"Dear old Georgetown"*, 81.

29. M. E. Martin to Willie, September 3, 1859, Smith-Cotton papers, Western Historical Manuscripts collection.

30. While there is some vagueness and an occasional inconsistency about genealogy in the biography of George Smith, the sources I have relied on are clear and consistent: the grave markers in the family plot in the Sedalia cemetery and the chart taken apparently from a family Bible in the George R. Smith papers in the Missouri Historical Society.

31. M. E. Smith in Harding, *Life of George R. Smith*, 292–295.

32. *Ibid.*, 323.

33. *Ibid.*, 387.

34. See the official records in the Recorder's Office: Book K page 407, March 7, 1865 as well as other references in what amounts to a very complex series of property transactions, and the divorce petition in the circuit Court Clerk office, Record E page 584, May 4, 1866. I am especially grateful to William B. Claycomb for sharing his knowledge of these records.

35. M. E. Smith in Harding, *Life of George R. Smith*, 387–388.

40. M. E. Smith to Cousins John and Ottie, March 16, 1903, Smith-Cotton Papers, Western Historical Manuscripts Collection.

41. The following discussions of this significant and widespread phenomenon provide substantial insight: John S. Haller, Jr., "Neurasthenia: The Medical Profession and the 'New Woman' of Late Nineteenth Century," *New York State Journal of Medicine*, February 15, 1971, 473–482; Carroll Smith-Rosenberg, "The Hysterical Woman: Sex Roles and Role Conflict in 19th Century America," *Social Research*, 39 (Winter 1972), 652–678; Ann Douglas Wood, " 'The Fashionable Diseases': Women's Complaints and Their Treatment in Nineteenth-Century America," *Journal of Interdisciplinary History*, IV (Summer 1973), 25–52; and a related discussion of innovative theory of the nervous system at the time, Charles E. Rosenberg, "The Place of George M. Beard in Nineteenth-Century Psychiatry," *Bulletin of the History of Medicine*, XXXVI (May–June 1962), 245–259.

42. Smith-Rosenberg, "The Hysterical Woman," 663.

43. M. E. Smith to S. E. Cotton, June 28, 1873, Smith-Cotton Papers, Western Historical Manuscripts Collection.

44. M. E. Smith to S. E. Cotton, May 20, 1873, Smith-Cotton Papers, Western Historical Manuscripts Collection.

45. *Ibid*.

46. *Ibid*.

47. See Ann Douglas Wood, " 'The Fashionable Diseases'," 28: "Doctors in America throughout the nineteenth century directed their attention to the womb in a way that seems decidedly unscientific and even obsessive to a modern observer."

48. M. E. Martin to G. R. Smith, December 4, 1868, Smith-Cotton Papers, Western Historical Manuscripts Collection.

49. M. E. Smith to G. R. Smith and S. E. Cotton, January 10, 1878, Smith-Cotton Papers, Western Historical Manuscripts Collection.

50. In 1873 she wrote her sister "I can go home." "My name not being the same as that of those who have thrown this shadow over my life is a wonderful help to me." M. E. Smith to S. E. Cotton, May 25, [1873], Smith-Cotton Papers, Western Historical Manuscripts Collection. Also see Ragland, *"Dear old Georgetown"*, 80, for the note that the name change came in New Jersey.

51. M. E. Smith to S. E. Cotton, May 20, 1873, Smith-Cotton Papers, Western Historical Manuscripts Collection.

52. M. E. Smith in Harding, *Life of George R. Smith*, 388.

53. M. E. Smith to S. E. Cotton, May 20, 1873 and M. E. Martin to G. R. Smith, January 1, 1869, Smith-Cotton Papers, Western Historical Manuscripts Collection.

54. M. E. Martin to S. E. and H. S. Cotton, May 15, 1868, Smith-Cotton, Papers, Western Historical Manuscripts Collection.

55. M. E. Smith to Rosalie [Watson], December 3, 1882, Smith-Cotton Papers, Western Historical Manuscripts Collection.

56. S. E. Cotton to Prof. C. A. L. Totten, April 22, 1906, Smith-Cotton Papers, Western Historical Manuscripts Collection.

57. Both poems are in Ragland, *"Dear old Georgetown"*, 127, 133.

58. M. E. Smith to G. R. Smith and S. E. Cotton, January 10, 1878, Smith-Cotton Papers, Western Historical Manuscripts Collection.

59. M. E. Smith to Rosalie Watson, December 26, 1888, Smith-Cotton Papers, Western Historical Manuscripts Collection.

60. Ragland, *"Dear old Georgetown"*, 5.

61. M. E. Smith to S. E. Smith, June 5, 1855, Smith-Cotton Papers.

62. M. E. Martin to G. R. Smith, December 4, 1868, Smith-Cotton Papers, Western Historical Manuscripts Collection.

63. Isaac Errett to S. E. Cotton, April 4, 1872, Smith-Cotton Papers, Western Historical Manuscripts Collection.

64. M. E. Smith to S. E. Cotton, May 25, and June 28, 1873, Smith-Cotton Papers, Western Historical Manuscripts Collection.

65. M. E. Smith to Cousins John and Ottie, March 16, 1903, Smith-Cotton Papers, Western Historical Manuscripts Collection.

66. Mileta A. Smith to G. R. Smith [1846], George R. Smith Papers, Missouri Historical Society.

67. M. E. Smith to S. E. Cotton, May 25, [1873], Smith-Cotton Papers, Western Historical Manuscripts Collection.

68. M. E. Martin to S. E. and H. S. Cotton, April 19, 1868, Smith-Cotton Papers, Western Historical Manuscripts Collection.

69. Ragland, *"Dear old Georgetown"*, 130.

70. *Ibid.*, 90.

71. *Ibid.*, 88–89.

72. Clara C. Hoffman to M. E. Smith and S. E. Cotton, August 12, 1891, Smith-Cotton Papers, Western Historical Manuscripts Collection.

73. Undated, unsigned typed reminiscence in Smith-Cotton Papers, Western Historical Manuscripts Collection.

74. See the correspondence from the Freedmen's Aid and Southern Education Society to the Smith-Cotton sisters, June 20, 1893 and November 24, 1893, Smith-Cotton Papers, Western Historical Manuscripts Collection.

75. Copy of letter, M. E. Smith to Jane Addams, December 4, 1899, Smith-Cotton Papers, Western Historical Manuscripts Collection.

76. Newspaper clippings in Smith-Cotton Papers, Western Historical Manuscripts Collection.

77. Ragland, *"Dear old Georgetown"*, 93.

78. U. S. Census, *Manufactures of the United States in 1860* (Washington, 1865), 307; U. S. Census, *Ninth Census—Volume III: Statistics of the Wealth and Industry of the United States* (Washington, 1872), 539; U. S. Census, *Report on the Manufactures of the United States at the Tenth Census*, Vol. II (Washington, 1883), 142; U. S. Census, *Report on manufacturing Industries in the United States at the Eleventh Census: 1890*, Part I (Washington, 1895), 496–497.

79. These work positions surfaced in news accounts in a variety of contexts, including work accidents, particular individuals noted for other activities, and letters to the editor. See for example the following reports which tend to emphasize the role of women as seamstresses and milliners and dressmakers and domestics: Sedalia *Weekly Bazoo*, April 10, 1877; September 18, 1883; July 9, 1889; a report on milliners and dressmakers in town (their topic of conversation ranging from the Murphy movement to the price of flour and the European war) in the Sedalia *Daily Democrat*, July 15, 1877; a letter to the editor from "Shop Girl" in the Sedalia *Weekly Bazoo*, May 9, 1882; and May Myrtle's essay on woman's influence in the Sedalia *Weekly Bazoo*, January 23, 1877 and her poems "Only a Working Girl," and "The Sewing Girl's Dream," in the Sedalia *Weekly Bazoo*, May 23, 1876 and November 29, 1881, although she used the name Rosa Pearle on the poems.

80. Sedalia *Weekly Bazoo*, November 30, 1886.

81. Sedalia *Weekly Bazoo*, January 9, 1877; May 27, 1879; February 14, 1882; September 26, 1882; June 26, 1883; July 8, 1884; July 15, 1884; January 12, 1889.

82. Sedalia *Weekly Bazoo*, May 2, 1882.

83. Sedalia *Weekly Bazoo*, September 13, 1881.

84. It would be tempting and of significant value to explore the world of the brothels in Victorian America. In this community a beginning to probe questions of location, clientele, mobility, and values could be made by examining the instances in which public attention focused upon their activities: Sedalia *Daily Bazoo*, November 8, 1870; July 18, 1871; Sedalia *Weekly Bazoo*, June 18, 1871; October 8, 1872; June 22, 1875; August 10, 1875; August 17, 1875; August 23, 1877; November 23, 1880; May 17, 1881; March 7, 1882; April 11, 1882; July 10, 1883; October 9, 1883; December 18, 1883; October 14, 1884; August 27, 1889; Sedalia *Daily Democrat*, August 8, 1885; November 7, 1885; December 19, 1885; December 25, 1885.

85. Sedalia *Weekly Bazoo*, October 9, 1883.

86. Sedalia *Weekly Bazoo*, March 7, 1882.

87. See for example the accounts and object lessons in these reports: Sedalia *Weekly Bazoo*, March 19, 1878; December 14, 1880; March 8, 1881; November 1, 1881; November 29, 1881; October 16, 1883; December 6, 1887.

88. Sedalia *Daily Democrat*, November 18, 1885; Sedalia *Weekly Bazoo*, January 15, 1889.

89. Sedalia *Weekly Bazoo*, June 14, 1887.

90. Draft of temperance speech in George R. Smith Papers, Missouri Historical Society and partially reprinted in Harding, *Life of George R. Smith*, 54–55.

91. See the pledge cards for the Sedalia CTU in the F. A. Sampson Papers, State Historical Society of Missouri, Columbia.

92. F. A. Sampson speech welcoming the state WCTU convention to Sedalia, probably June 13, 1878, in Sedalia CTU Papers, State Historical Society of Missouri.

93. G. R. Smith speech on temperance, 1843, in George R. Smith Papers, Missouri Historical Society.

94. M. E. Smith to Rosalie Watson, December 26, 1888, Smith-Cotton Papers, Western Historical Manuscripts Collection.

95. Ragland, *"Dear old Georgetown"*, 62.

96. Undated, unsigned typed reminiscence in Smith-Cotton Papers, Western Historical Manuscripts Collection.

97. Sedalia *Weekly Bazoo*, July 11, 1882.

98. Sedalia *Weekly Bazoo*, August 8, 1882; July 17, 1883; December 4, 1883; November 4, 1884.

99. Sedalia *Weekly Bazoo*, January 13, 1885.

100. Sedalia *Weekly Bazoo*, January 20, 1885.

101. Sedalia *Weekly Bazoo*, August 8, 1882.

102. Barbara Leslie Epstein, *The Politics of Domesticity: Women, Evangelism, and Temperance in Nineteenth-Century America* (Middletown, Conn., 1981), especially 128–133. By demurring at this point I do not mean to challenge Epstein's broader analysis which I find helpful in explaining phenomena like the crusading efforts of Sedalia women.

103. See the samples of her work cited in note 79 above.

104. Sedalia *Weekly Bazoo*, January 31, 1882.

105. Sedalia *Weekly Bazoo*, February 7, 1882.

106. See the letter from "Champion" to the Sedalia *Weekly Bazoo*, December 3, 1878, responding to May Myrtle's reservations about the WCTU. On the other hand, the minutes of the Sedalia CTU recorded her presence at a board meeting July 26, 1879. Sedalia CTU Minute Book, State Historical Society of Missouri.

107. Sedalia *Daily Democrat*, August 4, 1885; August 8, 1885.

108. *The Earth*, May 8, 1886.

109. *The Earth*, March 27, 1886.

110. See the discussion in Alma F. Vaughan, "Pioneer Women of the Missouri Press," *Missouri Historical Review*, LXIV (April 1970), 304–305.

111. *Rosa Pearle's Paper*, May 19, 1894.

112. *Rosa Pearle's Paper*, July 21, 1894.

113. *Rosa Pearle's Paper*, June 16, 1894.

114. *Rosa Pearle's Paper*, August 4, 1894.

115. *Rosa Pearle's Paper*, July 7, 1894.

116. *Rosa Pearle's Paper*, June 16, 1894.

Chapter XI: A Way of Life Forsaken?

1. *Truth*, March 7, 1889.

Index

Addams, Jane, 188
Agricultural Wheel, 165, 166
agriculture, 12–16, 149–169
alcohol and society, 21–22, 23, 71,
    120–122, 125, 187, 193–196
Ancient Order of United Workmen,
    126–128, 135–137, 141, 146, 166,
    205
apprenticeship system, 17
Arator, 8
Arrow Rock, 11
Ashley, William Henry, 7

Barlow, Mary, 86
Beaman, 90
Beard, Charles, 49
Beecher, Henry Ward, 74
Behrens, E. T., 146, 147, 240 n.26
Benton, Thomas Hart, 39
Bingham, George Caleb, 21–23, 25,
    227 n.37
Blackwater Township, 24
Blauner, Robert, 91
Blocher, David, 99, 100, 103, 110
Blue Lodges, 41–42
Boeker, William, 18
Bond, William, 123
Born, John, 158
Bowles, John, 6
Bridges, L. L., 246 n.38
Brown, Rev. Edwin T., 74–76, 115
Buchanan, Joseph R., 135, 241 n.33
Buncombe, 8
Burlington Railroad, 105

businessmen, and challenges of
    competition and consolidation,
    97–114

Calahan, Lillie, 191
Carnes, Monte, 141
charity, 20, 61, 77, 83–84, 126–128,
    184–189, 196–197
Children's Heathen Mission Society, 74
Citizens' Movement, 112
Civil War, 45–49, 153–154
Cook, Lizzie, 86, 116, 191
Cooper, Lelitha, 17
Cooper, William, 17
Cotton, Henry S., 185–186
craft system of production, 12–13,
    16–17; see also technology
Crandall, O. A., 246 n.38
Cravins, C. M., 18
credit, system of, 107, 153–157, 160,
    163, 168, 225 n.17; see also money

David _____ , a slave, 30
DeBernardi, G. B., 147, 165, 166–169
Debs, Eugene V., 144
deflation, 154–155, 160, 163, 168
Dresden, 98, 165, 166
Drew, Richard W., 136
drugs, 86–87
Dugan, Alice, 200
Dugan, Elizabeth, 199–201
Dugan, George, 199
Dunlap, Rev., 120

254

Earheart, J. D., 90
Edmondson, Caleb, 11
education, 17, 26–27, 62–63, 101–103,
    172, 199
Edwards, John N., 118, 119
Elder, Jay, 88–89
Eldon (home of William H. Field), 48
elections, ante-bellum, 21–25, 38, 39,
    44; 1862 and 1864: 49
Elk Fork Township, 24
Elm Spring (home of David
    Thomson), 9, 17, 26, 46

fairs, 158–159
farmers, ante-bellum, 10–19; and
    post-Civil War economy, 149–157;
    and social and political growth,
    157–169
Farmers' and Laborers' Union, 165
Farmer's Mill, 66
Faulhaber, G. L., 129
Ficks, Nels, 84
Field, William H., 48
Fink, Leon, 163–164
Fitzgerald, Hugh, 137–138, 144
Fitzhugh, George, 41
Fitzsimmons, James, 132, 134
Fuller, Aunt (Elizabeth Dugan),
    199–201

Gabriel, Aaron, 17
Gabriel, Nancy, 17
Gamble, Hamilton, 46
Garner, A. B., 123, 124
Gentry, Major William, 106, 158–159,
    245 n.29
George, Henry, 146, 165
George R. Smith College, 188
Georgetown, Kentucky, 8, 176
Georgetown, Missouri, 9, 11, 16, 37,
    44, 45, 46, 48, 54, 58, 80, 171, 172,
    174, 175, 178
ghosts and phantoms, 90–91, 176
Gluckman, Max, 91
Goodwin, J. West, 61, 87, 100,
    118–119

Goodwyn, Lawrence, 163
Gould, Jay, 104–106, 112, 140, 141,
    143
Gould Southwestern System, 81,
    107–113, 131–134, 136, 139–144
Grange, 159–162, 166
Grant, Ulysses S., 135
Green Ridge Township, 36
Greenback Party, 138, 147, 161,
    162–165, 166, 167, 168, 246 n.38

Hager, A. M., 108–109, 132, 136
Hammond, Mary, 86
Hancock, J. R., 62, 66
Heard, George, 33
Heath, John and Robert, 6
Heath's Creek, 6
Heath's Creek Township, 42
Hieronymous, John, 7
Hieronymous, Widow, 7
Hoberecht, William, 66
Hoffman, Clara C., 187
Homkomp, Clement, 147
Hornsby, Brinksly, 42
Houstonia, 87
Howard, Maggie, 191
Hoxie, Vice President, 108, 111, 113,
    140, 143
Hurst, James Willard, 99, 229 n.12
Hurt, Richard, 17

Independent Order of Good Templars,
    72, 194
Ingram, Nellie, 137
Ironquill, 69–70, 234 n.1
Irons, Martin, 110, 112, 136–139,
    142–143, 242 nn.43, 46

James, Frank and Jesse, 117–119, 239
    n.6
Jamison, John C., 109, 133
Jaynes, A. D., 61, 123, 124
Jenkins, Hiram, 6–7
Johnson, Richard M., 8
Jones, conductor, 90

Jones, John S., 229 n.3
Junction House, 116, 191

Kansas, slavery-free soil issue in, 39–42
Kansas Pacific Railroad, 105
Kehn, George, 126
Kehn, J. H., 126
Kelley, James, 121
Kemp, James, 22
Kemp, R. M. R., 150–151
Kemp, William R., 22
Kentucky Gaieties, 116
Klein, Emma, 190
Knights of Labor, 110–113, 134–145, 146, 147, 164, 165, 200
Knights of Labor Concert Company, 137, 145
Knights of Maccabees of the World, 146
Kruse, Henry, 107
Kumm, Louis, 117

Labor Exchange, The, 168–169
labor theory of value, 18, 82, 127, 167–169, 207; see also work, conception of
Laidlaw, Alexander Hamilton, 179–183
Lamont, 165
Law and Order League, 111, 142, 143
Lee, Dr., physician, 92
Lemmer, George F., 153
Lindsay, R. T., 98
Little Helpers, 74
Longwood, 8, 57
Love, James E., 47
lynchings, 42–43, 71

McLaughlin, Eliza, 91, 92
McVey, Absalom, 11, 16, 205
McVey, W. A., 21
Magann, James G., 63
Major, Lewis Redd, 25
Marlin, Thomas, 6–7

Marmaduke and Sappington, 8
Marmaduke, John S., 108, 109, 131
Marmaduke, M. M., 18
Marshall, Samuel, 18
Martin, George Smith, 177, 205
Martin, James W., 176, 178
Marvin, Asa C., 58, 103
materialism, and market-derived values, 93, 160, 198; and organized religion, 73–76; as masculine quality, 85, 170, 191, 193; and individualism, 33–35, 36–40, 207–208
Meyer, J. D., 147
Miller, Arthur, 211
Miller, John, 17
Mills, C. Wright, 210
Missouri, Kansas and Texas Railroad, 57, 67, 103, 105, 107, 111, 123, 124, 128, 130
Missouri Pacific Railroad, 62, 67, 75, 79, 97, 98, 103, 104, 105, 106, 107, 118, 119, 122, 124, 128, 129, 130; see also Pacific Railroad
Missouri Trust Company, 156
money, 154–155, 207; as system of exchange of commodities, 17–19; as system of speculation, 162–163, 167–168
Montgomery, Bacon, 32, 53, 59
Montgomery, Thomas J., 60
Morrison, John, 106
Morton, James, 125
Moses, T. W., 62
Muddy Creek, 6–7, 9, 205
Mumford, Lewis, 81
Murphy Temperance Movement, 120–122, 124, 125, 194
Murray, L. S., 108
Myers, John, 120
Myrtle, May (Elizabeth Dugan), 199–201

National Labor Union, 138
Nauman, John, 66
Nesbitt, James, 84
neurasthenia, 116

Newbill, John G., 17
Newkirk, Cyrus, 61, 103, 106
Nichols (railroad agent), 118
non-material values, 206–207; and
  worker religion, 75–77, 115, 235
  n.10; and female culture, 85, 191,
  193, 198; and supernatural, 91–92;
  and farmers, 149–150, 160,
  166–168, 169; and secret societies,
  41–42, 72–73, 126–128, 134–135,
  159, 160, 161–162

Otterville train robbery, 118–119

Pacific Railroad, 38–39, 43–45; see also
  Missouri Pacific Railroad
Page, Fred, 132–133
Page, Rev., 120–122, 124
Parker, Albert, 61
Parks, Clara, 191
paternalism, and limits of, 25–32,
  76–78, 119, 127, 128–130
Patrons of Husbandry, see also Grange
Pearle, Rosa (Elizabeth Dugan),
  199–201
Pemberton, George M., 17
Pemberton, Mason, 24
Perry, Eugene, 143
Pettis County Agricultural and
  Mechanical Society, 158
Pierce, Reverend, 90
Pin Hook (see also St. Helena), 8
Pinkerton agents, 108
Pomeroy, Marcus M. "Brick," 76–78
Postal, 8
Powderly, Terence V., 113, 141,
  142–143, 144, 242 n.43
Powell, William H., 29
Price, Sterling, 39, 43, 47, 48

Ragland, N. M., 187
railroads, 36, 103–106; financial bonds
  of, 38–39, 55, 58, 97–99; and
  system of time, 80–81; see also
  specific railroad companies

Railway Employees' Benevolent
  Association, 141
Ramsey, H. M., 54, 206
Rees, Mrs. Thomas Prince Earl, 47
religion, 69–78; black, 31–32; and
  work ethic, 73–76, 234 n.6; and
  anti-materialist ethic, 75–78, 115
Retail Grocers Association of Sedalia,
  106–107
Rice, T. M., 163, 164
Rickman, John B., 108, 109
roads, early Pettis County, 20–21,
  226–227 n.34
Rollins, James, 21, 41
Romaine, Nicholas T., 146, 168, 209
Rosa Pearle's Paper, 200–201

St. Helena, 8, 205
St. Louis, Kansas City and Northern
  Railroad, 104–105
Sam _____ , a slave, 42–43
Schmidt, Herman, 121
secret societies, 41–42, 72–73,
  126–128, 134–135, 159–162; see also
  specific organizations
secularization, 70–71, 73–74, 84–85,
  193, 198, 208–209
Sedalia, founding of, 44–50; post-Civil
  War development of, 55–58, 60–64
Sedalia Board of Education, 103
Sedalia Board of Trade, 62, 64, 66,
  67, 71, 76
Sedalia Co-operative Store Society,
  159–161
Sedalia, Lexington, and St. Louis
  Railroad, 57, 58
Sedalia Library Association, 62, 76
Sedalia Lyceum, 72
Sedalia Mills, 66
Sedalia Savings Bank, 159
Sedalia Trades and Labor Assembly,
  137–139, 147
Sedalia, Warsaw, and Southern
  Railroad, 106, 159
Sedville (original name of Sedalia), 44
Shannon, Fred A., 149, 156–157
Sibley, E. K., 136

slavery, 9, 24–25, 28–32, 39–43, 173
Smith, David Thomson, 46, 171, 176, 188, 206
Smith, George R., 11, 16, 21, 26, 28, 32, 33, 36–45, 57–58, 59, 61, 170, 171–173, 174, 186, 187, 193–194, 196
Smith, Martha Elizabeth (Martin), 11, 12, 16, 21, 26–27, 29, 30, 36, 170, 171, 172, 173, 174, 175–185, 186–189, 189
Smith, Melita Thomson, 46, 171, 173–174, 186
Smith, Sarah Elvira (Sed), 44, 170, 172–175, 185–189
Smith Manufacturing Company, 66
Smith-Rosenberg, Carroll, 181
Snedaker, Charles, 107
steam engines, see also technology, revolution in
Stevens, E. W., 112
Stevens, Robert S., 77, 103–104
Stotts, Mary, 13
strikes, of 1877: 123–125; of 1880: 128–130; of 1885: 107–110, 131–135; of 1886: 110–113, 139–145; critique of, 167
suicide, 84, 86–87
supernatural, 31–32, 87–93

Talmage, A. A., 104, 105, 122–123
tax (railroad bond) revolt of 1869, 58–60, 98; of 1876, 98–99
Taylor, John, 116
Tebo and Neosho Railroad, 57, 58, 103
technology, revolution in, 64–68; agricultural, 152–153
temperance, see also alcohol and society
Texas Pacific Railroad, 110, 111, 139, 140
Thatcher, Captain, 118
Thomas, Keith, 90, 92
Thomson, General David, 8–9, 13, 15, 17, 25–28, 31, 36, 46, 174, 205
Thomson, Manlius, 25

Thomson, Marion, 25
Thomson, Melcena, 25, 26
Thomson, Melita, 25, 171; see also Melita Thomson Smith
Thomson, Mentor, 21, 22, 25, 45, 48
Thomson, Mildred (Major), 25
Thomson, Milton, 25, 26, 33
Thomson, Monroe, 25
Thomson, Morton, 17, 25
Tilly, Charles, 7
time, perception of, 14–16, 64–68, 80–81, 85
tramps, 82–83
Trevellick, Richard, 138

unemployment, 82–83
Union Labor Party, 146, 147, 165
Upchurch, J. J., 126

Van Wagner, J. M., 74–75, 121, 124
Vest, George G., 42–43, 45

Wabash Railroad, 105, 107
Walshe (foreman), 79, 81, 128–130
Wasson, Thomas, 8
Weber, Max, 234 n.6
West, Mollie, 191
Whyte, William H., 210
Wieman, H. B., 137–138, 146
Willard, Frances, 165, 187
Williams, H. Martin, 164
Wilson, T. L., 58
Womack, John, Jr., 211
women, and limits of ante-bellum paternalism, 26–27; and social transformation, 84–87; and medicine, 179–183; and market, 189–193; and responses to new social order, 170–202
Women's Benevolent Association, 193
Women's Christian Temperance Union, 187, 194, 195, 196, 199, 201
Wood, Clifton and Watson, 8
Wood, James C., 48
Wood, Joseph, 71, 194

Wood, Mrs. M. E., 101
work, conception of, 12–14, 15–16, 30, 73–74; *see also* labor theory of value
work, industrial processes of, 79–82
work-discipline, 81–82
work ethic, capitalist, 40, 74–76, 84, 99, 100, 127, 200, 235 n.7
workers, institutions and values of, 115–148
Working Women's Home, 196–197

Wright, Isaac, 164, 246 n.40

Younger brothers, 118–119

Zimmerman, Jacob, 66